The Coach's Strength Training Playbook

Featuring the Tier System

Joe Kenn

COACHES CHOICE™

ISBN: 1-58518-869-7
Library of Congress Control Number: 2003109501

Book layout: Jennifer Bokelmann
Cover design: Kerry Hartjen

Coaches Choice
P.O. Box 1828
Monterey, CA 93942
www.coacheschoice.com

Dedication

To Angie, Joe, and Peter – my inspiration

Acknowledgments

I'd like to thank the following people:

My parents, Joe and Carol, and my sister Dorianne for their unconditional support.

Cheyenne Pietri, Mark Uyeyama, Rich Gray, and Adam Miller, former assistants who believe in this system of training and have had a tremendous amount of input into its success.

Gary Craner, Tammy Pascoe, and Jeff Lien, Boise State University Athletic Training Department. Dave Tate, Elite Fitness Systems. Louie Simmons, Westside Barbell Club. Chris Doyle, Head Football Strength and Conditioning Coach, University of Iowa. Martin Rooney, Parisi School of Sport. Ron Pfeiffer, Professor, Boise State University.

Dr. Ken Leistner. Jeff Connor, PowerLift. Tom Proffitt and Bill Jacobs, Hammer Strength. Greg Sellers, MetRx. Mike Pratapas, Tom Kleinlein, Frank Mansuetto, Shane Johnson.

Coaches Dirk Koetter, June Daugherty, "Sam" Sandmire, Ron McBride, Pokey Allen, Tom Mason, Keith Flynn, Greg Patton, Ed Jacoby, Randy Mayo, Rod Jensen, and Darlene Bailey. My coaches: Bill Dooley, Al Groh, Rich Mollo, Dan Rocco, Whitey Jordan, Cliff Yoshida, Jerry McManus, Joey Bullock (my strength coach), and Mike Stamile.

Foreword

Joe Kenn is a strength coach, but more importantly, he is a "strength guy." Many coaches, both on the collegiate and professional levels, have the intellect, the education, and the time in various weightrooms to be knowledgeable. Coach Kenn, however, has the passion, a lifetime love of lifting weights, and the conviction that properly applied resistance exercise can change lives. I know because Joe Kenn and I grew up in the same neighborhood, attended the same high school, and have had many of the same weight training experiences.

Coach Kenn's passion came as a result of a childhood desire to be muscularly larger and stronger. It grew as he did, as the consistent weight training began to pay physical and psychological dividends. His passion was fueled, as his football ability increased proportionately to his growing strength and physical stature. He left a high school career for one in college, convinced that weight training would, could, and should make the difference between being "one of the players" at Wake Forest University, and being "the best player he could possibly be." Hours in the classroom gaining practical knowledge of the human body were augmented by hours in the weight training facility. Joe listened to his coaches and learned. Furthermore, he asked questions and always followed his own intuition. Entering the college coaching profession in the area of strength and conditioning, he continued to learn, continued to experiment, and, at all times, continued to be on his own path as a dedicated strength and conditioning professional.

This path wound through Boise State University, the University of Utah, and presently to Arizona State University. At every stop, the athletes under his charge benefited from his commitment to excellence—excellence in his own performance as a professional, excellence demanded of his players, and excellence in doing his best professionally each and every day. In time, Joe's theories and ideas formed the basis of his "Tier System," an organizational construct that pulled together his approach to systematic and functional strength training, and his belief in what would best serve his athletes. *The Coach's Strength Training Playbook* is a compilation of what Joe has learned, what he has implemented, and what he has found to work. Over the years, Coach Kenn's legendary work ethic and intensity have been contagious. With the underpinning of his program based on sound, fundamental physiological principles, Coach Kenn's total package gives those that utilize it an instant advantage. Organization and implementation, total information, and motivating inspiration—these are the defining attributes of strength and conditioning coach Joe Kenn. These are also the distinguishing features of *The Coach's Strength Training Playbook*.

—Dr. Ken E. Leistner

Preface

Unless you are willing to expand your mind from the conventional models of program design, stop! Read no further; this information is not for you. On the other hand, if you are an individual who is willing to think outside the traditional models of strength training, then I feel this strength-training application is one that will interest you. I urge you to read on.

This model of training is slightly different then some of the more mainstream programs being written today. I feel what I accomplished with this specific training protocol was to balance out all the positive traits of the three strength disciplines, weightlifting, powerlifting, and body building, and to develop a style that can use all three theories, methodologies, and exercises to form a program that will help improve athleticism.

After several revisions to this information (1995, 1997, 1999), I felt it was time to share what we have accomplished with this program. I have had the distinct privilege to work at three universities implementing this style of training: Boise State University, the University of Utah, and Arizona State University, with positive results coming at all three programs, and with numerous athletes from various sports showing improvement in their athleticism.

This is our coaching playbook for strength training program design. It is written in a manner to help coaches who are interested in this style of training to have a handbook that will lead them through the steps of a successful year-round training program. This model is primarily for individuals who coach sports that require a great deal of maximum and explosive strength (i.e., football, wrestling, basketball, track and field, gymnastics). Also, it can be manipulated to help improve strength in sports such as tennis, golf, cross-country etc.

I refer to the actual design of a specific program as the X's and O's of strength training. This is a playbook. It will serve as a reference when designing specific programs for a sport.

As mentioned earlier, this is the fourth revision to these training principles and probably will not be the last. I have continued to study and research all the methodologies that are being used today and how that material may benefit our athletes. With that being said, we always have something to learn. I go by the slogan absorb, modify and apply when it comes to incorporating new and innovating ideas to the main model of training.

This subject matter of this manual will deal specifically with my theories as they relate to strength-training program design. Other factors of training will be mentioned only when necessary.

Good luck,

Joe Kenn

Contents

Disclaimer

The information in this book is being offered for education and information purposes. There is inherent risk with any physical activity.

Anyone who participates in strength training should be required to schedule a physical exam from a physician before partaking in this strenuous task. This manual is a teaching and education tool. It should be noted that those who voluntarily participate in this style of training understand it is a dangerous activity and that the author and publisher assume no liability for injury.

1

Overview

The development of a yearly plan for strength training has become a crucial aspect in the success of individuals as well as teams. Because of the increased importance of an athlete being conditioned year-round, a properly planned program has increased the role of the strength and conditioning coach (from here on, this person will be called the S/C coach). A team or individual that is functionally stronger and in better condition generally wins the competition. Stronger athletes usually have followed a structured yearly training program, one that includes all aspects of strength, mobility, flexibility, nutrition, conditioning, agility, and speed development.

It is imperative that the S/C coach be aware of the numerous training principles and applications that are available. The more information available, the more it allows you to make confident decisions when designing your program. This will ultimately enable you to create a program that will affect the athletes' performance in a positive way.

Strength Training

In any sport, the development of whole-body strength has become more and more essential to sport coaches, whose longevity at their current posts is based on the success of their athletes and their team. The strength programs that these athletes participate in help twofold in the goal of winning. First, a stronger athlete is a better athlete; and second, a stronger athlete is a healthier athlete. The ability of an athlete to improve performance, decrease the chance of injury, or decrease recovery time if an injury does occur is extremely important when championships are on the line. That is why the S/C coach's role in the development of athletes has become more influential.

There are different avenues to take when creating a strength-training program that will improve athletic ability. Which ones are correct and which ones are the most successful we may never know because many teams have won championships with various styles of training.

The program in this book has considered all the methods that have been available for review. The methodology of the program is a combination of all the training principles that are being used today on the professional, university, and high-school levels. This type of training has been termed athletic-based strength training, and the training model is known as the tier system.

The tier system is a true conglomeration of numerous types and styles of training that many coaches use or have used. You will see derivatives of the sports of weight lifting, powerlifting, and bodybuilding. These sports are the strength disciplines. Training principles from the Westside Barbell Club (Coach Louie Simmons and Dave Tate), traditional periodization, and high-intensity training (HIT) are interwoven to complete the package. The principles of HIT and events from strongman training are used in the auxiliary training programs.

There are two main segments that are important in the planning of a successful strength-training program. The first is the development of the annual training plan through the theory of periodization. The second is designing the actual strength program through the tier system model. The annual plan allows the coach to set up the direction and the specific time periods for specific programs and goals throughout the year. When this plan is completed, the coach then begins the development of the cyclical plan for each program. This will prepare the athletes for the demands that are placed on them during different stages of the competitive year.

Most sports have a multiple-game season that may last four months or longer. These sports may also have a spring or fall practice schedule in which sport-specific drills may take precedence over strength training. If these situations are not taken into account before the actual development of a specific program takes place, the individual designing the program is looking for trouble. It is imperative that the program planner looks at the big picture first, and then looks at specific blocks of time during the year to specifically work on progressing the athletes toward the upcoming competitive season.

The second segment is where the program planner begins listing exercises that may be implemented into the training program, and then chooses those exercises that will benefit the athlete in the most efficient manner. Once the exercises are finally chosen, they are strategically placed in the weekly template to create an athletic-based strength-training program.

As mentioned earlier, this is truly an atypical program. Some of the traditional principles of exercise order and traditional periodization have been broken. When the tier system was designed and this type of training was named athletic-based strength training, its designers were not looking to set a trend; they were looking for the most efficient way to tie in all the great aspects of the different types of training and mold them into one model.

It is imperative that strength professionals keep an open mind to the numerous ways that exist to train athletes. The ability to recognize other programs' success and take the time to study and evaluate their structures will allow you to make your program better.

As mentioned earlier, this manual will cover the author's design model for strength training. There will be references to other components of athletic development only when needed.

Overview of the Program

Mission Statement

To achieve athletic excellence through a systematic training approach that will enhance both mental and physical performance. The strength and conditioning coaching staff will enhance each individual athlete's athletic potential through a structured program that includes all aspects of physical development and injury prevention.

Overall Program Philosophy

The strength and conditioning staff will enhance every athlete's performance to reach his potential. Each individual athlete has an impact on the success of the sports program. When an athlete is putting in the time and effort to succeed, the strength and conditioning staff is equally committed to giving the same effort and more to help that athlete.

The goals of the training program are:

- Work
- Team building
- Development of the athlete
- Injury prevention

Work

Several factors should be evaluated in the program when it is related to the word *work*.

- *Increase work capacity*–raising the athlete's ability/volume of purposeful activity in a given period of time.
- *Work intensity*–the athlete shows eagerness and strong concentration.
- *Work effort*–the athlete is attempting to achieve his objectives.
- *Work ethic*–the athlete's moral principles, pride.

Team Building

Team building means developing a group working together. Most coaches will predominately deal with teams, so group work is extremely important to the overall objective of the program. When possible, it is recommended to train in large group or team settings because these intangibles of success can be established:

- Unity
- Competitiveness
- Camaraderie
- Peer review
- The power of one–one mission, one goal

Development of the Athlete

Athletes use strength training as one of the major pieces of their overall physical development. Unlike powerlifters and weight lifters, who actually compete in the exercises they train with, most athletes have been recruited to play a specific sport or position that utilizes strength training as a way to improve their level of fitness and athletic ability. The position or sport coach works on the specific skills necessary to succeed on the playing field of choice.

Exercises that increase mobility are extremely important to the development of athletes. In the strength disciplines, most training activities are completed in a linear plane, with little or no foot movement (weight lifting is the only discipline where the feet move, but is very specific to the catch phase of the lifts). Therefore, the choices of movements in training can be narrower in scope. Also, strength athletes do not have the concern of the conditioning aspect in their sports. Specific conditioning demands have a major influence on the strength programs that are developed during the annual plan.

Injury Prevention

- Several factors in this book's program relate to injury prevention:
- Functional strength training

- Functional conditioning
- Functional flexibility
- Proper nutritional guidance
- Rest and recovery
- Needs assessment – injury-prone areas pertaining to a specific sport

The Five Bullet Points of Athletic-Based Strength Training

The following five bullet points show the main components of the tier system strength-training program. The training templates, speed of movement, and workout duration are based on these five points.

- Training movements rather than body parts
- Whole-body training sessions versus split training sessions
- Explosive versus nonexplosive movements
- Variety
- Tempo

Training Movements Rather Than Body Parts

Most athletes who are successful have the innate ability to control their body in space. Movement training is an important factor in improving body control. The days of concentrating on specific body parts are over. No one is going to care how big your athletes' arms and chests are if they are sitting next to you on the bench. By emphasizing movement patterns, the program planner can develop a better functional training program that will transfer the improvements from the strength-training program to the competitive setting.

Closed chain or ground -based exercises should make up approximately 75% (or more) of your overall exercise choices per program. These exercises are those in which athletes are standing on their feet producing force against the ground. The more force that athletes can apply to the ground, the faster they can run, jump, and change direction. The use of free-weight movements involving barbells and dumbbells is more effective when this type of training is being considered. Free weights also allow us to train in multiple planes of movement within one exercise set. These movements can be forward/backward, left/right, up/down, rotational, and angular.

Exercises that have multiple joint actions are highly utilized in this program. Most athletic skills are multi-joint movements that are timed in a synchronized fashion. Exercise variations of the back squat and variations of the clean, jerk, and snatch help to improve these movement patterns. These movements also have an extension component within them. Extension involves three major joints: the ankle (plantar flexion), knee, and hip. These three joints, when moved from the flexed to extended position, create the explosiveness needed to fire off the line of scrimmage, serve a tennis ball, or dunk a basketball. Training multiple-joint movements has proven to have a higher carryover value to sports than single-joint isolation movements.

The implementation of unilateral lower body (single leg) movements is another emphasis of this program. During competition, the athlete is very seldom on both feet at the same time. Single leg strength becomes an important factor in the lower body development of the athlete, where balance and stabilization are issues. Also, when performing single leg movements such as step-ups and lunges, the athlete actually opens and closes the kinetic chain, which is similar to running. During the support phase, the leg is in contact with the ground (closed chain), then leaves the ground (open chain) during the recovery phase, and then comes back into contact with the ground during these movements. When athletes run, their body is supported by one leg 80% of the time.

Dumbbell training is an important factor when training unilateral upper-body movements. Using dumbbells for upper body development gives athletes the same advantages as unilateral training for the lower body. Dumbbells allow S/C coaches to train arm movements individually. This helps develop more stabilization strength in each shoulder, as well as develop torso stabilization, overall body balance, and awareness during standing movements. Because more muscle fiber recruitment is necessary when training with dumbbells as compared to barbells in upper body movements, more muscle force is applied to the resistance. This program also implements exercises performed on balance boards, balance beams, and stability balls. This helps improve proprioception, body balance, and core stabilization.

Whole-body Training Sessions Versus Split Training Sessions

The concept of whole-body training sessions evolved from researching high-intensity training (HIT) programs. HIT programs are based on two to three days per week of training. Each standard session is comprised of one exercise per body part, and each exercise is performed for one set for a prescribed number of repetitions. In some cases the exercise of choice for a body part may be a single joint/isolation movement. An example of this type of program would look like this:

- Neck
- Shrug
- Leg curl
- Leg press
- Leg extensions

- Heel raise
- Chest press
- Row
- Lateral raise
- Triceps pushdown
- Biceps curl
- Torso

Although there is a place for single joint movements in this program, as stated before, athletic movement is made up of synchronized multiple joint actions. This program is based on movement related to athletic activity, and most movements of the program, therefore, are multiple joint in nature.

Instead of developing a whole-body approach based on body parts and performing one set per exercise, movement categories were developed that break down the exercises based on the number of joints that are involved in a particular movement. These categories are total-body movements, lower-body movements, and upper-body movements. Total-body movements represent exercises that include movements of all the major joints of the body performed in a synchronized manner. Lower-body movements are those exercises that focus on the movements that originate from the torso down. Upper-body movements focus on movements above the torso. These movements are then performed for 2 to 10 sets.

It is extremely important to note that in most athletic situations, the whole body is active in movement. The question must be raised: why would the S/C coach prefer to split the body into lower-body and upper-body sessions or push/pull sessions? These movements are all interwoven into one during performance. In every sport-related movement the body uses a synchronized movement pattern that involves all the major joints of the body. Although the term *sport specificity* should be related only to exact drills that are performed on the playing field, the body must be conditioned through resistance exercise similar to the demands faced in competition.

It is the author's contention that the most efficient way to strength train would be on a three-day-per-week, whole-body program. This allows for improved recovery as well as being able to implement the running emphasis (speed or conditioning) of the cycle on non-strength training days. In addition to these three strength sessions per week, most athletes will have an additional two to four running sessions per week.

Explosive Versus Nonexplosive Movements

This program makes no separation between explosive or nonexplosive movements. It is agreed that some exercises may need to be performed faster than others, but based on the rate of force development that an athlete can generate, any exercise can be trained as slow or as fast as you would like. In most sports, success is based on who can arrive at point B from point A the fastest; therefore, it is important to have an explosive approach to concentric bar speed. The terms *maximum concentric acceleration or progressive acceleration during the positive phase (concentric) of the movement* should be emphasized. This is usually implemented for all multijoint movements in this program, unless an athlete is recovering from injury or performing a prehabilitation program; then you may want to concentrate on a slower movement speed.

During the concentric phase of the movement, it is recommended that athletes attempt to accelerate the bar in the fastest time possible (it is understood that there will be a deceleration phase before lockout, or at the midpoint of a pulling movement). This is an acquired taste, because most athletes' first experience in strength training was based on bodybuilding principles and tempo training. In the sport of bodybuilding, the goal is the aesthetics of lean body mass and definition, and not necessarily maximum strength development.

Another point on explosive versus nonexplosive movements is based on years of watching athletes attempt submaximal and maximal lifts in the strength- training program. During this process of evaluating bar speed, whether a lift was classified to be explosive or nonexplosive in the past, after approximately 85% of the athlete's one repetition maximum, the bar begins to slow down due to the increased load. As the load increases, speed will decrease; however, the athlete must continue to drive the bar as fast as possible at all times.

Variety

Athletics is based on a tremendous amount of movement in different planes of action. It is imperative that athletic-based strength training programs include as many variations of movement as possible to train the muscles in as many planes as possible. A free weight–dominated approach allows for extreme variety. Remember, training on all three planes of movement: sagital, frontal, and transverse, as well as unilateral movements, are crucial in athletic-based strength training. Every two to four weeks, it is recommend that changes should be made to the exercises of the weekly schedule. This allows S/C coaches to change movement angles and stay within the philosophy of building a functionally stronger athlete.

Tempo

One of the goals of the program is to increase work capacity. This can be done in a daily session by decreasing rest time, always standing during workout sessions, complexing, coupling, or combining movements, or super/tri-setting exercises. It is understood that most research says that a three-minute rest between sets is necessary to increase strength. Unfortunately, most athletes never get this amount of rest between successive bouts of performance in a competition. For example, in football, an average series is 5 plays with a rest interval of 35 seconds. This athlete will repeat this type of performance for approximately 17 series, for a total of 85 plays. Obviously some series may be as short as 1 play and as long as 15, so it is important that the athlete is trained with a limited rest period in between sets to be prepared for numerous bouts of repetitive exercise. By reducing the rate of recovery between sets, you are allowing for more muscle fiber to be recruited for each set thereafter.

The goal is to complete the main session of the workout in 60 minutes or less, regardless of the total number of sets prescribed. This program builds in an anaerobic conditioning effect during strength sessions. This will help increase the athletes' work capacity.

2

Annual Plan Development

Periodization

The development of a properly outlined yearly training regimen has a tremendous effect on the individual and team's success. With this in mind, the theoretical principle of periodization plays an important role in the S/C coach's decision making throughout the training year.

Periodization is the principle of developing long-term (yearly) training outlines for a specific sport. The main concept of periodization is that of breaking down the training year into "periods." Each period has specific goals and program guidelines. The periods are set to allow the athlete to be physically and mentally ready for upcoming competitions.

There are numerous factors that must be considered in the development of a successful periodization model. Volume, intensity, frequency, exercise selection, exercise order, recovery, linear speed development, change of direction, plyometric training, basic skill development, aerobic conditioning, and anaerobic conditioning are some of the main factors that must be accounted for.

Although nothing is set in stone, a periodization outline allows a coach to have the framework for the specific goals for the training year. This allows the coach to have a plan in place, and if necessary, make minor adjustments to future programs.

Periodization has been interpreted in several different ways since it surfaced as one of the primary factors for the success of the Eastern bloc sports system. For the competitive Olympic athlete, a periodization model can last as long as four years.

The following periodization format was developed to simplify many of the advanced models and to take into consideration the academic/training calendar of most high-school and college-age athletes. Many amateur U.S. athletes are student-athletes on the high school and university levels, and most models don't take this into consideration. Since many athletes have competitive seasons annually, the entire training year is referred to as the annual plan.

The Annual Plan

The annual plan is unique to each sport. A frequently asked question by most sport coaches is, when does the year begin? Some believe the annual plan starts when the school year starts, and ends when school lets out for the summer. Some think it starts January 1 and ends December 31. Others believe it starts when competitions begin. Although these seem to be logical answers to the coach, these answers are incorrect. There are also some coaches that do not even consider the importance of an annual plan and just repeat training regimens one after the other. Failure to plan is planning to fail.

When Does the Annual Plan Begin?

The annual plan is based specifically on the sport that the program is being designed for. The annual plan begins the day after the last competition of the previous season and ends the day of the last competition of the upcoming season. This allows for a gradual increase in the development of the athlete from one program phase to the next without unnecessary breaks that would hinder improved performance.

Uncontrollable Factors of the Annual Plan

Before one begins to develop the annual plan for a specific sport, there are several factors that need to be considered before the actual running programs and strength programs (cycles) are developed. Before the actual design of the annual plan can be started, a list of uncontrollable factors must be created.

Uncontrollable factors are those factors that the S/C coach cannot manipulate when designing the annual plan for a sport. These factors can lead to the S/C coach adjusting programs and cycles because these factors were not accounted for when the annual plan was developed. To save time, before you begin the development of the annual plan, think about the factors that you must account for in the year. Most of these factors are dates that fall within the academic calendar (see Figure 2-1).

These factors have the ability to alter a particular program and cycle. For example, say an S/C coach creates an eight-week cycle for a sport, with week eight being a test week. Unfortunately for the S/C coach, week eight falls during spring break, and all the athletes will not be in school for that week. Therefore, the strength coach cannot perform the testing at that time and now must adjust not only the evaluation week, but also the eight-week program and the remaining schedule of the annual plan.

```
Type of school year - semester or quarters
School holidays
Length of semester or quarter breaks
Fall break
Spring break
Examination schedule at the end of semesters or quarters
When does the semester or quarter begin?
Sport - length or season
Sport – Is it a split semester season? - Example basketball
Sport - Does the sport include 2 a day practice in the pre competitive phase?
Sport - Does the sport implement a spring or fall schedule/practice?
Play-Offs – length of participation
Tournaments – length of participation
Bowl Preparation
Student Athlete Discretionary Time
```

Figure 2-1. Examples of uncontrollable factors of the annual plan

Stages of the Annual Plan

There are three main stages we implement into the annual plan: rejuvenation, developmental, and competitive (see Figure 2-2). Within these three stages, specific programs are developed based on the time periods determined during the 52-week training plan. Each stage and subsequent program has goals and objectives that are established to enhance the athletes' performance for the most important competition schedule of their sport.

Stages	Rejuvenation	Developmental	Competitive
Programs	Post Season	Spring	Pre Season
	Off Season	Summer	In Season
		Fall	Championship Season
		Winter	

Figure 2-2. Main stages and programs of the annual plan

The Rejuvenation Stage

The first major stage of the annual plan is the rejuvenation stage. This stage begins the day after the last competition of the previous year. The duration of this stage is typically between two and eight weeks. A shorter stage is generally a biproduct of a longer competitive stage. In most team sports (professional, college/university, high school), teams that are extremely successful usually have a shorter rejuvenation stage because they have qualified for play-offs, tournaments, or bowl games. The rejuvenation stage begins the new competitive year.

During this stage it is important to maintain a general level of fitness while also giving the athlete time to psychologically and biologically rest, relax, and regenerate. This is accomplished by implementing training strategies that are atypical to the specific programs characteristics of the developmental and competitive stages.

The rejuvenation stage is the ideal time to begin intense rehabilitation of injuries that may have occurred during the year's competitions. In this case, these individuals will have a program designed specifically for developing strength in the injured area. Each injured athlete should schedule an individual appointment with the athletic trainer to implement a specific rehabilitation routine for the affected area(s). The S/C coach will then meet with the athletic trainer to discuss the alternatives available for the athlete's training plan.

The majority of the program protocols for rehabilitation will be implemented from an auxiliary training file that has numerous rehabilitation and prehabilitation programs. This will allow the athlete to be at or near 100% health for the developmental stage that follows. Obviously, this discussion pertains to athletes who have minor injuries. The major injury (surgical) rehabilitation process may consist of more time then the two to eight weeks of the rejuvenation stage.

The rejuvenation stage can be broken down into two different programs, the postseason and the off-season. Depending on the length of the rejuvenation stage, the postseason program may not be included. When both programs are implemented, it is best to divide the number of weeks equally for each program. If this phase has an odd number of weeks such as seven, three weeks should be given to the postseason program and four weeks to the off-season program. The off-season program is more conducive to the training that will occur during the developmental and competitive stages. Therefore, when the total number of weeks in the rejuvenation stage is odd, it is recommended that more time be invested in the off-season program.

During this stage, most athletes are on semester break and are away from campus. It is important to note this when developing the exercise plan for these programs. Athletes may not have the same equipment at home as they do at your facility.

The coach's involvement during this stage is minimal. After the review of technique for the foundation exercises and the introduction of new exercises have been accomplished, the coach is on the floor for safety or spotting concerns. This gives the athlete more control over the pace and choices of exercises without the interference of the coach.

This is the only time during the annual plan where the athlete will focus on individual body parts (postseason program) rather than movement patterns related to strength development. The athlete is encouraged to experiment with different training apparatuses for a more multidimensional training effect, which we are trying to encourage during this stage. This will give the athletes the opportunity to train their bodies differently then our typical training programs.

• The Postseason Program

Depending on the length of the rejuvenation stage, the postseason program may not be implemented. If the rejuvenation stage is four weeks or longer, the postseason program (see Figure 2-3) will be the first training program of the annual plan. If the rejuvenation stage is shorter, this program is omitted.

Strength training during this program is broken down into three sessions per week; in other words, every other day. There are two parts to each session: an exercise technique section, followed by traditional circuit training (body parts). The exercise technique section is implemented to perfect exercise technique of our main exercises, and to introduce new exercises that will be included in the developmental stage.

The traditional circuit program is outlined for the athlete with the corresponding body part and number of reps to be completed for each. The athlete can choose any exercise that represents that body part movement. We implement three circuits during the week, a short circuit (six to nine exercises), a moderate circuit (9 to 12 exercises), and a long circuit (12 to 15 exercises).

Training percentages are not affixed to any exercise during this program. Athletes should choose a load that allows them to perform each rep with proper technique. They should be able to finish one to two reps after the goal rep is achieved.

• The Off-Season Program

The off-season program (see Figure 2-4) will always be included in the annual plan. The length of the rejuvenation stage will determine if this is the first or second program of the training year.

During this program the athlete will train on a four-day split, with Day 1 and Day 4 being lower-body-emphasis workouts and Day 2 and Day 5 being upper-body-emphasis workouts. Days 3, 6, and 7 are recovery days.

Work Out 1	Work Out 2	Work Out 3
Rack Holds 3 x 5 sec.	OH Squat Holds 3 x 5 sec.	OH Squat Holds 3 x 5 sec.
Hang Clean Progression Set 3x5 Rep1 – RDL	Squat Progression Bwt Squat – Wall or Rack x 15	Press/Jerk Progression Set 2x5 Rep1 – Standing Press
Rep2 – Shrug Pull	Free Hand Squat w/ bar x 15	Rep2 – Push Press
Rep3 – Power Pull	Zercher Squat 2 x 12 pause	Rep3 – Power Jerk
Rep4 – High Catch Clean	Front Squat 2 x 12 pause	Rep4 – Split Jerk – Dominant Leg
Rep5 – Clean to Front Squat	Back Squat 2 x 12 pause	Rep5 – Split Jerk – Alternate Leg
Each Rep start with cadence	Snatch Grip Progression Set 3x3	Repeat Behind Head
Ready – erect position	Rep1 - RDL	Each Rep start with cadence
Set – Athletic Position	Rep2 – Shrug Pull	Ready – erect position
Hit – perform movement	Rep3 – Power Pull	Set – Athletic Position
From the Deck Progression Set 3x3	Each Rep start with cadence	Hit – perform movement
Rep1 – Clean Deadlift	Ready – erect position	Bench Progression
Rep2 – Shrug Pull	Set – Athletic Position	Floor Press 2 x 12
Rep3 – Power Pull	Hit – perform movement	Bench Press 2 x 12
Each Rep start with cadence	Block Snatch Grip Progression Set 3x3	Grip7 Bench Press 2 x 12
Set – Proper Deck Position	Rep1 – Block Deadlift	
Hit – perform movement	Rep2 – Shrug Pull	
12 Exercise Circuit-repeat 1-3	Rep3 – Power Pull	
1 – Hamstring x 12	Each Rep start with cadence	
2 – Leg Press/V Squat/Bear x15	Set – Proper Block Position	10 Exercise Circuit-repeat 1-3
3 – Quadriceps x 12	Hit – perform movement	1 – Leg Exercise x 12
4 – RDL – Hammer x 12		2 – Back Exercise x 12
5 – Back x 12	7 Exercise Circuit – repeat 1-3	3 – Back Exercise x 12
6 – Chest x 12	1 – Chest Exercise x 12	4 – Shoulder Exercise x 12
7 – Shoulder x 12	2 – Back Exercise x 12	5 – Shoulder Exercise x 12
8 – Triceps x 12	3 – Shoulder Exercise x 12	6 – Chest Exercise x 12
9 – Biceps x 12	4 – Triceps Exercise x 12	7 – Triceps Exercise x 12
10 – BWT exercise x 12	5 – Biceps Exercise x 12	8 – Biceps Exercise x 12
11 – Back x 12	6 – Leg Exercise x 12	9 – Leg Exercise x 12
12 – Torso x 15	7 – BWT Exercise x max	10 – BWT Exercise x 12

Figure 2-3. Sample postseason template

Work Out 1	Work Out 2	Work Out 4	Work Out 5
Hang Clean 3-5 x 5-6	Bench Press 3-5 x 8-12	Push Jerk 3-5 x 5-6	Grip1 Incline Press 3-5 x 6-10
Back Squat 3-5 x 8-12	Choose Horizontal Movement 4 x 12	Front Squat 3-5 x 6-10	Choose Horizontal Movement 4 x 12
Choose Multiple Joint Single Leg Movement 2 x 12 each leg	Choose Vertical Push and Pull Exercise 3 x 12	Choose Multiple Joint Single Leg Movement 2 x 12 each leg	Choose Vertical Push and Pull Exercise 3 x 12
Choose Posterior Chain Exercise 3 x 12	Choose Elbow Flexion and Extension Exercise 2 x 12	Choose Posterior Chain Exercise 3 x 12	Choose Elbow Flexion and Extension Exercise 2 x 12

Figure 2-4. Sample off-season template

A total-body exercise will be included in the lower-body sessions and will be performed as the first exercise of the daily rotation. The athlete still has the ability to make exercise choices in some cases, but the program is more conducive to the programs of the developmental stage. This program will not include training percentages but will have set/rep schemes assigned to each exercise.

• The Rejuvenation Stage Conditioning Program

During the rejuvenation stage, conditioning is primarily aerobic and athletic in nature (see Figure 2-5). The athletes have the choice of two different categories of conditioning sessions: general conditioning activities, or athletic conditioning exercises.

General Conditioning Activities 20-30 mins.	Athletic Conditioning Exercises
• Stationary Bike • Treadmill • Stair Stepper • Nordic Trak • Rower	• Basketball – full or half court • Racquetball • Handball • Tennis • In Line Skating • Any sport activity non related to your specific sport is acceptable

Figure 2-5. Rejuvenation conditioning options

Aerobic activities are considered general conditioning activities. These activities include long-distance jogging, stair climbing, stationary bike riding, stationary rowing, treadmill work, and using other endurance machines available to the athlete. This workout should last between 20 and 30 minutes.

Athletic conditioning exercises are considered nonsport-specific activities. Athletes should be encouraged to participate in a sport activity not related to their specific sport. Some examples are racquetball, in-line skating, basketball, and handball. Conditioning will become more specific in the later programs of the annual plan. Conditioning during this phase should be 2 to 3 times per week. The athletes choose how many times per week they condition, as well as what activities they partake in.

• The Secondary Rejuvenation Stage

A secondary rejuvenation stage can occur during the annual plan. This stage would usually occur after a strength-testing period or during semester- or quarter-ending classroom examination weeks.

The Developmental Stage

The developmental stage follows the rejuvenation stage. It is the second stage of the annual plan, and continues the building of future champions. This phase can vary between 18 to 30 weeks in duration depending on the sport. The objectives of this phase are to enhance the athlete's level of fitness, strength, flexibility, conditioning, agility, and speed.

This phase should be between one to two times as long as the competitive phase, but in some cases with team sports it might be as short as two to three months. Volume of training is based on the goals of each program.

To simplify matters on program names, the programs during this stage are classified by the seasonal equinoxes of the year (see Figure 2-6). Depending on when the rejuvenation stage ends and the competitive stage begins will determine whether the athlete will be in a spring, summer, fall, or winter developmental program.

Developmental	Programs
Spring Program	March 21st – June 21st
Summer Program	June 22nd – September 22nd
Fall Program	September 23rd – December 21st
Winter Program	December 22nd – March 20th

Figure 2-6. Developmental programs

During this stage, programs designed during the dates March 21 to June 21 will be referred to as spring development. The summer development program will be between June 22 and September 22. The fall development program will be between September 23 and December 21. The winter development program will be between December 21 and March 20.

In some cases, because of the academic calendar and non-competitive practices, a team's program may be a combination of two seasons, or a season may be split in half. For example, consider the members of a football team. During the spring development program, the athlete has to compete in spring practice, followed by semester exams. A 10 to12 week program leading to the beginning of two-a-day practices generally follows this. Based on this model's approach to long-term planning, this scenario would be broken down into three programs. The athlete would participate in a spring I development program, followed by a secondary rejuvenation stage, and then a spring II/summer development program that would carry him through the second half of spring and the first half of summer.

The objectives of the early developmental stage programs are to increase the athlete's work capacity and general physical preparation, and to improve technical and basic skills. General as well as specific strength training exercises that will enhance athletic ability in the sport should have a higher priority than the specific skills that are required for the individual's success in that sport. This may change if a spring or fall practice schedule is implemented during this stage.

The length of a program and the specific goals of the running program will determine the type of strength training that will be implemented during this stage. The running sessions during this stage are geared toward the goals of the specific program. Most of the drills will include linear runs, change-of-direction drills, and interval training. It is also a time where technique and basic running mechanics are focused on.

During the latter part of the developmental stage, the athlete is making the progression to the competitive stage. Therefore, the type of program designed is more specific to the needs of the athlete's sport.

Most of the strength exercises used are directed specifically to improving overall athletic ability. This is done without negating the antagonistic muscle groups that help in balance and stabilization. This is also a good time to implement hybrid exercises into the program. Hybrid exercises allow for greater muscle activation, and in some cases increased range of motion, which is imperative as the athletes get closer to competition.

The majority of exercises implemented should be of high quality and facilitate a general transfer of movement patterns for the individual to have a maximum training effect. Hopefully, this will develop an optimal link between skills developed in strength training and running sessions, and the position-specific skills of the sport.

Running during the latter part of this stage is geared toward sport-specific movement patterns and anaerobic interval programs that pertain to the energy system of that sport. During this type of running program it is imperative that the S/C coach coordinate with the sport coach for drills and movement actions of the specific sport.

The Competitive Stage

During the competitive stage, the goal is to continue to improve on the level of physical preparation developed during the developmental stage. Although this is a difficult task come championship time, the goal is to have the best-prepared and conditioned teams on the field or court. The objectives of the competitive stage are achieved through competitions, sport-specific skills and exercises, and strength training.

The overall volume of work for the strength-training program during the competitive stage is reduced minimally. The goal is to continue to drive the athlete to improve strength during this stage. Actual practice sessions are now the focal point of training, with the strength session secondary. The duration of this phase could be between three and five (or more) months, depending on the sport.

The competitive stage is broken down into three programs. This stage will begin with a preseason program, followed by an in season program. If a team is fortunate to play in a NCAA event, bowl game, or play-off game this will be considered the Championship Season program.

• The Preseason Program

The goal of the preseason program is to have the athlete participate in scrimmages and exhibition meets. This will allow the sport coach and the S/C coach to evaluate and assess the athlete or team's level of preparation for the main competitions.

During this program, strength training is either metabolic circuit (movement) based or standard training sessions. This determination is dependent on the length of the program and the team's practice schedule.

The implementation of a metabolic circuit will occur for sports that include two-a-day practices during this program. Metabolic circuits are implemented because of the amount of work done during practice. These circuits are four to six exercises long, based on movements that will help in flexibility and muscle recovery. Volume, intensity, and time are decreased in a circuit. This can help give the athlete more time to recover between practices during this strenuous period. Conditioning is sport specific and handled on the field, court, or mat if necessary.

• The In Season Program

The in season program is dedicated to the elevation of the skills and performance for the specific sport of choice. Strength training exercises during this program are geared toward speed and strength development.

The number of strength training sessions per week is dependent on competitions that an athlete participates in. Depending on the competition schedule, two to three strength-training sessions per week are recommended, with three being optimal. The goal of the strength-training program is to exceed the amount of strength developed during the developmental stage. Conditioning is handled on the field, court, or mat.

• The Championship Season Program

The championship season program will be a continuation of the in season program if tournaments, play-offs, or bowl preparation begins right after the in season. If there is a break between the last in-season competition and the first competition of the championship season (usually four weeks for a bowl game), the athlete will train similar to the program during the developmental stage until approximately 10 to 14 days before the competition. With a longer period of time between competitions, raising the volume during the first two weeks of training will help increase work capacity and further enhance the overall conditioning levels of the athlete.

For step-by-step instructions on how to establish an annual training plan, refer to Appendix A.

3

Training Cycles

Basic Terminology

Volume is a measurement of the total amount of repetitions. This can be per movement, per training session, per week, per month, or per year.

Intensity is the percentage of load based on an athlete's repetition maximum of a performed exercise. This book refers to this as training intensity.

When the three main training stages and specific programs have been established, it is now time to set the specific training goals for each time period. It is recommended in an athletic-based model that strength-training goals per program be based on the goals of the running plan for the same time period. It is truly important that the goals of both areas, running and strength training must coincide for the training results to be successful. The running plan established for this model of strength training has four categories of emphasis: plyometrics/speed development (category 1), metabolic conditioning/practice (category 2), anaerobic conditioning/interval training (category 3), and general conditioning (category 4). Depending on the running category that is emphasized for a particular period, the strength-training cycle will have similar goals.

For example, say a football team trains at a high volume of yardage during the first training cycle of the spring II/summer program, category 3. The volume per workout is usually between 2200 and 2500 yards. Because the demands on the body are quite different than the shorter and more explosive emphasis of our plyometric/speed development program, it would be counterproductive to train the athlete in the strength program at a lower-volume, high-intensity cycle. This would not lead to optimal results. The strength program for this running plan should emphasize high-volume training to stimulate local muscle endurance to areas of the body that are being trained.

Cycle training is one of the foundations for a successful annual plan. It is the systematic scheme of increasing an athletes' strength from a base point A to a higher-level point B over a designated period of time.

Micros, Mesos, and Macros

Microcycles

The microcycle represents the smallest unit of measurement in our annual plan's development of strength-training cycles. The microcycle is an individual training week. Microcycles are based on a Sunday through Saturday workweek. This weekly structure allows for the variations of exercises, volume, intensity, and frequency for each individual training session of the week. Blocking the days per week into a microcycle allows for the tracking of the total number of training sessions, as well as weekly averages in volume and intensity.

Individual microcycles have been named based on the type of training for the week. There are six different types of training blocks that can define a weekly training period.

Base

A base microcycle refers to the first week of the cycle. This week may also be considered an introduction microcycle. During this week new training goals, the addition of new exercises, or both are implemented into the program.

Load

Depending on the type of cycle being implemented, the next one or two microcycles will be considered load microcycles. During this microcycle, the training intensity is increased from the previous week. Load microcycles will have the highest total volume and intensity of a mesocycle (see the section on mesocycles later in this chapter). When two load weeks follow each other, they will increase in a step-load progression based on training intensity.

Unload

This is a recovery/regeneration microcycle. It is strategically placed following base and load microcycles to give the athlete the ability to recover. This block is implemented to restore energy, remove fatigue, and to relax psychologically. During unload weeks, the sets, reps, or both are decreased per training session.

Performance

The performance microcycle is an evaluation week. The athlete will be tested in specific exercises/drills identified for that particular sport. The number of tests performed is based on the particular goals of the performance microcycle and where it falls in the annual plan.

Competition

The competition microcycle involves the athletes participating in actual competitions for their sport. These microcycles may fall in succession, every other week, or once every several weeks, depending on the sport.

Variation

The variation microcycle can follow a performance microcycle or can be implemented during the rejuvenation stage of the annual plan. This is an unload microcycle, implementing a variety of exercises not included in the athlete's specific training program. The type of training performed during a variation block is usually a circuit or a program that is atypical to the tier system. The implementation of a variation microcycle into the developmental stage usually means a transition from one cycle to another, a program change, or a stage change.

Active Rest

The active rest microcycle is a cycle where the athlete is not required to participate in strength-training workouts. Sometimes it is necessary to give the athlete complete rest from strength training to ensure recovery. Generally, five to seven days of rest will not affect the athlete's strength levels. After seven days, the athlete may begin to detrain and strength levels may begin to diminish. This microcycle is generally implemented during either classroom examinations, after a season, or during holidays. During active rest periods, it is still in the athlete's best interest to engage in some light physical activities.

Both the variation and active rest microcycles may be used as training modes during a secondary rejuvenation period.

Mesocycles

The linking of microcycles together to determine a training effect is considered a mesocycle. Mesocycles vary between two and four weeks in our methodology. The length of the mesocycle is based either on the type of cycle we are implementing or the training level of our athlete. Depending on the strength level of our athletes, or program goals, a standard four-week or two-week mesocycle will be implemented.

Optimally, when using intensity-based cycles, four-week mesocycles work more efficiently.

Basic Intensity Cycles

There are six types of training effects (see Figure 3-1) that can be chosen from for a specific cycle. The type of training cycle that will be implemented depends on the specific goals and needs of the program. Each cycle type has a specific role in the physical development of an athlete. Also, depending on the cycle used, a corresponding set scheme is implemented.

Strength Cycle	Training Range	Total Body Reps per Set*	Total Body Volume	Lower/ Upper Body Reps per Set	Lower/ Upper Body Volume
General Conditioning	60% - 67.5%	6	18	10	30
Strength Endurance	60% - 67.5% 70% - 77.5%	5-6 4-6	30 24	12-15 8-10	60-90 40-60
Developmental Strength	70% - 77.5% 80% - 87.5%	4-6 2-4	24 20	6-10 3-6	20-48 12-30
Metabolic Strength	80% - 87.5% 90% - 95%	Cluster Cluster	20 10	Cluster Cluster	15-30 10-15
Explosive Strength*	55% - 65% 70% - 75%	3-6 3-6	18-30 12-24	3-6 3-6	18-30 12-24
Maximum Strength	90+%	1-2 or **Multiple Rep Max**	4-10	1-3 or **Multiple Rep Max**	3-12

Figure 3-1. Basic intensity cycles for foundation exercises

• General Conditioning (Gen-C)

A general conditioning cycle is implemented when introducing strength training to novice participants or athletes coming off of serious injury. It is incorporated to keep the load low and the repetitions at a range where proper technique and execution can be stressed for strength-training exercises. We use a stable three-set scheme for gen-C. This is a three-set cycle with the same load and repetitions per set (see Figure 3-2).

• Strength Endurance (S-End)

A strength endurance cycle is implemented when there is a need for local muscular endurance during training. The volume is high and serves as a base for higher-intensity training. S-end training is an excellent progression for newcomers after they have gone through the technique development from a gen-C cycle. Also, S-end training may be used for athletes who need to add additional muscle mass. S-end training is also implemented when the running plan is conditioning based with a high volume of yardage. A descending set cycle is used for strength endurance. The highest training intensity for the session is performed first, and then each set after is decreased by 2.5%. The repetitions stay the same (see Figure 3-2).

Gen-Cond Stable 3	S-End Descending	Dev-S Advanced	Max-S Progressive	Met-S Cluster	Exp-S Prilepin
65% x 10	65.0% x 12	82.5% x 4	67.5% x 3	82.5% x 4cl-20	75% x 3
65% x 10	62.5% x 12	82.5% x 4	72.5% x 3	82.5% x 4cl-20	75% x 3
65% x 10	60.0% x 12	82.5% x 4	77.5% x 3	82.5% x 4cl-20	75% x 3
	57.5% x 12	82.5% x 4	82.5% x 5	82.5% x 4cl-20	75% x 3
	55.0% x 12	82.5% x 4	82.5% x 5	82.5% x 4cl-20	75% x 3
	52.5% x 12	82.5% x 4	82.5% x 5	82.5% x 4cl-20	75% x 3
					75% x 3
					75% x 3

Figure 3-2. Set and rep schemes

• Developmental Strength (Dev-S)

Developmental strength is the primary strength mode of the developmental stage during traditional training. The volume is lower than the S-end cycle, while the average intensity is slightly higher. The dev-S cycle will prepare the athlete for the conversion to either the more rigorous maximum strength or explosive strength cycles. The two primary set schemes for this mesocycle are advanced stable or progressive stable sets. The advanced stable scheme is a six-set cycle, where intensity and repetitions stay the same. The progressive stable scheme is also a six-set cycle where the first three sets ascend to the top three sets, which are performed for the top training intensity of the day, and the reps remain the same. The repetitions of the first three sets are usually half the volume of the top sets (see Figure 3-2).

• Metabolic Strength (Met-S)

In most competitive sports, the ability to maintain a high level of strength, play after play or point after point, is critical. Most sports have multiple bouts of exercise followed by a short rest period in between. The athletes who can recover the fastest between rest intervals and maintain the highest level of strength are usually the ones who will win the battles. The met-S cycle takes this into account by using a set/rep principle called a cluster. A cluster set is one in which each rep of the set is an individual rep, with a short rest time between. For example, some use a 20 to 35 second rest in within a cluster, with a 90 to 120 second rest in between sets. This allows the athlete a short recovery period followed by an all-out single at a particular load. Cluster sets are primarily used as sets of 3 to 5 reps, but for testing purposes, a cluster set could go as high as 10 to 15 reps. The set and rep cycle is similar to the advanced stable scheme, with the exception of the rest period between reps (see Figure 3-2).

• Explosive Strength (Exp-S)

Synonymous with power, the explosive strength cycle is a low to moderate intensity phase. Speed of movement is a strong factor in our program. We try to develop many different types of strength. The goal is not how much the athlete can move, but how fast. Training cycles are primarily based on the Prilepin table (see Figures 3-2, 3-3, and 3-4).

PERCENT - RANGE	REPS per SET	OPTIMAL VOLUME	VOLUME - RANGE
55-65	3-6	24	18-30
70-75	3-6	18	12-24
80-85	2-4	15	10-20
90+	1-2	7	4-10

Figure 3-3. Prilepin table

%	Reps per Set	Volume Low	2 sets	3 sets	4 sets	5 sets	6 sets	7 sets	8 sets	9 sets	10 sets
55-65	3t6	18		x6			x3				
70-75	3t6	12	x6	x4	x3						
80-85	2t4	10				x2					
90+	1t2	4	x2		x1						
%	Reps per Set	Volume Optimal	2 sets	3 sets	4 sets	5 sets	6 sets	7 sets	8 sets	9 sets	10 sets
55-65	3t6	24			x6		x4		x3		
70-75	3t6	18		x6			x3				
80-85	2t4	15				x3					
90+	1t2	7						x1			
%	Reps per Set	Volume High	2 sets	3 sets	4 sets	5 sets	6 sets	7 sets	8 sets	9 sets	10 sets
55-65	3t6	30				x6	x5				x3
70-75	3t6	24			x6		x4		x3		
80-85	2t4	20				x4					x2
90+	1t2	10				x2					x1

Figure 3-4. Prilepin set rep chart

Some terms that are often mentioned in the context of the explosive strength cycle are:

Starting strength—the measurement of how fast and forceful the athletic motion is at the beginning. The ability to turn on as many muscle fibers as possible instantaneously. Starting strength can be improved by implementing a pause at the midpoint of movements. This takes away any momentum of the eccentric phase and makes the athlete develop a forceful motion at this position of the exercise.

Explosive strength—is the greatest amount of force developed in a very brief time period. The athlete's ability to leave the muscle fibers turned on over a longer period of time

Speed-strength—how well an athlete applies force with speed. A combination of starting strength and explosive strength. Speed in more vital over strength.

Strength-speed—rapid movements against heavy loads. Strength is more vital than speed.

During this cycle, the focus is on increasing bar velocity and acceleration, and improving speed of movement. The goal is for the athlete to apply a maximum amount of force to the resistance and move it as fast as possible during the concentric phase of the exercise. A coaching point during this or any other type of training cycle is preaching maximum concentric or progressive acceleration on all movements, but during this type of training this is the absolute goal.

• Maximum Strength (Max-S)

Maximum strength training is used when the goal is to improve repetition maximums. The one-repetition max is preferred by some because it is the only true indicator of what athletes can accomplish as their limit in a specific exercise. It is understood that many coaches may not feel comfortable with this and they may choose a repetition maximum and calculate an estimated one-rep max. An advanced or progressive stable set cycle is used during this mesocycle (see Figure 3-2).

Macrocycles

Once recognized as the entire training year, macrocycles are defined as the linking of two or more four-week mesocycles within the same training program. These types of cycles are usually found in the traditional cycling plan. Macrocycles generally occur during the developmental stage, when there is a long uninterrupted training block. A macrocycle may also occur during the competitive stage, when there are successive competitions weekly. Long-term cycles such as macrocycles are usually used when the training age is low or to establish a solid strength base before graduating to a more advanced design. In a macrocycle, each four-week block has a specific type of strength that is focused on.

Four types of training cycles can be implemented within the tier system's annual plan. They are the traditional cycle, the performance cycle, the elite cycle, and the performance elite cycle. The goals of the program, the training level of the athlete, or both determine the choice of cycle.

The Traditional Cycle (TTC)

The traditional cycle (see Figure 3-5) follows our interpretation of the modified progressive overload principle as well as typical traditional periodization. For a muscle to increase strength, it must be stressed beyond its present capacity. The overload (resistance) must be progressed gradually over time with a built-in time for recovery (reduction in load and volume) so the athlete can adjust to the increased demands placed on the body without fatigue, staleness, overtraining, or all of the above becoming an issue.

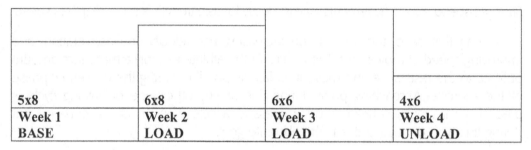

5x8	6x8	6x6	4x6
Week 1	Week 2	Week 3	Week 4
BASE	LOAD	LOAD	UNLOAD

Figure 3-5. Four-week TTC mesocycle

A traditional cycle is usually a long-term cycle that gradually progresses the athlete to a higher level of strength. A traditional macrocycle will usually consist of two to three four-week mesocycles progressing the athlete from a high-volume, lower-intensity phase to a low volume, high- intensity phase (see Figure 3-6). Unload weeks occur at every fourth week (adding in a week of recovery and regeneration), as the athlete makes the transition to the next cycle.

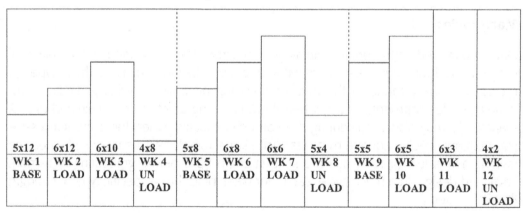

5x12	6x12	6x10	4x8	5x8	6x8	6x6	5x4	5x5	6x5	6x3	4x2
WK 1	WK 2	WK 3	WK 4	WK 5	WK 6	WK 7	WK 8	WK 9	WK 10	WK 11	WK 12
BASE	LOAD	LOAD	UN LOAD	BASE	LOAD	LOAD	UN LOAD	BASE	LOAD	LOAD	UN LOAD

Figure 3-6. 12-week TTC macrocycle

• The Complete Cycle

A complete cycle (see Figure 3-7) is a traditional cycle that has a performance microcycle and a variation microcycle following a four-week block of training that includes a base, two loads, and an unload microcycle. The length of a complete cycle can be either six weeks (1 mesocycle), 10 weeks (2 mesocycles), 14 weeks (3 mesocycles), or 18 weeks (4 mesocycles).

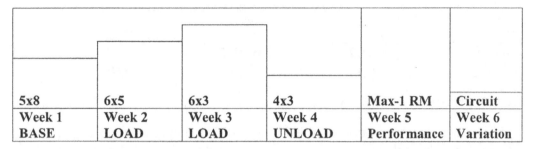

5x8	6x5	6x3	4x3	Max-1 RM	Circuit
Week 1	Week 2	Week 3	Week 4	Week 5	Week 6
BASE	LOAD	LOAD	UNLOAD	Performance	Variation

Figure 3-7. Six-week complete cycle

An incomplete cycle is a cycle in which the program planner has to restructure or eliminate elements of the complete cycle. This is done when there are an odd number of weeks to work with. In the traditional cycle all assistance movements follow the same repetition scheme as the foundation exercise for that particular movement category.

For example, if the rep scheme for a lower-body foundation movement is 12 reps per set, all other lower-body movements are performed for 12 reps per set. One four-week mesocycle in the traditional approach has one goal, either strength endurance, base strength, explosive strength, or maximum strength.

First-year athletes and those who have a low training age primarily use traditional cycles. The traditional approach of cycling, where there is one strength goal focused on per mesocycle, prepares the athlete both mentally and physically for the more advanced training that will follow.

This cycle is also used during periods where the emphasis of the running plan is high volume. Traditional cycles are used to develop a solid foundation before embarking on our advanced training cycles.

The Performance Cycle (PTC)

The performance cycle (see Figure 3-8) is also a four-week-based cycle, but these cycles do not have to be linked together as in the traditional cycle model. When implementing a PTC, there is anticipation of a new record being achieved during week-four training sessions. This record is usually a multiple repetition maximum based on a training intensity from a previous one-repetition maximum. If the athlete is "on," the coach may decide to go off the designated plan for the session and go after a new one-repetition maximum. This cycle along, with its elite counterpart, are the primary cycles implemented during the developmental stage of the annual plan for advanced athletes.

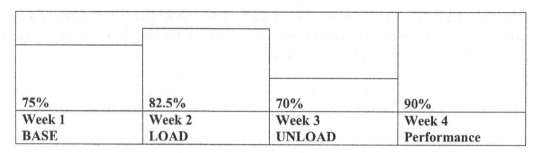

75%	82.5%	70%	90%
Week 1	Week 2	Week 3	Week 4
BASE	LOAD	UNLOAD	Performance

Figure 3-8. Four-week PTC mesocycle

The major difference between the TTC and PTC occurs in weeks 3 and 4. In the TTC, week 3 is the highest training intensity of the cycle, with week 4 being the unload week. In the PTC, week 3 is the unload week following the week 2 loading. Also in the PTC, the unload week is strategically placed at week 3 because the coach is preparing the athlete for week 4 performance tests. During the performance microcycle several (1 to 3) movements can be evaluated for record purposes. The similarity of the two cycles is based on the repetition scheme for all exercises of the same movement category. They are identical throughout the microcycle. Performance cycles are based on the training methodology of United States Weightlifting.

The Elite Cycles

The elite cycles are based on a non-traditional cyclical approach. Within one microcycle/mesocycle, strength endurance, explosive strength, and developmental or maximum strength training methods will be trained together. This may be the ideal way to train the advanced athlete because in traditional periodization, the athlete does not maintain/improve on the progress of the previous cycle.

It has been determined that all these types of strength are interwoven together to achieve success, so why not train them at the same time, rather than separate four-week blocks? The non-traditional approach allows the athlete to continue to improve elements of each type of strength without having to totally switch priorities, therefore losing the desired effects of past training cycles.

For example, in a 12-week traditional approach, weeks 1 to 4 would generally be a strength endurance cycle, while weeks 9 to 12 would be a maximum strength cycle. By the time the athletes reach week 9, the benefits of weeks 1 to 4 would be minimal at best. In a non-traditional approach, depending on the rotation of the daily session, each movement category has a different training goal. Low-volume, high-intensity work; high-volume, low-intensity work; and explosive training are all included into a microcycle.

The elite cycles are based on a three-emphasis rotation of cycles: effort, speed, and volume. Each is performed every training session with a corresponding movement category. The elite cycles (advanced elite in particular) are based on the conjugated periodization approach used by Westside Barbell Club.

• Effort Cycles

Effort exercises are of two different types: percentage-based and repetition-max-based. The percentage-based cycle is based on the foundation movements of our program. For the advanced elite cycle some rotate supplemental exercises every two weeks trying to set new records for a prescribed amount of repetitions. These repetitions are usually between 1 and 5. This is the only difference between the performance elite and advanced elite cycles.

The Performance Elite Cycle (PETC)

The performance elite cycle (see Figure 3-9) is similar to the PTC, with the exception of the sets and rep schemes. Foundation rather than supplemental movements are used for the PETC. For the PETC, the sets and rep schemes come from the Prilepin volume table. The Prilepin table is based on a rep-per-set scheme that optimizes the greatest amount of speed and strength per set (see Figure 3-3).

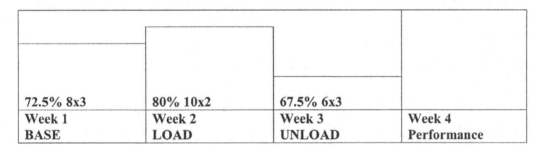

72.5% 8x3	80% 10x2	67.5% 6x3	
Week 1	Week 2	Week 3	Week 4
BASE	LOAD	UNLOAD	Performance

Figure 3-9. Four-week PETC mesocycle

The Prilepin table is used for all of the total-body-based percentage cycles. Prilepin discovered that when athletes perform more than the maximum allowed reps per set at a certain percentage, the bar speed slowed and power output decreased (see Figure 3-4). When using this table for the PETC, it is recommended that athletes train at the high end of the volume scale.

• The Advanced Elite Cycle (ETC)

The advanced elite cycle is based on a two-week mesocycle for effort exercises (see Figure 3-10). By rotating exercises bimonthly, a high level of training (90% and above) can be maintained for a greater period of time than by traditional means of training. In a traditional outline, after training at 90% or above for three weeks on the same exercise, the athlete will begin to reach a state of diminishing returns.

	Floor Press		Board Press		Close Gr Bench		Stand Press		Incline Press
Floor Press Effort 1	Effort 1	Board Press Effort 2	Effort 2	Close Gr Bench Effort 3	Effort 3	Stand Press Effort 4	Effort 4	Incline Press Effort 5	Effort 5
WK 1 Intro	WK 2 Max	WK 1 Intro	WK 2 Max	WK 1 Intro	WK 2 Max	WK 1 Intro	WK 2 Max	WK 1 Intro	WK 2 Max

Figure 3-10. Multiple rotation of ETC – upper body

The advanced elite cycle is primarily used during the competitive stage of training. It may be used during the developmental stage of training when the athlete has sports practice, or for the highly trained athlete who has been in an organized program for three-plus years.

Depending on the emphasis of the program, the effort exercise is either the first or second emphasis of the daily/weekly plan. Week one introduces the exercise to the athlete, and they work for a higher repetition maximum. Week two's work is based on the repetition max set done the previous week or from a previous record set. The athletes continue to increase the load until they can no longer achieve the repetition goal (see Figure 3-11).

Week 1 Total/Lower Body	Week 2 Total/Lower Body	Week 1 Upper Body	Week 2 Upper Body
Set 1 – x3-5	Set 1 - x3	Set 1 - x5	Set 1 - x3
Set 2 – x3-5	Set 2 - x3	Set 2 - x5	Set 2 - x3
Set 3 – x3-5	Set 3 - x3	Set 3 - x5	Set 3 - x3
Set 4 – x3-5	Set 4 – x1-3	Set 4 - x3	Set 4 - x1
Set 5 – x3-5	Set 5 – x1-3	Set 5 - x3	Set 5 - x1
Set 6 – x3-5	Set 6 – x1-3	Set 6 - x3	Set 6 - x1

Figure 3-11. Repetition cycle for effort exercises

The total/lower body cycle begins with week one working up to a three- or five-repetition maximum. Week two, the athlete works up to a one or three repetition maximum based on the movement choice. The upper body cycle begins with week one working up to a three- repetition maximum. Week two, the athlete works up to a one to three repetition maximum.

In the case that the athletes do not set a new record from a previous training session, that is ok. They still must work to the heaviest load they can for that particular session. This is based on the maximum effort philosophy. Athletes must work to the highest level they can achieve on that particular day regardless if it is a record or not.

After the movement and repetition maximum are recorded, when the athletes return to a repeated movement, their goal is to break the previous cycles repetition record. Again, by rotating the movements every two weeks, athletes are able to stay above a 90% workload longer than the usual three weeks under traditional cycling principles. This will allow them to maintain a higher level of maximum strength throughout the annual plan. The supplemental movements used for effort are chosen based on their importance of improving the maximum strength of our foundation movements. It is recommended using this approach to rotate three exercises per lower and upper body.

Speed

The speed emphasis comes from the definition of the explosive strength cycle. Similar to the effort cycle, this will be either the first or second emphasis of the training session based on the goals of the program. Speed cycles are set up as three-week waves for total- and lower-body movements and as two-week cycles for upper-body movements (see Figure 3-12). Exercises used for speed training are total body (dead lift, power clean from the deck, or high pull from the deck), lower body (pause squat or box squat), and upper body (bench press with varied grips). During the movement, the athlete's goal is to move non-maximal loads with the greatest amount of speed possible.

Week	Total Body	Squat	Bench - bands	Bench - chains	Bench - naked
One	8-10x1 @ 60-65%	5-8x2 @ 45-50%	8x3 @ 45-50%	8x3 @ 50-55%	8x3 @ 55-60%
Two	8-10x1 @ 65-70%	5-8x2 @ 47.5-52.5%	8x3 @ 45-50%	8x3 @ 50-55%	8x3 @ 55-60%
Three	8-10x1 @ 70-75%	5-8x2 @ 50-55%			

Figure 3-12. Speed cycle chart

The total body movements incorporated in the program are usually referred to as the explosive movements, but by utilizing maximum concentric acceleration with lower- and upper-body movements, an explosive action can be created with these lifts also. Maximum concentric acceleration is a principle in which the athlete performs a repetition with a controlled negative and then accelerates the bar from midpoint through the concentric portion of the lift. By using this method of training, coaches are improving the efficiency of the movement.

Based on Dr. Fred Hatfield's compensatory acceleration training (CAT), this method of training results in athletes not backing down when their leverages improve. When performing this type of training, the athletes are giving maximum effort throughout the full range of motion of the concentric portion of the lift. Obviously, right before the completion of the lift, the bar must begin to decelerate to avoid injury. This is much different from the tempo type of training that most bodybuilders use to maximize the hypertrophy (muscle building) effects of strength training.

Another principle used in our goal of increasing explosive strength output is accommodating resistance. During this type of training, chains, bands, or both are used to overload the top end of the exercises. Based on biomechanics, the athlete is stronger in limited range of motion movements, especially at lock out. The author implements the use of chains and bands during squat and bench press training to help the athlete develop bar acceleration throughout a greater range of motion during the concentric phase of the movement. As the bar gets closer to completion, the athlete is in a much more advantageous position for overload. Bar weight alone will lead to a longer deceleration phase because of the progressive speed being built. The added load as leverages improve allows the athlete to continue to accelerate the bar longer while the resistance is getting heavier at lockout. By increasing the acceleration phase of the movement, coaches are able to increase the rate of force development through a greater range of motion.

Chains unload at the midpoint of the movement and load during the ascent phase of the movement, allowing the athlete to accelerate a lighter load at the midpoint and drive through a heavier load at lockout. The bands continue to keep added resistance on the bar, which also allows the athlete to build up rapid eccentric strength. This creates a stretch reflex component similar to plyometric training, as well as increasing the resistance (load) at the top end of the movement. The training age and strength level of the athlete determines the amount of added resistance from either chains or bands.

Volume

The volume emphasis is the third emphasis of the rotation. The rep range is based on the S-end mesocycle guidelines. Volume work complements the overall training program. Most exercises used for volume training are chosen based on their ability to improve range of motion and joint integrity. The types of exercises used for this cycle are based on the stage of training the team is in. In some cases, sets may be done to momentary muscular failure but most of the time the load and rep scheme are set so the athlete has 1 to 2 reps left.

By combining all three types of strength development into one training session/one microcycle, the coach allows the athlete to prepare the body in a better functional training plan that will enhance his abilities and levels of strength in a highly efficient way, when compared to traditional cycling. Although both cycle models are used, the non-traditional approach has the ability to produce a higher productive training mode for the advanced level athletes.

See Appendix B for examples of actual training cycles.

4

The Tier System

The objective when developing the tier system was to create an athletic-based strength-training model for athletes. This system of training would focus on the athletic ability and development of football players, basketball players, track and field athletes, gymnasts, wrestlers, and any other athlete who uses strength training as one of the focal points for improved performance. This training system was developed to replace the more common protocols that were based on models and principles of the three strength disciplines, weight lifting, powerlifting, and bodybuilding. Training in a particular discipline's modality may be counterproductive to the overall development of athletes. The goals of the three disciplines are extremely different from one another, let alone the goals of high school, college, and professional sport programs.

Of course, one must realize that these three disciplines play an important role in the development of athletes who participate in sports. In any sport, strength is a key ingredient and is extremely valuable to the athlete's improved performance. Every high school, college, and professional S/C coach across the country is using exercises and training methods of these disciplines to help enhance athletes' ability to succeed.

One of the many goals and objectives of the tier system was to evaluate the principles and protocols of all three disciplines and develop a model of training that would enhance an athlete's strength level to help improve overall athletic ability. Each strength discipline has an important influence in the development of an athlete if used in combination with one another and utilized in a thought-out approach.

The tier system model is based on using exercises and principles from all three disciplines integrated within one program. One aspect of the tier system is training the athlete on a rotation of movements rather than body parts. Exercises are classified in three main classifications and then further categorized within the main categories.

In brief, there are three major movements that can be accomplished during a specific exercise: total body, lower body, or upper body. Exercises are evaluated by what joints are involved during the execution of a movement and placed into one of these three categories. Movement planes, limb involvement, and movement actions further break down exercises.

A second aspect of the tier system is the "whole body" approach to training sessions. Although the majority of the exercises would be the same, this style of training is atypical relative to the split routines commonly seen in athletic strength training today. Split routines usually have alternating lower- and upper-body training days, with a day off in between. One of the tier system's training principles is based on body action. Since most physical activity involves using a synchronized movement pattern from the ankle to the neck joint in almost every task, why wouldn't the athlete want to train the body in a similar manner? In one training session, movements that revolve around developing the whole body are implemented into each session.

The tier system is primarily a multijoint movement program. Athletic movement is made up of multiple joint actions of muscles. Although single-joint or isolation exercises are important in developing muscles that stabilize movements or in assisting with other muscle actions, they are not as important in the tier system format as multijointed, whole-body movements. This is why single-joint or isolation movements are primarily used during auxiliary training.

Prior to 1998, four functions of the tier system were to:

- Rotate the order of exercises based on movement and strength developed.
- Implement a variety of exercises to develop the prime movers of the sport at numerous joint angles.
- Prioritize these exercises based on the type of movement and strength developed, and place them in order of importance.
- Control volume by regulating the number of work sets that can be performed based on the level of tier and type of exercise that coincides with it.

Although the approach now is similar, these four points of emphasis have changed slightly. The term "strength developed" is used in both the first and third items in the bulleted list and needs to be examined more closely. Like most programs, this program was built around the distinction that there are slow, nonexplosive lifts and fast, explosive lifts. Explosive lifts were those from the sport of weight lifting, and nonexplosive lifts came from powerlifting and bodybuilding.

As the program evolved, the implementation of the principles of the rate of force development, compensatory acceleration, maximum concentric acceleration, and progressive acceleration became greater, it was determined that the athlete could train any exercise as fast or as slow as needed. It was found that any exercise can be trained as fast or as slow as needed based on applying a great amount of force against a given resistance. Since this has been added to the development of the athlete and program, the terms "explosive" and "nonexplosive" have been dropped because one of the primary objectives for athletic strength development is to move the load as fast a possible during the concentric phase of the movement. Athletes should be specifically told what the speed of movement is going to be before attempting the exercise for the prescribed number of repetitions.

Also, in terms of movement speed, as athletes were evaluated during this new training outlook, the 85% rule was established. This rule states that regardless of how you classify a movement (fast or slow), after the athlete reaches approximately 85% intensity or higher on a particular movement, the concentric portion slows down anyway. This was the main reason the term explosive movement was changed to total-body movement.

When the slow, nonexplosive lifts and fast, explosive lifts categories were restructured, this also changed a major factor in the rotation of exercises. When the tier System was being developed, a conditioning aspect was built into the program in reference to explosive movements. In most strength training protocols, it is said that you should train fast movements before slow movements. Although this sounded logical for weightlifters, most athletes need to perform multiple explosive types of movements over a long duration of time. That is why explosive movements were rotated throughout the microcycle, to train fast under a state of fatigue.

As most football coaches will say, "We need to be explosive in the fourth quarter." The fourth quarter is the final 15 minutes of the game; no mention of the first quarter usually occurs in staff meetings. Now we train every movement with special attention to concentric bar speed.

In the second bullet point, the main training sessions were strictly based on what was perceived as the prime movers of the sport. This was more of a focus on upper-body movements. Since most sports are pushing dominant (wrestling would be and exception), all upper-body movements were predominately pressing movements. Stabilization, antagonistic work, or both were usually saved for the auxiliary training program. The focus now is more on a balanced relationship between pulling and pressing movements. This is based on repetition volume per microcycle.

As mentioned in the fourth bullet point, volume control was primarily based on our traditional approach to cycling, where repetitions were matched for each exercise per movement category. Volume control is still a precedent, but we now monitor volume by both exercise order and the type of strength being developed.

As the system has evolved, the four new functions of the tier system are:

- Rotate the order of exercise based on movement.
- Implement a variety of movements to train in numerous planes within a microcycle.
- Prioritize movements based on big movements and functional movements.
- Control volume by exercise order and emphasis on specific strength developed.

Big movements refer to barbell exercises that activate a large amount of muscle action. Functional movements focus on independent limb action. Without developing a solid strength base in the big exercises, it would be hard to utilize functional exercises as a means to increasing athletic ability.

Some examples of lower body big exercises are the back squat and the front squat. Some examples of lower body functional exercises are the lung and the step-up.

The Tier Programs

The tier system revolves around three main training sessions per microcycle. These sessions are primarily rotated in either a Monday, Wednesday, and Friday, or a Tuesday, Thursday, and Saturday schedule. Auxiliary programs (discussed later) may be included into the microcycle at the coach's, athlete's, or both's discretion.

There are two main training templates developed around the tier system philosophy: a three-day template and a two-day template. The two-day template is used primarily during the competitive stage for sports that have multiple competitions during a microcycle. This template is used when it is unlikely that the athlete will be able to participate in strength training for the typical three sessions.

What Is a Tier?

The simplest definition is a tier represents a ranked exercise. In the basic tier programs, a daily training session can consist of three or five tiers. These numbers represent the number of exercises that are to be completed during the main session of the daily plan.

Each tier has four predetermined factors. Three of these factors, movement category, exercise classification, and strength development emphasis, restrict the choice of exercise per tier. The fourth factor is volume. Each tier has a predetermined number of sets prescribed based on the level of the tier and the template being implemented.

Coding the Programs

From a coaching standpoint, the programs are coded to describe the type of tier program being used. Tier programs are named on a number and letter basis. The name of the program is based on the number of days per week the athlete trains, the number of exercises per session, and if there is any auxiliary work that is mandated in the microcycle. Below is a list of tier programs.

3x5	primary program 1
3x3	primary program 2
3[A]x3	
3x3[A]	
3[A]x5	
3x5[A]	
2x3	
2x3[A]	

The first number before the "x" represents the days per week the athlete trains. The second number represents the number of mandatory exercises that are to be completed in the main session of the daily plan. The letter "A" represents auxiliary training. An "A" designation before the "x" tells the coach and athlete that there will be an additional day of training for auxiliary work. An "A" after the "x" tells the coach and athlete that auxiliary work will be completed at the end of the daily plan's main session, as well as the posterior chain movement, before the athlete completes the post-workout routine. For example, each individual tier represents a mandatory exercise. Therefore, a 3x5-tier program tells the coach and athlete that the athlete is performing a strength-training program that involves 3 workouts per week, with 5 mandatory exercises required per training session.

The variations of the 3x5 program are the primary strength-training programs for the tier system. A traditional or elite 3x5 template will be used, depending on the goals of the designated program, the training level of the athlete, or both. These programs are highly utilized during the developmental stage.

3x3 programs are usually used in several ways. One way is during the competitive stage, when the athlete has only one competition per microcycle and 3 training sessions can still be obtained. With the increased demand on skill development, time invested in strength training is decreased, so more attention can be placed on practice and strategic planning. These programs may also be used when training time is reduced because of noncompetitive official practice sessions (for example, spring football practice, fall baseball practice).

Also, using a 3x3 program with auxiliary work after the main session is an ideal way to develop athletes who participate in noncontact sports where they can concentrate on strength development and prehabilitation of specific joints. This is also beneficial for high school athletes who participate in weight training classes that last approximately 45 minutes in duration.

Building a Tier Program

The following subsection will describe how the rotation of the tier programs was developed. The majority of this information is the premise of the traditional template. Several basic changes separate the traditional and elite templates of training.

Developing Movement Categories

• Basic Terminology

Bilateral movement—a barbell, dumbbell, or any other resistance exercise. When performing these movements, the limbs involved work together simultaneously.

Unilateral movement—a barbell, dumbbell, or any other resistance exercise. When performed, these exercises have independent limb action. This can be done by alternating limbs or performing single limb sets.

Exercise Pool

The first step of the program design is to determine which exercises are being considered for a specific program. This list is considered the exercise pool (see Figure 4-1). This is the first process that should be considered when designing a strength program.

There are two questions the program planner must ask when creating the exercise pool: Can I teach it, and do I have the necessary equipment to safely implement this particular exercise? Once you have answered these questions, you can now create *your* pool.

Everyone's pool will be different based on the answers to the above questions. This pool will consist of all the exercises that are being considered for the specific program. This does not necessarily mean all of the exercises will be used, but it allows the program planner to evaluate each exercise and its importance to the program.

In many cases, when designing an athletic-based program, a mini-pool may be developed for a specific program based on a more comprehensive pool. This comprehensive pool should list every exercise plus variations that you can teach and may use at some point in the annual plan. These lists can easily be over 1000 exercises with variations. See Appendix C for an example of a comprehensive exercise pool.

Exercises	Exercises
Power Clean	Jerk
Back Squat	Push Jerk
Bench Press	Push Press
Standing Shoulder Press	Step Up
Front Squat	Lunge
Hang Clean	Bent Over Row
Incline Press	Dumbbell Clean
Dips	Dumbbell Snatch
Pull Ups	Romanian Deadlift
Leg Press	Straight Leg Deadlift
Clean Pull	Incline Press
Power Snatch	Leg Curl
Hang Snatch	Leg Extension
Snatch Pull	Low Back Extension
Triceps Extension	Single Leg Squat
Biceps Curl	Close Grip Bench Press
Dumbbell Bench Press	Dumbbell Incline Press

Figure 4-1. Sample mini-pool

It should also be noted that when reviewing and analyzing the needs of a specific sport, there are some exercises that may not be worth the risk to an athlete. These are exercises that, although may be very good movements, may not be the "best" choice for a particular sport.

For example, in tennis training, although hip extension is a focal movement for the tennis athlete, it may not be in the best interest of the athletes for the coach to have them perform full pull-and-catch movements such as the power clean to help develop hip extension. This exercise may not be worth the risk of injury. The stress to the athlete's wrist from the force of catching the bar in a racked position could lead to injury. The hand and wrist are tremendously important to the tennis athlete, and therefore an alternative exercise may be best suited to enhance hip extension and reduce the risk of injury. The alternative may lie with a dumbbell or barbell power pull or shrug pull where hip extension is still emphasized without the catch phase of a clean movement. These are questions that need to asked and answered when developing athletic-based programs.

In the tier system, any exercise that is being considered for a specific program will be placed into one of three general movement categories (see Figure 4-2). These three categories are total-body, lower- body, and upper-body movements. Once the exercises are placed into one of the three general categories, it is listed as a specific movement based on joint action or movement plane.

Category T	Category L	Category U
Power Clean	Back Squat	Bench Press
Hang Clean	Front Squat	Incline Press
Clean Pull	Leg Press	Close Grip Bench Press
Power Snatch	Step Up	Dumbbell Bench Press
Hang Snatch	Lunge	Dumbbell Incline Press
Snatch Pull	Romanian Deadlift	Standing Shoulder Press
Jerk	Straight Leg Deadlift	Bent Over Row
Push Jerk	Single Leg Squat	Dips
Push Press	Leg Curl	Pull Ups
Dumbbell Clean	Leg Extension	Triceps Extension
Dumbbell Snatch	Low Back Extension	Biceps Curl

Figure 4-2. Sample exercise pool per movement categories

The whole-body training approach is based on having at least one exercise per movement category in each training session. The focus is on movements that will help improve athletic ability and reduce the chance of injury rather than develop specific areas of the body. This type of training is more beneficial for an athlete than typical body-part training.

• Category T—Total-Body Movements

Total-body movements are represented by exercises that involve the following movements: knee extension, hip extension, plantar flexion, and shoulder elevation. Also, flexion and extension of the elbow may be involved in certain exercises. The movement of all these joints at one time in a synchronized fashion is related to the actual movements performed in sports at any level. Total-body exercises are primarily derived from the sport of weightlifting. Total-body exercises are excellent movements for incorporating large-scale muscular activation.

• Category L—Lower-Body Movements

Lower-body movements are represented by exercises that involve the following movements: knee extension, hip extension, and plantar flexion. Lower-body exercises are those exercises that will help increase strength in the lower back, quadriceps, hamstrings, gluteus muscle group, hip extensors, flexors, adductors, and abductors, and the muscles of the lower leg (calf and ankle).

• Category U—Upper Body Movements

Upper-body movements are represented by exercises that involve the following movements: rotation at the shoulder joint, elbow flexion, and extension. Upper-body exercises are those exercises that will help increase strength in the chest, upper back and trapezius, shoulder region, and arms (triceps, biceps, and forearms).

• Movement Categories (Specific)

Once an exercise has been assigned a general category, it is then placed in a specific group within the category. These specific groupings are based on the movement, actions, or both of the exercise.

❑ Category T Exercises

Total-body exercises are grouped into three subcategories: pulling, pushing, or hybrid movements (see Figure 4-3). Pulling movements are categorized as full pull and catch, and extension movements. Full-pull-and-catch movements are similar to classical weightlifting exercises, where the load is caught in the traditional completion of the clean or snatch. Extension movements are completed when hip, knee, and/or ankle (plantar flexion) are fully extended at the completion of the movement. Pulling movements can either begin from the ground or can be partial range of motion exercises.

Pulling	Movements	Pushing	Movements	Hybrids
Full Pull and Catch	Hang Clean	**Presses**	Push Press	Hang Clean/Jerk
	Power Snatch	Unilateral	DB Push Press	Snatch/Overhead Squat
Unilateral	Split Clean			
Extension	Deadlift	**Jerks**	Split Jerk	
	Power Pull		Push Jerk	

Figure 4-3. Category T – exercise breakdown examples

Pushing movements are categorized as either presses or jerks. Exercises are considered pressing movements when the athlete completes the movement with the knees and hips fully extended. In jerk movements, the athlete rebends the knee and hip and catches the load in a flexed-knee position. Both movements are started with a slight bend of the hips and knees to create the initial drive. These exercises are started with the bar racked across the chest and shoulders, or supported on the back and shoulders.

Hybrid movements are those exercises that combine two distinct movements within one repetition. Total-body hybrids always begin with the first movement being a total-body movement. The second movement may be a total-, lower-, or upper-body exercise.

Total body exercises can also be unilateral movements. This can be done with the use of dumbbells for independent limb actions of the arms as well as using a split-catch technique. The split catch is a technique where the athlete splits the legs in a lunge position to catch the clean or snatch, and then recovers to the standing position.

❏ Category L Exercises

There are seven major groupings for lower-body movements. Exercises can be designated as: in place, horizontal, vertical, posterior chain, flexion or extension, and hybrids (see Figure 4-4). In-place, horizontal, and vertical movements are based on leg and foot action. In-place movements are those exercises in which the athlete is in a position where foot placement is in a stable fixed position. These exercises can either be single leg (unilateral) or double leg (bilateral) movements.

In	Place		Horizontal		Vertical	Posterior	Chain	Flexion	Extension	Hybrid
bilateral	Back Squat	forward/ backward	Lunge	Up/Down	Hi Step Up	Bent Leg	Glute Ham Raise	Leg Curl	Leg Extension	Goodmorning/ Back Squat
unilateral	Split Squat	Lateral	45 degree Lunge	Lateral	Xover Step Up	Str Leg	Back Ext			Front Squat/Push Press

Figure 4-4. Category L – exercise breakdown examples

Horizontal and vertical movements are single-leg movements where one foot leaves the ground and moves to a secondary position. Horizontal movements primarily come from variations of lunges, where movements are forward and backward. Vertical movements primarily come from variations of step-ups and step-downs, where movements are up and down and the athlete's movement limb is either stepping up or down from an object.

Movements that occur in the transverse plane or move outside the typical linear paths of forward/backward or up/down are considered lateral variations. These also come from variations of our lunge and step-up progressions.

Posterior chain exercises represent movements that occur at the low back, glutes, hamstrings, and spinal erectors. Posterior chain exercises are also broken down into bent legged or straight legged, and can be either a double- or single-leg movement. In athletics, this area of the body has been overlooked for a long time. Strength in this portion of the power zone is imperative. If the posterior chain, torso/abdominal region (the power zone) is not strong, it does not matter how strong the athlete's limbs are.

Single-joint movements that involve flexion and extension of the hip, knee, and ankle are used during auxiliary training, or during pre/post workout routines when necessary. We prefer to use multiple-joint actions to develop these movements in a more athletic way.

Lower-body hybrids are multiple exercises performed within one repetition, where the first movement is a lower-body movement. The second movement may be a total-, lower-, or upper-body exercise.

❑ Category U Exercises

There are six subcategories for upper-body movements. They are horizontal, vertical, extension, flexion, shoulder rotation, and hybrids (see Figure 4-5).

	Horizontal		Vertical	Extension		Flexion		Shoulder Rotation	Hybrid
Push-Bi	**Bench Pr**	Push-Bi	**Standing Press**	Bilateral	**Pushdown**	Bilateral	**BB Curl**	**Fly**	**Shoulder Press/ Overhead Squat**
Push-Uni	**DB Incline Pr**	Push-Uni	**DB Press**	Unilateral	**DB Extension**	Unilateral	**DB Curl**	**Lateral Raise**	**Upright Row/Overhead Press**
Pull-Bi	**Bent Row**	Pull-Bi	**Pull Down**						
Pull-Uni	**DB Row**	Pull-Uni	**SA Chin**						

Figure 4-5. Category U – exercise breakdown examples

Horizontal and vertical movements are based on arm position from the body's anatomical starting point. Horizontal movements are those movements where the arm is held at approximately 90 degrees from the shoulder joint. When the athlete's arms are at 180 degrees from the shoulder joint, or in the overhead position, these are considered vertical movements.

Differentiating horizontal and vertical pushes or pulls is based on the concentric muscle contraction or positive action of the movement. If the concentric action occurs when the resistance or load is moving away from the body, this is considered a push. When the resistance is coming toward the body, this is considered a pull.

Flexion and extension exercises are single joint movements that occur at the elbow, wrist, and neck. Shoulder rotation exercises include the following movements: elevation, retraction, depression, rotation, protraction, abduction, adduction, and extension of the shoulder region. Most of these exercises will be single-joint movements.

Upper-body hybrids are multiple exercises performed within one repetition, where the first movement is an upper-body movement. The second movement may be a lower- or upper-body exercise.

Similar to total-body movements, most upper-body exercises could be done both bilaterally and unilaterally. Also, the utilization of dumbbells for movements increases range of motion as well as increases the activation of the stabilizing muscles during the execution of the movement.

Exercise Classification

After the pool has been completed, the next step is to classify the exercises. Each exercise is classified as a foundation, supplemental, major-assistance, or secondary-assistance exercise. This is extremely helpful in ordering the exercises in proper sequences for the tier system, as well as prioritizing exercises per category (see Figure 4-6).

	Category T Pulling Movement	Category T Pushing Movement	Category L	Category U
Foundation	Power Clean	N/A	Back Squat	Bench Press
Supplemental	Hang Clean Power Snatch Hang Snatch	Jerk	Front Squat Leg Press	Incline Press Close Grip Bench
Major Assistance	Clean Pull Snatch Pull Dumbbell Clean Dumbbell Snatch	Push Jerk Push Press	Step Up Lunge Romanian Deadlift Single Leg Squat	Dumbbell Bench Dumbbell Incline Shoulder Press Bent Over Row Dips Pull Ups
Secondary Assistance	N/A	N/A	Leg Curl Leg Extension	Triceps Extension Biceps Curl

Figure 4-6. Exercise classification examples

• Foundation Exercises

Foundation exercises are multijoint barbell exercises. Preferably, one exercise per movement category should be a foundation exercise. These exercises are usually evaluated for repetition maximums. Generally, foundation exercises are chosen based on the fact that they will give the best indication of overall strength development for the specific movement category.

In the case of improving athletic ability, the same exercises may be used for multiple sports. Foundation exercises should remain the same throughout multiple annual plans so the coach can chart individual and team improvement. In the case of changing foundation exercises, make sure you establish a sound justification for making the switch, and clearly evaluate the positives versus negatives in how it will affect both individual and team improvement.

Foundation exercises are those exercises upon which the rest of the program is going to be built. Also, foundation exercises are those exercises that the program planner believes will emphasize the development of the particular movement category it is associated with in the most efficient manner. In a nutshell, foundation exercises are those exercises that you think of after you ask yourself the question, if you could only train one exercise per movement category for a particular sport, what would it be?

In the case of testing two exercises from the same movement category, you must determine which one will be the primary and which one will be the secondary foundation exercise. When choosing to implement two foundation exercises for a category, one exercise should give the best indication of overall strength for that specific category. Testing two movements per category in a given testing period is not recommended.

The exercise chosen as the primary foundation exercise is always a tier 1 exercise in the weekly rotation of exercises. The secondary foundation exercise becomes the tier 2 exercise if used for that movement category (see later in this chapter for a more detailed discussion of tier 1 and tier 2 exercises).

Some examples of primary foundation and secondary foundation exercises follow:

Total body—Power clean from deck	Primary foundation
Total body—Hang clean	Secondary foundation
Lower body—Back squat	Primary foundation
Lower body—Front squat	Secondary foundation
Upper body—Bench press	Primary foundation
Upper body—Incline press	Secondary foundation

Commonly used main foundation exercises for strength-training programs are listed in Figure 4-7. Obviously, in some situations you may want to use an exercise not listed in this table, based on needs analysis of the sport and working with the head sport coach to determine the true goals of the strength program.

Total Body	Lower Body	Upper Body
Hang Clean	Back Squat	Bench Press
Power Pull from Deck/Hang	Front Squat	Standing Press

Figure 4-7. Main foundation exercises

• Supplemental Exercises

Supplemental exercises have taken on new meaning in our training theory. Referred to as special exercises by the Westside Barbell Club, these exercises are still used to add variety and complement the corresponding foundation exercise. They have also taken an identity of their own.

In sports where maximum strength is of great importance, supplemental exercises are used as secondary test movements throughout the annual plan. This is done to improve strength continuously. When these exercises are used in this manner, they are rotated bimonthly. Using supplemental exercises in this mode allows for challenging and competitive training sessions.

Supplemental exercises are extremely important, as they enhance the athletes' overall strength by training similar muscle actions as the foundation exercises in slightly different movement planes and angles.

These exercises are primarily multiple-joint barbell exercises. Depending on the type of training template used, they may be either tier 1 or tier 2 exercises (see later in this chapter for a more detailed discussion of tier 1 and tier 2 exercises). Foundation and supplemental exercises are also known as the big exercises. These exercises increase the athlete's strength level.

• Major Assistance Exercises

Major assistance exercises can benefit the athlete in two different ways. Major assistance exercises assist in the development of the muscle or muscle groups that are used in the execution of foundation and supplemental exercises. Also, since some of the exercises work as stabilizers and use the antagonistic muscle groups of the prime mover exercises, they help avoid muscular imbalances that can lead to injury.

Major assistance exercises can also be classified as functional exercises when that definition applies. These exercises are those that primarily allow independent-movement actions of the limbs. This is an extremely important factor when using strength training as a building block for improving athletic ability. These types of exercises help in the development of mobility and help maintain or improve the athlete's flexibility. They can also aid in the improvement of balance, coordination, and proprioception. These movements, in terms of athletic development, cannot be overlooked. They serve as a true complement to the foundation and supplemental exercise of the program.

Major assistance exercises also comprise the gymnastic movements, i.e., body-weight exercises. A lost art in most training scenarios, these purely functional exercises use movements that are primarily body weight–oriented.

Major assistance exercises are usually multijoint barbell, dumbbell, or alternative resistance exercises. These exercises are usually rotated in two- or four-week blocks as tier 3,4, or 5 movements (see later in this chapter for more information about these movements). These exercises play an important role in the elite training template for the volume and mobility tiers.

• Secondary Assistance Exercises

Secondary assistance exercises are single-joint exercises and act as stabilizing exercises for the foundation and supplemental exercises. These exercises apply direct resistance to a specific muscle group. They are primarily used in the auxiliary program and pre/post workout routines. They may also be implemented individually for those athletes who may either be in rehabilitation or prehabilitation. They can also be used to strengthen weaker muscle groups that may affect performance.

Movement Category Sequence, Daily Sequence, and Weekly Sequence

• Movement Category Sequence

One of the major intentions of the tier system was to rotate the order of exercises based on movements. This would accomplish four important goals in the development of the microcycle strength-training sessions.

The first goal was to develop a sequence in which each category would receive an equal number of exercises per microcycle. For example, a 3 x 5 program has a total of 15 mandatory exercises per week. Five will come from each of the three movement categories, giving each a 1/3 distribution.

The second goal was to emphasize the development of the hips and legs. Two-thirds of the movement category distribution (one-third from total-body movements and one-third from lower-body movements) will improve strength levels in this region of the body. The level of strength developed from the torso down is the foundation of the athlete's success.

The third goal was to develop a sequence that would allow each category to be the priority emphasis for one of the daily training sessions of the microcycle. This would allow the foundation exercise for a specific category to be the first exercise of the daily session. The athlete should recognize this and understand this is *the* movement of the session.

The fourth goal of the movement sequence was to rotate the movements so that two exercises from the same category would not be performed back-to-back in a daily training session. This primarily affects the 3x5 tier programs. This was done to allow for built-in recovery from exercise to exercise within one category to the next.

To determine the movement sequence for the microcycle, first determine which movement category closely relates to athletic movement. Second, determine which movement category is the primary group for strength development. In other words, which category has one exercise that is needed to drive the rest of the program? Third, think about how the running plan per microcycle would affect the strength sessions.

Based on these three points, the movement sequence for the microcycle was developed in this manner (see Figure 4-8). The first training session of the week would be a total-body priority session. The synchronized movement patterns of total-body exercises have the most correlation in terms of athletic movement. Usually the lower-body session is going to lead off with the back squat. The back squat may be the most important movement in terms of strength development. If an athlete could only train one exercise a week, this would be the exercise recommended. It truly is the king of all exercises. The third and final session of the week would be the upper-body priority session.

	Session T Day 1	Session L Day 2	Session U Day 3
EMPHASIS	Category T Total Body	Category L Lower Body	Category U Upper Body

Figure 4-8. Microcycle movement sequence

The running plan also had an affect on the sequencing of the movement categories. A secondary factor in establishing this sequence was to eliminate the possibility of having a running session on the same day as the priority lower-body training emphasis. Since most running programs are four-day alternating programs, with a day off after two consecutive sessions, the plan was for the lower-body training session to be performed on non-running days. It is the belief of many coaches that when an athlete runs and trains heavy squats on the same day, athletes tend to back off on one or the other, depending on their strong points.

For example, think about football training. Most of the big skill athletes (linemen) would tend to back down during the running session knowing that they had a big squat workout ahead of them. Skill athletes (wide receivers, running backs, cornerbacks, safeties) would train hard during the running session and try to back off during the squat workout. As much as we would like to say this doesn't happen, it does; it is human nature. This is one reason why this training sequence was developed.

Plus, in the majority of most developmental stage programs, the lower-body day falls on Wednesday. It has been known in the business industry for some time that the most productive workday of the week is Wednesday. Why would a coach not want his athletes training on this day? Although total-body movements are extremely beneficial to improving athletic ability, the primary movement of any program should revolve around the squat. The strength gained through this one exercise is a key ingredient to the improvement of total-body movements, upper-body movements, and speed development.

After the microcycle sequence was completed, it was now necessary to construct a daily training session sequence (see Figure 4-9). This sequence would take into account the microcycle rotation as well as how the categories were ranked based on the influence of improving athletic ability.

EMPHASIS	Session T Day 1	Session L Day 2	Session U Day 3
Priority	Total Body	Lower Body	Upper Body
Major	Lower Body	Upper Body	Total Body
Minor	Upper Body	Total Body	Lower Body

Figure 4-9. Daily movement category sequence

Session T's (total body) rotation became identical to the microcycle rotation. A total-body movement is the emphasis of the day, followed by a lower-body and an upper-body movement. Session L's (lower body) emphasis is a lower-body movement followed by an upper-body and total-body movement. Session U's (upper body) emphasis is an upper-body movement followed by a total-body and a lower-body movement.

It was decided that the first movement of the day would be the priority emphasis, the second movement the major emphasis, and the third movement of the day the minor emphasis. This is the basis of the traditional training template. By sequencing the categories in this order, it allows each category to be the priority, major, and minor emphasis one time per microcycle.

Within the weekly sequence, categories are rotated in this order because a priority emphasis session should be followed by a minor emphasis session per category. Only the upper-body movement session does not conform to this standard. In this case, two consecutive nonlifting days follow the priority emphasis. This rotation will help promote a faster recovery from training session to training session for each category and will diminish the chance of the athlete overtraining.

The movement sequence rotates the same way during the tier programs. In the 3x3-tier program (see Figure 4-10), once the athlete has performed one exercise per category following the proper sequence for the daily session, the athlete has completed the required lifts for that session.

TIER	Session T Day 1	Session L Day 2	Session U Day 3
One	Total Body	Lower Body	Upper Body
Two	Lower Body	Upper Body	Total Body
Three	Upper Body	Total Body	Lower Body

Figure 4-10. 3x3 tier program (tier breakdown based on movement category sequence)

In the 3x5-tier program (see Figure 4-11), once the movement category sequence is completed with an exercise from each, the rotation begins again for that particular session. After the rotation has been completed, the priority emphasis category of the day is repeated followed by the major emphasis of the day. Tier 4 exercises repeat the Tier 1 movement category, and Tier 5 exercises repeat the Tier 2 movement categories. This gives you two priority emphasis exercises, two major emphasis exercises, and one minor emphasis exercise to be completed in a 3x5-tier program.

TIER	Session T Day 1	Session L Day 2	Session U Day 3
One	Total Body	Lower Body	Upper Body
Two	Lower Body	Upper Body	Total Body
Three	Upper Body	Total Body	Lower Body
Four	Total Body	Lower Body	Upper Body
Five	Lower Body	Upper Body	Total Body

Figure 4-11. 3x5 tier program (tier breakdown based on movement category sequence)

There are two ways that a 2x3 program can be implemented. One program only utilizes sessions T and L during the microcycle. Changes in the exercise classification and specific movement sequence are adjusted based on program goals. The second is to rotate sessions through multiple microcycles (see Figure 4-12).

Week	Training Session 1	Training Session 2
ONE	Session T	Session L
TWO	Session U	Session T
THREE	Session L	Session U
FOUR	Session T	Session L

Figure 4-12. 2x3 session rotation

Tier	Classification
One	Foundation
Two	Supplemental or Major Assistance
Three	Supplemental or Major Assistance
Four	Supplemental or Major Assistance
Five	Supplemental or Major Assistance

Figure 4-13. Tier breakdown based on exercise classification

Exercise Classification Sequence

There are corresponding classifications that also restrict the choice of movement per tier (see Figure 4-13). These exercises are placed in order by the movement category sequence of the daily training session, as well as their classification within the category they are affiliated with. Foundation exercises will always start the daily training session for the traditional template followed by supplemental exercises, major assistance exercises, or both. Secondary assistance exercises are not included in the main tier program, but they are an important part of the auxiliary training package.

Tier Level	Tier/Rotation	Classification	Movement
One	Total Body	Foundation	Foundation
Two	Lower Body	Supplemental	In Place Double Leg
Three	Upper Body	Supplemental Major Assistance	Horizontal or Vertical Movement – check for balance
Four	Total Body	Supplemental Major Assistance	Bilateral Extension, any Unilateral Movement, or and Total Body Hybrid
Five	Lower Body	Major Assistance	Horizontal, Vertical, or Unilateral Hybrid [H to V or V to H] opposite movement of Session L Tier 4

Session L Exercise Classification and Movement Rotation

Tier Level	Tier/Rotation	Classification	Movement
One	Lower Body	Foundation	Foundation
Two	Upper Body	Supplemental Major Assistance	Horizontal or Vertical Movement – check for balance
Three	Total Body	Supplemental Major Assistance	Any Overhead, Any Extension, or TB/TB, TB/LB, LB/TB hybrid
Four	Lower Body	Major Assistance	Vertical, Horizontal, or Unilateral Hybrid [V to H or H to V]
Five	Upper Body	Supplemental Major Assistance	Horizontal or Vertical Movement – check for balance

Session U Exercise Classification and Movement Rotation

Tier Level	Tier/Rotation	Classification	Movement
One	Upper Body	Foundation	Foundation
Two	Total Body	Supplemental Major Assistance	Bilateral Full Pull and Catch, Jerk (unilateral option), or Bilateral Extension
Three	Lower Body	Supplemental Major Assistance	In Place Double or Single Leg, or Vertical or Horizontal
Four	Upper Body	Supplemental Major Assistance	Horizontal or Vertical Movement – check for balance
Five	Total Body	Major Assistance	Choice Any Unilateral Movement

[Based on Traditional Template]

Figure 4-14. Weekly exercise classification and movement rotation

Each tier has a choice of exercise variations based on classification and movement (see Figure 4-14). Choices have been given for some tiers because each sport may have different needs. This allows for a variety of exercises to be done for the same tier throughout the year, attacking and strengthening the body's joints at different angles.

The upper-body rotation for this model is based on rotating horizontal and vertical pushes and presses. The goal is to have a balance between pushes and pulls based on work set volume. The foundation exercise does not factor into the rotation. When setting up this rotation, it is important that, whichever movement is chosen for tier 2, the complete opposite is placed in tier 4. This rotation is formulated from an eight-week plan rotating the movements throughout tiers 2 to 5 (see Figure 4-15). This rotation can and will be altered when implementing bracketing techniques to specific tiers (see the discussion of bracketing later in this chapter).

Weeks 1&2	Session T	Session L	Session U
Tier 1 – 6 sets			Foundation
Tier 2 – 5 sets		Horizontal Pull	
Tier 3 – 4 sets	Horizontal Press		
Tier 4 – 3 sets			Vertical Press
Tier 5 – 2 sets		Vertical Pull	

Weeks 3&4	Session T	Session L	Session U
Tier 1 – 6 sets			Foundation
Tier 2 – 5 sets		Vertical Press	
Tier 3 – 4 sets	Vertical Pull		
Tier 4 – 3 sets			Horizontal Pull
Tier 5 – 2 sets		Horizontal Press	

Weeks 5&6	Session T	Session L	Session U
Tier 1 – 6 sets			Foundation
Tier 2 – 5 sets		Horizontal Press	
Tier 3 – 4 sets	Horizontal Pull		
Tier 4 – 3 sets			Vertical Pull
Tier 5 – 2 sets		Vertical Press	

Weeks 7&8	Session T	Session L	Session U
Tier 1 – 6 sets			Foundation
Tier 2 – 5 sets		Vertical Pull	
Tier 3 – 4 sets	Vertical Press		
Tier 4 – 3 sets			Horizontal Press
Tier 5 – 2 sets		Horizontal Pull	

Figure 4-15. Upper body horizontal/vertical push/pull rotation

For most tiers, there are numerous movement choices. The choice made for each particular tier is based on the particular goals and needs for the specific sport. The tremendous amount of variety in this program allows for more challenging training sessions and keeps the athletes mentally motivated.

Tier 1 represents the foundation exercise for the movement category that has the priority emphasis of the day. Tier 1 exercises are first in the exercise order and are usually cycled off of a previous repetition maximum. A foundation exercise may be substituted for another exercise in tier 1 if the coach is implementing a repeat session.

Tier 2 exercises are classified as supplemental or major assistance exercises. Tier 2 exercises are always second in the exercise order and represent the major emphasis of the day. If a secondary foundation movement is used, this exercise is cycled from a previous repetition maximum.

Tier 3 exercises will either be classified as a supplemental or a major assistance exercise. Tier 3 exercises are always the third exercise in the exercise order and represent the minor emphasis of the day. In a three-tier program, this would be the last required lift of the session.

Tier 4 exercises are fourth in succession and are either supplemental (upper-body only) or major assistance exercises. Tier 4 exercises represent the same category as tier 1, the priority emphasis of the day.

Tier 5 exercises are also supplemental (upper-body only) or major assistance exercises. They are the fifth exercise of the day and represent the same movement category of tier 2, the major emphasis of the day. These exercises are cycled similar to the major assistance exercises in tiers 3 and 4. In a five-tier program this would be the last required lift of the session.

Cycles for tier 2 to 5 exercises are either repetition-based or percentage-based from the foundation exercise. When a coach is choosing opposite movement patterns for tier variation, he should keep in mind these patterns should involve pull/push movements for total- and upper-body movements, or horizontal/vertical movements for lower-body movements. Because of the numerous joints involved in the completion of a total-body lift, this category would never have secondary assistance exercises.

Ranking the Pool Based on Tier Considerations

Now that the movement sequence and exercise classification have been established, the program planner must rank in order the top three or five exercises per category. These exercises should be ranked based on importance to the improvement of athletic ability, relationship to the foundation movement, and how they coincide with the classification sequence and the goals of the program.

Once the five exercises per category are chosen, they are now plugged into the tier that coincides with its ranking. If the coach is implementing a 3x3-tier program, the first three exercises per category will be used, and so on for a 3x5. Remember that the exercises will be dispersed throughout the three training sessions of the microcycle (see Figure 4-16).

Session	T	Session	L	Session	U
Tier Level	Rotation/Rank	Tier Level	Rotation/Rank	Tier Level	Rotation/Rank
1	*Total 1*	1	*Lower 1*	1	*Upper 1*
2	*Lower 2*	2	*Upper 2*	2	*Total 2*
3	*Upper 3*	3	*Total 3*	3	*Lower 3*
4	*Total 4*	4	*Lower 4*	4	*Upper 4*
5	*Lower 5*	5	*Upper 5*	5	*Total 5*

Figure 4-16. Order of exercises per movement category

As stated earlier, one of the keys of the tier system is exercise variety. This is to develop joint strength and stability at different movement planes. The majority of movements will change either bimonthly or monthly to ensure variation, and reduce staleness and over training possibilities.

Volume in Work Sets

As well as the movement categories and classification of exercises, each tier has a predetermined amount of work sets that are recommended for that exercise (see Figure 4-17). The work sets per tier for the traditional model were manipulated based on the type of exercise; order in the workout; and the heavy, moderate, and light training sessions per week. The elite model is similar, with the difference being the emphasis on effort, speed, and volume versus the heavy, moderate, and light principle. Daily and weekly volume is maintained by the number of work sets allotted per tier and the reps per set based on the training cycle being used. Each tier has a preset number or range of work sets that correlates with the order of the session (traditional) or the strength emphasis of the tier (elite).

Work set volume was chosen over repetition volume because coaches implement several types of intensity cycles during the annual plan, depending on the goals of the specific program. This allowed the designers of the program to design the foundation training intensity cycles off of six work set routines and then deduct training sets from the cycle per tier level.

In the traditional model, where repetitions per set match every exercise per category, the volume can be manipulated on a standard heavy, moderate, and light training session approach. The movement sequence of the tier system allows the athlete to gain what may be the most efficient use of this approach. The following section examines the typical heavy, moderate, and light training approach (see Figure 4-18) and then proceeds to tier system adjustments.

This is an example of a typical three-day-per-week training cycle with one peak, the heavy day. In this particular cycle, the athlete is performing a 5x5 routine for three exercises, the clean, the squat, and the bench press. On each day this will be the exercise order.

Tier Level	3x3 Traditional	3x5 Traditional	Olympic Sports High School option	3x5 Elite-Effort	3x3 Elite-Speed
One	6	6	5	6-10	8-10
Two	5	5	4	5-8	5+
Three	4	4	3	3-4	2-3
Four		3	2	2	
Five		2	2	2	

Figure 4-17. Volume (based on work sets per tier)

Volume Intensity	DAY 1		DAY 2		DAY 3
HEAVY	5x5 @ 85%				
MODERATE					5x5 @75%
LIGHT			5x5 @ 65%		
	Clean, Squat, Bench		Clean, Squat, Bench		Clean, Squat, Bench

Figure 4-18. Typical heavy, moderate, light training microcycle

• Day One Workout

Day one's workout is considered the heavy day of the week. The athlete's goal is to complete 5 sets of 5 repetitions at 85% of a 1 repetition maximum for each exercise. The athlete methodically progresses through the clean, to the squat, and finally to the bench press. At this load, there is a high probability that the athlete will not achieve the repetition goal for each set in the latter stages of the squat and bench press portion of the workout. Therefore this session would not have accomplished its goal, as the athlete was unable to achieve all the repetitions required.

• Day Two Workout

Following the heavy session for the week, day two's workout is considered the light session. The athlete is required to perform the same set/rep scheme as day one, but the training intensity has been reduced to 65%. The athlete is able to cruise through this workout with little stress to the body. In most cases this workout is too easy, and not much has been accomplished in the terms of improving athletic ability.

• Day Three Workout

The moderate day of the week falls on day three. The training intensity for this session is 75%. As with the other two sessions, the athlete's goal is to perform 5x5 at each exercise. This session seems to be ideal. The athlete accomplishes the goal reps for each exercise, and the workload is favorable for strength development.

The majority of individuals evaluating this microcycle would agree that one of the three sessions was what could be considered a quality session, day three (the moderate training day). As the tier system was being developed, this scenario was closely examined. Since the moderate day was determined to be the most efficient and productive session of the week, how could the program be designed where the workload of each session would mimic the moderate day?

After reviewing the daily rotation of the movement categories and establishing set patterns per tier, the following three-peak microcycle was developed for the traditional model (see Figure 4-19). This three-peak microcycle is based on each movement category having a "heavy emphasis" on separate training sessions.

Volume/Emphasis	Session T Day 1	Session L Day 2	Session U Day 3
Heavy/Priority			
Moderate/Major			
Light/Minor			
Key	Total Body	Lower Body	Upper Body

Figure 4-19. Three-peak microcycle based on heavy, moderate, and light sessions

As mentioned earlier, the first three tiers represent the priority, major, and minor emphases of the session. With this in mind, the priority movement of the session was classified the heavy emphasis; the major movement, the moderate emphasis; and the minor movement, the light emphasis. This rotation created a moderate approach to the training session that would allow the athlete to train in heavy, moderate, and light sessions within one workout and allow for a more efficient plan of training throughout the microcycle.

• Heavy, Moderate, and Low Volume Sessions

By manipulating volume, coaches can coincide the amount of work sets with the emphasis of the session. That makes the priority emphasis a high-volume workout, the major emphasis a moderate-volume workout, and the minor emphasis a low-volume workout. For example, if a total-body movement was the priority emphasis for the daily training session, the amount of the work sets for this category would be the greatest (see Figure 4-17).

Approximately 43% of the total work sets are allocated for the priority emphasis for the daily session. About 33% percent of the total work sets are allocated for the major emphasis of the day, and about 23% of the total work sets are allocated for the minor emphasis of the day. By implementing a heavy-, moderate-, and low-volume workout for each category, this gives the athlete ample time to recover from session to session and decreases the chance of overtraining.

In the elite model, the same three-peak microcycle is implemented, but the emphasis is on the type of strength developed (see Figure 4-20). Sets and reps are based on the strength goal of the tier. Effort represents the highest training intensity for the movement category. Speed represents the lowest training intensity, with the most emphasis is on force development. Volume represents the highest repetition volume per set, with emphasis on strength endurance and increasing lean body mass.

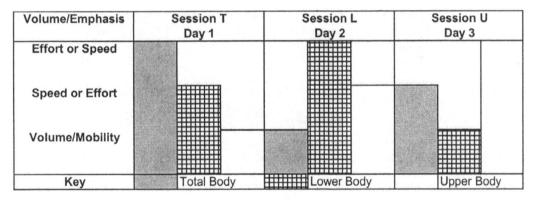

Figure 4-20. Three-peak microcycle based on strength developed

The Traditional Template

The traditional template is based on a three-peak microcycle (see Figure 4-19). Each of the movement categories represents one of the peaks. The daily sessions revolve around a priority, major, and minor emphasis for each category, as well as the manipulation of volume for each category based on the emphasis for the session. A rotational sequence of the three categories determines which category is the priority emphasis, major emphasis, or minor emphasis for that particular session (see Figure 4-21).

This rotation allows the foundation exercise to be emphasized as the primary exercise for each session. The rotation allows the athlete to prepare both physically and

Session T				
Tier	**Emphasis**	**Category**	**Classification**	**Exercise**
One	Priority	Total Body	Foundation	*Hang Clean*
Two	Major	Lower Body	Supplemental	*Front Squat*
Three	Minor	Upper Body	Supplemental	*Standing Overhead Press*
Four		Total Body	Major Assistance	*Shrug Pull from Deck*
Five		Lower Body	Major Assistance	*Walking Lunge*

Session L				
Tier	**Emphasis**	**Category**	**Classification**	**Exercise**
One	Priority	Lower Body	Foundation	*Back Squat*
Two	Major	Upper Body	Supplemental	*Incline Press*
Three	Minor	Total Body	Major Assistance	*Snatch Grip Power Pull*
Four		Lower Body	Major Assistance	*16" Step Up*
Five		Upper Body	Major Assistance	*Chin Ups*

Session U				
Tier	**Emphasis**	**Category**	**Classification**	**Exercise**
One	Priority	Upper Body	Foundation	*Bench Press*
Two	Major	Total Body	Supplemental	*Power Jerk*
Three	Minor	Lower Body	Major Assistance	*Split Squat*
Four		Upper Body	Major Assistance	*Bent Row*
Five		Total Body	Major Assistance	*Dumbbell Snatch*

Figure 4-21. Example of a 3x5 traditional tier program

mentally for the demands placed on the body for the duration of a practice or competition.

Priority Emphasis

A movement category is the priority emphasis of the day when the first exercise for the training session is a tier 1 foundation exercise. The total volume of work sets for the category is higher than that for the other two categories. Intensity is the highest for this category during this session, as it relates to percentage of repetition maximum. Priority emphasis exercises will be tier 1 and tier 4, depending on the length of the program.

Major Emphasis

A movement category will be the major emphasis of the day when the first exercise of the training session is a tier 2 supplemental exercise. The total volume of work sets for this category is considered moderate. Major emphasis exercises will be incorporated in tier 2 and tier 5 exercises, depending on the length of the program.

Minor Emphasis

A movement category will be the minor emphasis of the day when the first exercise of the training session is a tier 3 supplemental or major assistance exercise. The total volume of work sets for this category is considered light.

As mentioned earlier, traditional training is based on linear periodization. Repetitions per set are solely based on the repetition cycle of the foundation lifts. For example, if the repetitions per set for the back squat is 10, every lower-body movement will perform sets of 10 repetitions per exercise.

This program automatically allows for the varying of exercises/movements throughout a microcycle. If the program is implemented correctly, the goal is to never repeat the exact same exercise within the three-day rotation. This allows for true athletic strength development. This is focusing on whole-body development rather then specific increases in one particular movement or developing specific body parts.

The Elite Template

The elite template is also based on a three-peak volume microcycle (see Figure 4-21). Each of the movement categories represents one of the peaks. The daily session revolves around an effort, speed, and volume/mobility emphasis for each category, as well as the manipulation of volume for each category based on the emphasis for the session. A rotational sequence of the three categories determines which category is the effort emphasis, speed emphasis, or volume/mobility emphasis for that particular session (see Figure 4-22).

This rotation allows the program planner to emphasize a specific strength developed per movement category during each session. This rotation allows the athlete to develop the three main strength emphases of physical development, which are maximum strength, explosive strength, and strength endurance within a daily session and an individual microcycle.

The elite template evolved from the traditional template based on the growing influence of the training philosophy of Westside Barbell Club and also their conjugated approach to periodization. Most of the principles that are applied are similar to the basic principles of the tier system model and the traditional template. The elite template is recommended as the primary training template of the annual plan for advanced-level athletes. A 3x5 program is used primarily during the developmental stage, and the 3x3 program during the competitive stage.

Session T Tier	Emphasis	Category	Classification	Exercise
One	Effort	Total Body	Foundation	*Hang Clean*
Two	Speed	Lower Body	Supplemental	*Pause Squat*
Three	Volume	Upper Body	Supplemental	*Standing Overhead Press*
Four	Mobility	Total Body	Major Assistance	*DB Hang Clean*
Five	Mobility	Lower Body	Major Assistance	*Walking Lunge*

Session L Tier	Emphasis	Category	Classification	Exercise
One	Effort	Lower Body	Foundation	*Back Squat*
Two	Speed	Upper Body	Supplemental	*Varied Grip Bench Press*
Three	Volume	Total Body	Major Assist	*Snatch Grip Power Pull*
Four	Mobility	Lower Body	Major Assist	*16" Step Up*
Five	Mobility	Upper Body	Major Assist	*Chin Ups*

Session U Tier	Emphasis	Category	Classification	Exercise
One	Effort	Upper Body	Foundation	*Bench Press*
Two	Speed	Total Body	Supplemental	*Clean from the Deck*
Three	Volume	Lower Body	Major Assist	*Split Squat*
Four	Mobility	Upper Body	Major Assist	*DB Row*
Five	Mobility	Total Body	Major Assist	*Dumbbell Snatch*

Figure 4-22. Example of a 3x5 elite developmental tier program

Heavy, Moderate, and Light Versus Effort, Speed, and Volume

The major difference between the traditional and elite model is the approach to cyclical training. Where the goal in the traditional template is to maintain volume through a rotation of heavy, moderate, or light training movements within a session (traditional cycling), the elite model is based on a rotation of strength development (see Figures 4-23 and 4-24). The goal in the elite template is to improve maximum strength, explosive strength, and strength endurance (hypertrophy) within a daily session and within the microcycle. This is done based on an individual cyclical approach for the first three tiers of the elite model.

Tier Level/Emphasis	Strength	Session T	Session L	Session U
One – Effort	Developmental/Maximum	Total	Lower	Upper
Two – Speed	Explosive	Lower	Upper	Total
Three – Volume	Endurance	Upper	Total	Lower
Four – Mobility		Total	Lower	Upper
Five - Mobility		Lower	Upper	Total

Figure 4-23. 3 x 5 elite template movement sequence – emphasis

Tier Level/Emphasis	Strength	Session T	Session L	Session U
One – Speed	Explosive	Total	Lower	Upper
Two – Effort	Developmental/Maximum	Lower	Upper	Total
Three – Mobility	Endurance based	Upper	Total	Lower

Figure 4-24. 3 x 3 elite template movement sequence – emphasis

• Effort

The effort tier is either a tier 1 or tier 2 exercise, depending on the plan. The effort movement represents the exercise per movement category that will have the highest workload in terms of training intensity. Effort work is geared around either training on a cyclical system based on standard percentage-based cycles for foundation movements, or is based on repetition maximum training utilizing a constant rotation of supplemental exercises. The effort tier replaces the heavy emphasis.

• Speed

The speed tier is always the opposite of the effort tier. If effort is a tier 1 movement, then speed is tier 2, and vice versa. The speed tier replaces the light emphasis. During this tier, the load is low and bar speed is at a high priority. During this tier, the training goal is to improve strength-speed and speed-strength.

Exercises used for speed development per movement category are very selective. Each category has set choices (see Figure 4-25). Coaches can use bands, chains, or a combination of both as additional means to improve strength-speed for lower- and upper-body exercises.

Total Body Movements	Lower Body Movements	Upper Body Movements
Clean from the Deck	Box Squat	Varied Grip (4 grips) Bench Press
Power Pull from the Deck Deadlift	Pause Squat	

Figure 4-25. Elite template speed movements

• Volume

Tier 3 is the volume tier in a 3x5 program, and a volume/mobility tier in a 3x3 program. This tier replaces the moderate training session. As you can guess, repetitions are the highest per set in this tier, as compared to tiers 1 and 2. This tier complements the work from tiers 1 and 2 by improving strength endurance and increasing lean body mass. In the 3x3 program this tier's movement is related to mobility training, so exercises chosen are generally those that are independent limb movements. These movements are used to improve athletic ability, stabilization, body awareness, and range of motion.

• Mobility

Tiers 4 and 5 are specifically geared to mobility strength training. Most of these exercises would be classified as major assistance/functional exercises. Each tier has two prescribed work sets, and the repetition volume per set will be similar to tier 3's workload. These movements really give this template a great balance of strength development, and the exercises implemented in these tiers are extremely beneficial in improving athletic ability.

In this template, total-body movements are trained slightly different then lower- and upper-body movements. When using the foundation movement as the effort exercise, a coach can base his workload off a standard training intensity cycle. When using a supplemental movement, it is recommended that you primarily train for conditioning (according to Louie Simmons) and perform a higher volume emphasis during this tier. The program planner may also choose to take a supplemental movement for a one rep maximum.

This elite template is truly an athletic-based training approach, as it improves four very important components of athletic development within one session/microcycle:

- Strength–maximum
- Strength–explosive
- Strength–endurance
- Mobility

Tier Rotations and Repeat Tiers

Tier Rotations

Although it is highly recommended to maintain the total-body, lower- body, upper-body rotations throughout the microcycle, in some cases it may be in the best interest of the program planner to rotate the sessions within one training day. This is extremely helpful when your facility has limited equipment and your group is large.

For example, one group may start on Session T, another on Session L, and a third on Session U. This allows the athletes to maintain a good training pace. The rotation of exercises allows for little interference between groups. As group T moves from platform work to lower-body movement, group L moves from the squat rack to upper-body movement, and the U group moves from the bench to the platform. This is a very good way to break up large groups within a facility that does not necessarily have an abundance of equipment.

Repeat Tiers

In some cases, where one movement category is not as involved in a particular sport, the program planner may restructure the tier program and have a repeat session. This generally occurs in the sports such as soccer and track (sprints, jumps, distance) where upper-body movements are not as critical as the total-body and lower-body movements.

	Day 1	*Auxiliary*	*Day 2*	*Day 3*
Standard 3 day	Session T		Session L	Session U
Standard 3 day + auxiliary session	Session T	Session A	Session L	Session U
Track	Session T		Session L	Session T
Soccer	Session L		Session T	Session L
Variations	L U T L U T L L U U		U T U T L U T U E L	T L L U T T L L U U

Figure 4-26. Tier rotations

When implementing repeat sessions, most of the time the session in which the upper-body movement is the priority is usually removed, and an additional total-body or lower-body emphasis session is substituted. When structuring a program with a repeat tier, the two sessions that are repeated are going to be the first and last sessions of the microcycle, with the single session being the middle training day.

The repeat session follows the same order and rotation as normal. It is up to the program planner to manipulate the adjustments to exercise classification and specific movement patterns based on the first session of the microcycle.

As mentioned earlier, you may include auxiliary training after the three main sessions. If you decide to add the auxiliary day as a fourth training day, it should be implemented on the Tuesday or Thursday opposite session U.

Additional Principles of Tier Training

The following five principles, complex sets, combo sets, super sets, tri sets, and coupling, are ways to increase work capacity within a specific session. Complex, combo, super, and tri sets each add additional work to the training session, with the goal being to complete the workout in the same time allotment that was determined without the extra movements and sets. Coupling does not add workload but decreases overall workout time by pairing tiers together.

The Complex Set

The complex set is based on training a plyometric exercise following a strength-training movement. This occurs for the first two tiers of training only. This is usually implemented during the developmental stage. After the athlete completes the strength training movement, the rest interval is 15 to 18 seconds before the plyometric activity is performed. Performing the activity too soon after the strength movement will lead to a loss of the nervous system effect and, after 30 seconds, the athlete will lose the strength training effect (according to Martin Rooney).

The Combo Set

The simplest pairing of exercises within a single tier is a combo set. This is primarily a principle for lower- and upper-body movements. A combo set is the combination of any two upper- or lower-body movements into the same tier. This means double the work for that tier emphasis of the session.

The Super Set

The pairing of antagonistic muscle groups is the simplest definition of super setting. This is a set rule in the tier system. In tier system training there are primarily three types of superset pairings: horizontal push/horizontal pull, vertical push/vertical pull (these represent upper-body movements), and flexion/extension. Flexion/extension movements can occur at the hip, knee, and elbow joint.

The Tri Set

The tri set is a minicircuit of three exercises. The tri set principle can be implemented after the main session in conjunction with the posterior chain movement of the session. During a tri set, a coach may include a weighted torso movement and a horizontal or vertical pull movement within the posterior chain tier. Tri sets are usually warranted when there is a tremendous amount of horizontal and vertical pressing movements occurring during the tier programs. Rest time between exercises for the combo, super, and tri sets are done within 30 seconds of the first exercise of the set.

Coupling

Coupling is a principle used in the tier system for two reasons. One is to increase work capacity within the daily session, and the second is to create a whole-body training effect. Coupling is a specific tier-system principle in which two exercises are paired in succession. These movements are always lower- and upper-body tiers. By coupling these two tiers, a total-body action can be simulated. Similar to the above set schemes, these exercises are done within 30 seconds of one another.

Three opportunities to couple lower and upper body movements exist within the traditional 3x5 training model:

- Session T   couple tier 2 and tier 3
- Session L   couple tier 4 and tier 5
- Session U   couple tier 3 and tier 4

The elite 3x5-training model has only one opportunity to couple a lower and upper body movement:

- Session L   couple tier 4 and tier 5

This is because tiers 1 to 3 in the elite model have different strength emphasis goals compared to the same goals per tier for the traditional model. Two rules of thumb when utilizing these principles are:

- In the traditional model, foundation exercises are never used in bracketing movements. In the elite model, effort exercises are never bracketed.
- Total body movements, regardless of tier position, are not utilized. They already give us a whole-body training effect.

Auxiliary Training

Auxiliary training is a very important part of the weekly plan. It accomplishes many goals and objectives as it relates to improving athletic ability. This type of training can be structured as a separate training day, performed after the main session of the daily workout, or performed as minicircuits in extra workouts.

Auxiliary training is used to improve work capacity, general physical preparedness (GPP), specific physical preparedness (SPP), and weak areas. These programs are also used in both the prehabilitation and rehabilitation of athletes. Auxiliary training, when implemented correctly, can be done 5 to 7 times per week under supervision from the program planner.

Extra Workouts

With the emphasis on the overall development of the body during the main session of the strength-training program, auxiliary training has become an integral part of injury prevention, conditioning, and improving weak points. Auxiliary training is based on individual one-on-one instruction with the athlete and coach.

Each program is based on no more than 20 minutes of work performed in a circuit approach with HIT training principles involved. These workouts are fast-paced and highly demanding in some instances. During auxiliary training, many movements may be done on a tempo approach rather then the speed emphasis of the concentric action, as stressed in the main tier programs.

Auxiliary training may include programs that develop general fitness, or GPP. These programs are generally flexibility programs, weight loss (aerobic training), power zone development, sled dragging, and the use of strongman events to elevate conditioning and whole-body strength.

Power zone development consists of movements that concentrate of the midsection of the body. Most of the work during these programs should focus on the stabilization of the hips, stomach, and back. Most people now refer to this as core training.

Strongman event training should be limited in load, as the goal in using this training is not to develop strongman competitors, but to enhance the athlete's overall development. Athletes who would partake in this type of extra training are generally football players, rugby players, wrestlers, and field-event athletes.

Specific physical preparedness (SPP), prehabilitation (prehab), and rehabilitation (rehab) types of training can also be done during this part of the weekly routine. Generally, routines that occur for these factors are based on the athlete's sport-specific need and relate to common injury-prone areas of the body.

Similar to SPP, prehab and rehab are the auxiliary programs useful in improving weak points. If the athlete has been evaluated and has a certain deficiency in a muscle group, this is a time when specific emphasis to that weak point can be addressed.

These programs can become a major emphasis in the overall structure of the microcycle. This is a highly successful program in helping achieve the program's overall goals of improving athletic abilities. To personalize each program for a specific sport, catchphrases can be used for the extra workout programs. See Figure 4-27 for some examples.

See Appendix D for step-by-step instructions for choosing exercises for a tier program.

Sport	Catchphrase
Football	Blitz packages
Basketball	Fast breaks
Wrestling	Take downs
Gymnastics	Perfect tens
Baseball/softball	Home runs
Tennis	Aces
Golf	Hole in ones
Volleyball	Spikes
Swimming/track	Sprints

Figure 4-27. Workout catchphrases

5

The Daily and Weekly Plans

The Daily Plan

The daily strength-training session consists of four parts; the pre-workout routine, the main session, the posterior chain tier, and the post-workout routine. Each has certain aspects that help the development of athletic abilities in the process of whole-body training. As a guide, the daily plan is based on a 90-minute training session. In reality, the athlete's goal is to train efficiently for 75 minutes max. Exceptional athletes who are extremely conditioned and efficient can complete the entire plan in less then 60 minutes.

When starting the session, three athletes per station when training is ideal. The most efficient ways for partners to work out are to train lightest to heaviest in terms of load per exercise. Lifter A goes from performing the exercise, to changing weights, to changing weights and spotting. Lifters B and C rotate based on start points. This gives the athlete ample time to recover and allows for smooth transitions between sets and exercises. The tier programs work the best in a self-contained power unit. This is because the use of a self-contained unit eliminates dead time by keeping the athlete in one designated area for the majority of the workout.

The Pre-Workout–10 Minutes

The pre-workout begins the daily session. It includes a general warm-up drill, power zone development, and dynamic flexibility/mobility drills.

The General Warm-Up Drill

This drill is generally a quick foot drill such as jump rope, agility ladders, minihurdles, and line drills. It is used to elevate the heart rate and dynamically warm up the body. This drill is usually three minutes in duration.

Power Zone Development

Power zone development or torso training has become a more integral part of the daily plan. Without a strong midsection, it is irrelevant how strong your limbs are. Our power zone development is based on training the abdominals, glutes, erectors, obliques, and hamstrings, or, everything from the mid-thigh to the bottom of the chest. This program will incorporate flexion extension, lateral flexion, stabilization, rotation, and posterior chain exercises to improve power zone strength. Abdominal and oblique training are performed before the main strength sessions, and glutes, hamstrings, and erector exercises (posterior chain) after the main session.

• Dynamic Flexibility/Mobility Drills

The dynamic flexibility program consists of hurdle mobility drills and lower- and upper-body movements done with the use of PVC, standard barbell, and mini-bands. Basic hurdle drills such as the walk over, lateral walk over, and duck under are used for hip flexibility. Overhead squats are a staple to the pre-workout plan. This is a great movement for hip, low back, and shoulder flexibility. Internal and external rotation, flys, and upright rows using the mini-bands improve upper-body dynamic flexibility. When the dynamic flexibility/mobility work is finished, the athlete now moves into the main session.

In addition to the above drills, if a specific sport has the head and neck involved in performance, include neck exercises in the pre- andpost- workout routines. Manual resistance, bands, or a resistance machine does this.

The Main Session–60 Minutes

The main session is the tier program that is being implemented. This section, when performed properly, should have a maximum time limit of 60 minutes for a 3x5 program. Allocate time for each tier to help the athlete keep the proper pace during the workout (see Figure 5-1).

Tier Level	Time Allotment
One	*22 minutes*
Two	*12 minutes*
Three	*10 minutes*
Four	*8 minutes*
Five	*8 minutes*

Figure 5-1. Basic time allotments

The goal in the main session is to improve work capacity by finishing the main session in the least amount of time. This is not to be accomplished by decreasing the technical efficiency of the exercises, skipping sets, or both. The more work the athlete can accomplish in a specific time period allows the body to adapt to the continuous stress that is added each week.

Posterior Chain Tier–10 Minutes

As mentioned earlier, with the increased importance of power zone development into our training principles, the posterior chain exercise of the session is of major importance. A tier program will always conclude the strength-training workout with a movement that specifically develops the hamstrings, glutes, and erectors. This is generally a three-set tier and the volume is usually high, 10 to 15 repetitions per set. Additional work may be implemented in this tier as a tri set or combo set. If a combo set is used in the posterior chain tier, the posterior chain exercise is combined with a resistance torso exercise.

The Post-Workout–10 Minutes

The post workout is the final part of the daily training plan. The post workout includes dynamic flexibility/mobility drills, joint integrity drills, and static flexibility movements.

Dynamic Flexibility/Mobility Drills

Basic hurdle drills similar to the pre-workout also are done at the completion of the session. A hybrid movement combining a barbell good morning and a snatch balance is used as the dynamic flexibility drill.

Joint Integrity Drills

Joint integrity is a section of the workout where the athlete performs several exercises or drills for the three main joints that are affected the most by injury during athletics: the ankle, knee, and shoulder. These exercises or drills are generally done for high volume and may include proprioception work.

Static Flexibility

To conclude the session, do static movements for the hip flexors, hamstrings, and chest and shoulder regions of the body (see Figure 5-2).

General Notes

When school is in session, each workout should begin by having the group come together for the goals, expectations, review of the workout, and miscellaneous information needed to begin. The majority of the training sessions end the same way. The group should break out together (team building). During the end of the session breakout, individuals should have the opportunity to speak about how the workout went, and coaches should give their input, discussing effort of the group and commending any outstanding performances.

Pre Work Out 10 minutes	Main Session 60 minutes	Posterior Chain Tier 10 minutes	Post Work Out 10 minutes
General Warm Up Power Zone Training Dynamic Flex/Mobility Neck/Traps – option	Tier 1 Tier 2 Tier 3 Tier 4 Tier 5	PC Tier – 3 sets Tri Set/ Combo Set option	Dynamic Flex/Mobility Joint Integrity Static Flex Neck/Traps - option

Figure 5-2. Daily plan

Some of the exercises and drills for the pre- and post-workout routines derive from physical therapy and athletic training protocols. The exercises from these disciplines for this portion of the daily plan are used to improve joint integrity and improving balance, coordination, and proprioception.

The Weekly Plan (Microcycle)

Figure 5-3 shows two examples of weekly plans that can be utilized. When doubling up on a training day with running and strength training, it is recommended that the team perform the running plan first and then proceed directly into the strength-training program (see Figure 5-4). This is primarily done with speed development sessions.

Monday	Tuesday	Wednesday	Thursday	Friday
AM Running Plan Speed Development	AM or PM Running Plan Conditioning	AM Strength Session L	AM or PM Running Plan Conditioning	AM Running Plan Speed Development
AM Strength Session T				AM Strength Session U
PM Extra Work Out option	AM or PM Extra Work Out option	PM Extra Work Out option	AM or PM Extra Work Out option	PM Extra Work Out option

Figure 5-3. Summer program microcycle

When performing a running session after a lifting session, at least three hours of recovery between the strength session and running session is recommended. Extra workouts are generally done three hours after the main workout of the day. If time is limited we will make exceptions.

Monday	Tuesday	Wednesday	Thursday	Friday
AM Strength Session T	PM Running Plan Speed Development	AM Strength Session L	PM Running Plan Speed Development	AM Running Plan Conditioning
PM Running Plan Conditioning				AM Strength Session U
PM Extra Work Out option	AM or PM Extra Work Out option	PM Extra Work Out option	AM or PM Extra Work Out option	PM Extra Work Out option

Figure 5-4. Winter program microcycle

Conclusion

Many ways to perform and develop a strength-training program for athletic development exist. The system outlined in this book is just one way. In a quest to continue to improve this program, it is necessary to embrace other programs of similar and different beliefs to make this program stronger. Athletes deserve coaches who are willing to strive to find out any and all information that may improve athletic performance.

This program is a true conglomeration of many of the programs that are being used today. The tier system is unique in some ways, and basic in others. It is still believed that there are some exercises and movements that cannot be omitted in the quest to improve strength in an athlete. But in athletics, the body is asked to do more then just stay in one place and react; therefore, many movements must be involved to improve athletic ability, which likely will lead to enhanced skill development when working with the coach.

The goals of a strength program should be simple: produce a sound training program for the athletes, evaluate all sports, develop programs that will strengthen injury-prone areas, have the athletes be the best-conditioned team competing, and give them the opportunity to win championships.

Championships are not won in the office, but won with athletes and coaches who give everything they have to become the best.

A

Charting Your Annual Plan

The development of the annual plan through the use of periodization should be a simple task. Too many coaches make this task far more agonizing then it really needs to be. This process has been simplified by taking into consideration what periodization is and how it relates to school-age athletes. Approximately 5 to 10 days after the previous in season or championship season should be used to review the previous plan and to develop the new annual plan for the specific sport being coached. A review day should follow every program. This allows the program planner to make adjustments to an upcoming program as well as record notes for the end-of-the-year recap.

To help put the information in Chapter 2 into an easily accessible way to create the annual plan, follow the step-by-step planning instructions that follow.

Developing your annual and cyclical plan should include these seven steps in order:

- Design a template.
- List calendar dates for weeks 1 to 52 (Remember: When does the training year begin?).
- Mark all competitions and uncontrollable factors.
- Break down your plan into the three main stages.
- Reduce your main stages to specific programs.
- Develop a running plan for each program.
- Develop a training intensity cycle(s) for each program—see Chapter 3.

These steps are shown in order on the following pages. Our template design was created using Microsoft Excel.

Annual Plan Development—Step 1

SPORT	1	2	3	4	5	6	7	8	9	10	11	12	13	14	15	16	17	18	19	20	21	22	23	24	25	26	27	28	29	30	31	32	33	34	35	36	37	38	39	40	41	42	43	44	45	46	47	48	49	50	51	52
Date (Sunday-Saturday)																																																				
STAGE																																																				
Program																																																				
Competition																																																				
Holidays																																																				
Uncontrollable Factors/Important Dates																																																				
Running Program Emphasis																																																				

Training Cycles	1	2	3	4	5	6	7	8	9	10	11	12	13	14	15	16	17	18	19	20	21	22	23	24	25	26	27	28	29	30	31	32	33	34	35	36	37	38	39	40	41	42	43	44	45	46	47	48	49	50	51	52
Microcycle ELITE/TRADITIONAL																																																				
Active Rest																																																				
Variation																																																				
Base																																																				
Load																																																				
Deload																																																				
Performance																																																				
Effort																																																				
Notes																																																				

KEY
Elite = Type of Training Template
ES = Elite template with emphasis on speed
EE = Elite template with emphasis on effort
Traditional = Type of Training Template
TR = Traditional template empahsis on volume

SADT = Student Athlete Discretionary Time

	1	2	3	4	5	6	7	8	9	10	11	12	13	14	15	16	17	18	19	20	21	22	23	24	25	26	27	28	29	30	31	32	33	34	35	36	37	38	39	40	41	42	43	44	45	46	47	48	49	50	51	52
Football	12	12	12	12	12	1	1	1	1	2	2	2	2	3	3	3	3	3	4	4	4	5	5	5	5	6	6	6	6	6	7	7	7	7	8	8	8	8	8	9	9	9	10	10	10	10	11	11	11	11	11	11
Date (Sunday–Saturday)	1	8	15	22	29	5	12	19	26	2	9	16	23	2	9	16	23	30	6	13	20	27	4	11	18	25	1	8	15	22	29	6	13	20	27	3	10	17	24	31	7	14	21	28	5	12	19	26	2	9	16	23
STAGE																																																				
Program																																																				
Competition																																																				
Holidays																																																				
Uncontrollable Factors/																																																				
Important Dates																																																				
Running Program																																																				
Emphasis																																																				
Training Cycles	1	2	3	4	5	6	7	8	9	10	11	12	13	14	15	16	17	18	19	20	21	22	23	24	25	26	27	28	29	30	31	32	33	34	35	36	37	38	39	40	41	42	43	44	45	46	47	48	49	50	51	52
Microcycle (ELITE/TRADITIONAL)																																																				
Active Rest																																																				
Variation																																																				
Base																																																				
Load																																																				
Deload																																																				
Performance																																																				
Effort																																																				
Notes																																																				

KEY
Elite = Type of Training Template
ES = Elite template with emphasis on speed
EE = Elite template with emphasis on effort
Traditional = Type of Training Template
TR = Traditional template emphasis on volume

SADT = Student Athlete Discretionary Time

Annual Plan Development—Step 2

Annual Plan Development—Step 3

Football	1	2	3	4	5	6	7	8	9	10	11	12	13	14	15	16	17	18	19	20	21	22	23	24	25	26	27	28	29	30	31	32	33	34	35	36	37	38	39	40	41	42	43	44	45	46	47	48	49	50	51	52
Date (mo.)	12	12	12	12	12	1	1	1	1	2	2	2	2	3	3	3	3	3	4	4	4	4	5	5	5	5	6	6	6	6	6	7	7	7	7	8	8	8	8	8	9	9	9	9	10	10	10	10	11	11	11	11
Sunday-Saturday	1	8	15	22	29	5	12	19	26	2	9	16	23	2	9	16	23	30	6	13	20	27	4	11	18	25	1	8	15	22	29	6	13	20	27	3	10	17	24	31	7	14	21	28	5	12	19	26	2	9	16	23

STAGE

Program

Competition / Holidays
bowl, bowl (wks 4–5); xx (wk 5); xx (wk 8); SG (wk 20); xx (wk 25); xx (wk 31); SADT (shaded); NAU, tba, Iowa, OSU, USC, UO, UNC, Ucla, CAL, Stan, WS, bye, UA (wks 40–52); xx (wks 40, 48, 50, 52)

Uncontrollable Factors / Important Dates
Fall, ex (wks 6–7); Spr, Sem (wk 8); Spr Br, Spr Prac, Spr Prac, Spr Prac (wks 15–20); Ex SADT (wks 24–25); Sum 1ex, Sum 2, Sum 2ex (wks 31–36); Fall Sem (wks 38–39)

Running Program

Emphasis

Training Cycles	1	2	3	4	5	6	7	8	9	10	11	12	13	14	15	16	17	18	19	20	21	22	23	24	25	26	27	28	29	30	31	32	33	34	35	36	37	38	39	40	41	42	43	44	45	46	47	48	49	50	51	52

Microcycle
ELITE/TRADITIONAL
Active Rest
Variation
Base
Load
Deload
Performance
Effort
Notes

KEY
Elite = Type of Training Template
ES = Elite template with emphasis on speed
EE = Elite template with emphasis on effort
Traditional = Type of Training Template
TR = Traditional template empahsis on volume

SADT = Student Athlete Discretionary Time

STAGE: REJUVENATION | DEVELOPMENTAL | COMPETITIVE

Football	1	2	3	4	5	6	7	8	9	10	11	12	13	14	15	16	17	18	19	20	21	22	23	24	25	26	27	28	29	30	31	32	33	34	35	36	37	38	39	40	41	42	43	44	45	46	47	48	49	50	51	52
Date Sunday-Saturday	12	12	12	12	12	1	1	1	1	2	2	2	2	3	3	3	3	3	4	4	4	4	5	5	5	5	6	6	6	6	6	7	7	7	7	8	8	8	8	8	9	9	9	9	10	10	10	10	11	11	11	11
	12	15	22	29	5	12	19	26	2	9	16	23	2	9	16	23	30	6	13	20	27	4	11	18	25	1	8	15	22	29	6	13	20	27	3	10	17	24	31	7	14	21	28	5	12	19	26	2	9	16	23

Program

Rows (left to right labels):
- Competition
- Holidays
- Uncontrollable Factors/ Important Dates
- Running Program Emphasis
- Training Cycles
- Microcycle — ELITE/TRADITIONAL
- Active Rest
- Variation
- Base
- Load
- Deload
- Performance
- Effort
- Notes

KEY
Elite = Type of Training Template
ES = Elite template with emphasis on speed
EE = Elite template with emphasis on effort
Traditional = Type of Training Template
TR = Traditional template empahsis on volume

SADT = Student Athlete Discretionary Time

Annual Plan Development—Step 5

Football	1	2	3	4	5	6	7	8	9	10	11	12	13	14	15	16	17	18	19	20	21	22	23	24	25	26	27	28	29	30	31	32	33	34	35	36	37	38	39	40	41	42	43	44	45	46	47	48	49	50	51	52
Date	12	12	12	12	12	1	1	1	1	2	2	2	2	3	3	3	3	3	4	4	4	4	5	5	5	5	6	6	6	6	6	7	7	7	7	8	8	8	8	8	9	9	9	9	10	10	10	10	11	11	11	11
Sunday-Saturday	1	8	15	22	29	5	12	19	26	2	9	16	23	2	9	16	23	30	6	13	20	27	4	11	18	25	1	8	15	22	29	6	13	20	27	3	10	17	24	31	7	14	21	28	5	12	19	26	2	9	16	23

STAGE: REJUVENATION — DEVELOPMENTAL — COMPETITIVE

Program: Post Season | Off Season | Winter | Spring I | 2nd | Spring II/Summer | Pre | In Season

Competition: bowl bowl ... NAU tba Iowa OSU USC UO UNC Ucla CAL Stam WS bye UA

Holidays: xx xx xx xx xx xx xx xx

Uncontrollable Factors/: Fall Fall | Spr | Spr Spr Spr | Spr Spr | Sum | Sum Sum | Fall
Important Dates: ex ex Sem | Br. Prac Prac Prac | Ex E: 1ex 2 | Sem

Running Program

Program Emphasis

| Training Cycles | 1 | 2 | 3 | 4 | 5 | 6 | 7 | 8 | 9 | 10 | 11 | 12 | 13 | 14 | 15 | 16 | 17 | 18 | 19 | 20 | 21 | 22 | 23 | 24 | 25 | 26 | 27 | 28 | 29 | 30 | 31 | 32 | 33 | 34 | 35 | 36 | 37 | 38 | 39 | 40 | 41 | 42 | 43 | 44 | 45 | 46 | 47 | 48 | 49 | 50 | 51 | 52 |

Microcycle

ELITE/TRADITIONAL

Active Rest

Variation

Base

Load

Deload

Performance

Effort

Notes

KEY
Elite = Type of Training Template
ES = Elite template with emphasis on speed
EE = Elite template with emphasis on effort
Traditional = Type of Training Template
TR = Traditional template emphsis on volume

SADT   SADT = Student Athlete Discretionary Time

Annual Plan Development—Step 6

Football	1	2	3	4	5	6	7	8	9	10	11	12	13	14	15	16	17	18	19	20	21	22	23	24	25	26	27	28	29	30	31	32	33	34	35	36	37	38	39	40	41	42	43	44	45	46	47	48	49	50	51	52
Date	12	12	12	12	12	12	1	1	1	1	2	2	2	3	3	3	3	3	4	4	4	4	5	5	5	5	6	6	6	6	6	7	7	7	7	8	8	8	8	8	9	9	9	10	10	10	10	11	11	11	11	11
Sunday-Saturday	15	22	29	5	12	19	26	2	9	16	23	30	6	13	20	27	4	11	18	25	1	8	15	22	29	6	13	20	27	3	10	17	24	31	7	14	21	28	5	12	19	26	2	9	16	23						

STAGE: REJUVENATION — DEVELOPMENTAL — COMPETITIVE

Program: Post Season | Off Season | Winter | Spring I | 2nd | Spring II/Summer | Pre | In Season

Competition	Holidays: bowl bowl	xx xx	SADT	xx	SG	xx	SADT	Sum 2ex	NAU fba Iowa OSU USC UO UNC Ucla CAL Stan WS bye UA

Competition numbers (In Season): 8 8 8 8 8 9 9 9 10 10 10 10 11 11 11
24 31 7 14 21 28 5 12 19 26 2 9 16 23

Uncontrollable Factors / Important Dates: Fall Fall (ex ex) | Spr Sem | Spr Prac / Spr Prac / Spr Prac / Spr Prac | Spr Spr / Ex Ex | Fall / Sem

Running Program Emphasis	General Conditioning / Athletic Conditioning	Category 1 / Complex Training / Speed Development	Category 2 / Metabolic / Practice	Cat 3 / Condo / Interv	Cat 3 / Condo / Interval	Category 2 / Category 1	Category 2 / Category 1	Cat 2	Category 2 / Sunday - Cat 1, Tuesday - Cat 2 - position / Wednesday - Cat 2 - special teams

Training Cycles: 1 2 3 4 5 6 7 | 8 9 10 11 12 13 14 15 | 16 17 18 19 20 21 22 | 23 24 25 26 27 | 28 29 30 31 32 33 34 35 | 36 | 37 38 39 40 41 42 43 44 45 46 47 48 49 50 51 52

Microcycle

ELITE/TRADITIONAL

Active Rest
Variation
Base
Load
Deload
Performance
Effort

Notes

KEY
Elite = Type of Training Template
ES = Elite template with emphasis on speed
EE = Elite template with emphasis on effort
Traditional = Type of Training Template
TR = Traditional template emphasis on volume

SADT | SADT = Student Athlete Discretionary Time

Football	1	2	3	4	5	6	7	8	9	10	11	12	13	14	15	16	17	18	19	20	21	22	23	24	25	26	27	28	29	30	31	32	33	34	35	36	37	38	39	40	41	42	43	44	45	46	47	48	49	50	51	52
Date	12	12	12	12	12	1	1	1	1	2	2	2	2	3	3	3	3	3	4	4	4	5	5	5	5	5	6	6	6	6	6	7	7	7	7	8	8	8	8	8	9	9	9	9	10	10	10	10	11	11	11	11
Sunday-Saturday	1	8	15	22	29	5	12	19	26	2	9	16	23	2	9	16	23	30	6	13	20	27	4	11	18	25	1	8	15	22	29	6	13	20	27	3	10	17	24	31	7	14	21	28	5	12	19	26	2	9	16	23

STAGE

| | REJUVENATION | | | | | | | | DEVELOPMENTAL | | | | | | | | | | | | | | | | | | | | | | | | | | | COMPETITIVE | | | | | | | | | | | | | | | | |

| Program | Post Season | Off Season | | | | | Winter | | | | | | | Spring I | | | | | | | 2nd Spring II/Summer | | | | | | | | | | | | | Pre | In Season | | | | | | | | | | | | | | | | |

Competition

| Competition | | bowl bowl | | | | | | | | | | | | | | | SG | | | | | | | | | | | | | | | | | | | | | NAU | tba | Iowa | OSU | USC | UO | UNC | Ucla | CAL | Stan | WS | bye | UA |

Holidays

| Holidays | | xx | xx | | | | xx | | | | | | | | | | | | | | | | | | | xx | | | | xx | | | | | | | | | | xx | | | | | | | xx | | | | | xx |

| Uncontrollable Factors/ | Fall Fall | | 1-to 1-9 | | Spr | | | | | | | | Spr Spr Spr Spr | | | | | | | Spr | Ex | | | | | Sum | | | | | | | | | Sum Sum | | | | | | | | | | | | | | | | | |
| Important Dates | ex. ex | | SADT | | Sem | | | | | | | | B- Prac Prac Prac Prac | | | | | | | Ex | | | | | | | | | | | | | | | 1ex 2ex | | | | | | | | | | | | | | | | | |

Running Program Emphasis

Running Program Emphasis	General Conditioning						Category 1							Category 2							Cat 3					Cat 3		Category 2					Category 2				Cat 2			Category 2												
	Athletic Conditioning						Complex Training							Metabolic/							Condo					Cond														Sunday - Cat 1, Tuesday - Cat 2 - position											
							Speed Development							Practice							Interv					Inter		Category 1					Category 1							Wednesday - Cat 2 - special teams											

Training Cycles

| Training Cycles | 1 | 2 | 3 | 4 | 5 | 6 | 7 | 8 | 9 | 10 | 11 | 12 | 13 | 14 | 15 | 16 | 17 | 18 | 19 | 20 | 21 | 22 | 23 | 24 | 25 | 26 | 27 | 28 | 29 | 30 | 31 | 32 | 33 | 34 | 35 | 36 | 37 | 38 | 39 | 40 | 41 | 42 | 43 | 44 | 45 | 46 | 47 | 48 | 49 | 50 | 51 | 52 |

Microcycle

| ELITE/TRADITIONAL | | | | | | | E | E | E | E | E | E | E | E | E | E | E | E | E | E | E | E | T | T | T | T | T | E | E | E | E | E | E | E | E | | | | E | E | E | E | E | E | E | E | E | E | E | E | E | E |
| | | | | | | | E | E | E | E | E | E | E | E | E | E | S | S | S | S | S | S | R | R | R | R | R | E | E | E | E | E | E | E | E | | | | S | S | S | S | S | S | S | S | S | S | S | E | E | S |

Active Rest

| Variation | V | V | V | | | | | | | | | | | | | A | | | | | | | A | V | | | A | V | | | | | | | | | A | V | V | | | | | | | | | | | | | | | |

Load

Base	80		70	80				75		85											68		80			75		70		75		75																				
Load	87		73	75	92			83		93												73	78			80		78		83		82																				
Deload			82				82	70	82	70			80															82	65		70																					

Performance

| Performance | | | | 5R | | | | | | 90 | | | | | 100 | | | | | | | | | | | | | | 85 | | 90 | | | | 90 | | | | | | | | | | | | | | | 90 | | | |

Effort

| Effort | | | | 5R | | | | | | | | | | | | E1 E1 E2 E2 | | | | | | | | | | | | | | | | | | | | | | | E3 E3 E4 E4 E5 E5 E6 E6 E7 E7 E8 E8 | | | | | | | | | | | | E9 |

Notes

Notes	technique	2 Day Split					Performance Elite							Advanced							Trad-			Perf		Performance					Performance					Cir-			Advanced Elite Cycle											
	circuit	Traditional												Elite							ional			Cycle		Cycle					Cycle					cuit			Seniors - Tier 1 Days 1&2, Day 3 Team WO											
	recover	Cycle												Cycle							Cycle															bands			Newcomers - Traditional S-End											
														S-End							S-End			Dev-S	Met-S			Met-S				Met-S																				

KEY

Elite = Type of Training Template
ES = Elite template with emphasis on speed
EE = Elite template with emphasis on effort
Traditional = Type of Training Template
TR = Traditional template emphsis on volume

SADT = Student Athlete Discretionary Time

B

Training Cycles

- Percentage-Based Cycles
- General Conditioning 4-week Cycle – Traditional – Total, Lower, Upper
- Strength Endurance 4-week Cycles – Traditional – Total
- Strength Endurance 4-week Cycles – Traditional – Lower, Upper
- Developmental Strength 4-week Cycles – Traditional 3 set – Total
- Developmental Strength 4-week Cycles – Traditional 6 set – Total
- Developmental Strength 4-week Cycles – Traditional 3 set – Lower, Upper
- Developmental Strength 4-week Cycles – Traditional 6 set – Lower, Upper
- Developmental Strength 4-week Cycles – Performance – Lower, Upper
- Prilepin Developmental 4-week Cycles – Performance

NINETY FIVE

	PrilipenH-1		PrilipenH-2		PrilipenO-1		PrilipenL-1		PrilipenL-2		1 set special		Advanced		Progressive		Wave		Wave-3		Descending		Ascending		Pyramid		HPyramid		Regress △	
	%	GR	%	GR	%	GR	%	GR	%	GR	%	GR	%	GR	%	GR	%	GR	%	GR	%	GR	%	GR	%	GR	%	GR	%	GR
warm up 1	55.0%	1t5	55.0%	1t5	57.5%	1t5	55.0%	1t5	55.0%	1t5	52.5%	x5	57.5%	1t5	42.5%	1t5	50.0%	1t5	45.0%	1t5			32.5%	1t5	22.5%	1t5	37.5%	1t5	57.5%	1t5
warm up 2	67.5%	1t5	67.5%	1t5	70.0%	1t5	67.5%	1t5	67.5%	1t5	67.5%	x4	70.0%	1t5	55.0%	1t5	62.5%	1t5	57.5%	1t5			45.0%	1t5	35.0%	1t5	50.0%	1t5	70.0%	1t5
warm up 3	77.5%	1t5	77.5%	1t5	80.0%	1t5	77.5%	1t5	77.5%	1t5	80.0%	x3	80.0%	1t5	65.0%	1t5	72.5%	1t5	67.5%	1t5			55.0%	1t5	45.0%	1t5	60.0%	1t5	80.0%	1t5
warm up 4	86.0%	1t5	86.0%	1t5	87.5%	1t5	85.0%	1t5	85.0%	1t5	87.5%	x2	87.5%	1t5	72.5%	1t5	80.0%	1t5	75.0%	1t5			62.5%	1t5	52.5%	1t5	67.5%	1t5	87.5%	1t5
work set A			92.5%	x1							95.0%	x2+																		
work set B	92.5%	x1	92.5%	x1	96.0%	x1									80.0%	x1	87.5%	x2	82.5%	x2			70.0%	x1					95.0%	x1+
work set C	92.5%	x1	92.5%	x1	96.0%	x1							96.0%	x1	85.0%	x1	96.0%	x1	90.0%	x1			75.0%	x1	60.0%	x10	75.0%	x5	95.0%	x1+
work set D	92.5%	x1	92.5%	x1									96.0%	x1	90.0%	x1	87.5%	x2	95.0%	x1			80.0%	x1	72.5%	x8	80.0%	x4	95.0%	x1+
work set E	92.5%	x1	92.5%	x1					92.5%	x1			96.0%	x1	95.0%	x1+	95.0%	x1	82.5%	x2			85.0%	x1	82.5%	x6	85.0%	x3	90.0%	xm4
work set F	92.5%	x1	92.5%	x1					92.5%	x1			96.0%	x1	95.0%	x1+	87.5%	x2	90.0%	x1			90.0%	x1	90.0%	x4	90.0%	x2	90.0%	xm4
work set G	92.5%	2x1	92.5%	2x1			92.5%	x2					95.0%	x1	95.0%	x1+	95.0%	x1	95.0%	x1			95.0%	x1	95.0%	x2+	95.0%	x1	82.5%	xm7
work set H	92.5%	2x1	92.5%	2x1			92.5%	x2					95.0%	x1	95.0%	x1+													70.0%	xm13

95% Training Cycles

NINETY TWO.FIVE

	PrilipenH-1		PrilipenH-2		PrilipenO-1		PrilipenL-1		PrilipenL-2		1 set special		Advanced		Progressive		Wave		Wave-3		Descending		Ascending		Pyramid		HPyramid		Regress △	
	%	GR	%	GR	%	GR	%	GR	%	GR	%	GR	%	GR	%	GR	%	GR	%	GR	%	GR	%	GR	%	GR	%	GR	%	GR
warm up 1	55.0%	1t5	55.0%	1t5	55.0%	1t5	55.0%	1t5	55.0%	1t5	47.5%	x5	55.0%	1t5	40.0%	1t5	47.5%	1t5	42.5%	1t5			30.0%	1t5	35.0%	1t5	35.0%	1t5	55.0%	1t5
warm up 2	67.5%	1t5	67.5%	1t5	67.5%	1t5	67.5%	1t5	67.5%	1t5	62.5%	x4	67.5%	1t5	52.5%	1t5	60.0%	1t5	55.0%	1t5			42.5%	1t5	47.5%	1t5	47.5%	1t5	67.5%	1t5
warm up 3	77.5%	1t5	77.5%	1t5	77.5%	1t5	77.5%	1t5	77.5%	1t5	75.0%	x3	77.5%	1t5	62.5%	1t5	70.0%	1t5	65.0%	1t5			52.5%	1t5	57.5%	1t5	57.5%	1t5	77.5%	1t5
warm up 4	86.0%	1t5	86.0%	1t5	86.0%	1t5	85.0%	1t5	85.0%	1t5	85.0%	x2	85.0%	1t5	70.0%	1t5	77.5%	1t5	72.5%	1t5			60.0%	1t5	65.0%	1t5	65.0%	1t5	85.0%	1t5
work set A			92.5%	x1							92.5%	x3+													45.0%	1t5	65.0%	1t5		
work set B			92.5%	x1	92.5%	x1									77.5%	x1	85.0%	x2	80.0%	x2			67.5%	x3					92.5%	x3
work set C	92.5%	x2	92.5%	x1	92.5%	x1							92.5%	x2	82.5%	x1	92.5%	x3	87.5%	x3			72.5%	x3	57.5%	x10	72.5%	x5	92.5%	x3
work set D	92.5%	x2	92.5%	x1	92.5%	x1							92.5%	x2	87.5%	x1	85.0%	x2	92.5%	x3			77.5%	x3	70.0%	x8	77.5%	x4	92.5%	x3
work set E	92.5%	x2	92.5%	x1	92.5%	x1			92.5%	x1			92.5%	x2	92.5%	x3	92.5%	x3	80.0%	x2			82.5%	x3	80.0%	x6	82.5%	x3	87.5%	xm5
work set F	92.5%	x2	92.5%	x1	92.5%	x1			92.5%	x1			92.5%	x2	92.5%	x3	85.0%	x2	87.5%	x2			87.5%	x3	87.5%	x4	87.5%	x2	80.0%	xm8
work set G	92.5%	x2	92.5%	x1	92.5%	x1			92.5%	x1			92.5%	x2	92.5%	x3	92.5%	x3	92.5%	x3			92.5%	x3	92.5%	x2+	92.5%	x1	70.0%	xm13
work set H	92.5%	x2	92.5%	x1	92.5%	x1			92.5%	x1			92.5%	x2	92.5%	x3														

92.5% Training Cycles

NINETY

	PhilipenH-1 %	GR	PhilipenH-2 %	GR	PhilipenO-1 %	GR	PhilipenL-1 %	GR	PhilipenL-2 %	GR	1 set special %	GR	Advanced %	GR	Progressive %	GR	Wave %	GR	Wave-3 %	GR	Descending %	GR	Ascending %	GR	Pyramid %	GR	HPyramid %	GR	Regress %	GR
warm up 1	52.5%	1t5	52.5%	1t5	52.5%	1t5	52.5%	1t5	52.5%	1t5	45.0%	x5	52.5%	1t5	37.5%	1t5	45.0%	1t5	40.0%	1t5							32.5%	1t5	52.5%	1t5
warm up 2	65.0%	1t5	65.0%	1t5	65.0%	1t5	65.0%	1t5	65.0%	1t5	60.0%	x4	65.0%	1t5	50.0%	1t5	57.5%	1t5	52.5%	1t5			35.0%	1t5			45.0%	1t5	65.0%	1t5
warm up 3	75.0%	1t5	75.0%	1t5	75.0%	1t5	75.0%	1t5	75.0%	1t5	72.5%	x3	75.0%	1t5	60.0%	1t5	67.5%	1t5	62.5%	1t5			45.0%	1t5			55.0%	1t5	75.0%	1t5
warm up 4	82.5%	1t5	82.5%	1t5	82.5%	1t5	82.5%	1t5	82.5%	1t5	82.5%	x2	82.5%	1t5	67.5%	1t5	75.0%	1t5	70.0%	1t5			57.5%	1t5	45.0%	1t5	62.5%	1t5	82.5%	1t5
work set A			90.0%	x1	90.0%	x1					90.0%	x3+																		
work set B			90.0%	x1	90.0%	x1																								
work set C			90.0%	x1	90.0%	x1							90.0%	x2	75.0%	x1	82.5%	x2	77.5%	x2			65.0%	x3	55.0%	x10	70.0%	x5	90.0%	x3
work set D	90.0%	x2	90.0%	x1	90.0%	x1							90.0%	x2	80.0%	x1	90.0%	x3	85.0%	x2			70.0%	x3	67.5%	x8	75.0%	x4	90.0%	x3
work set E	90.0%	x2	90.0%	x1	90.0%	x1			90.0%	x1			90.0%	x2	85.0%	x1	82.5%	x2	90.0%	x3			75.0%	x3	77.5%	x6	80.0%	x3	90.0%	x3
work set F	90.0%	x2	90.0%	x1	90.0%	x1			90.0%	x1			90.0%	x2	90.0%	x3	90.0%	x3	77.5%	x2			80.0%	x3	85.0%	x4	85.0%	x2	85.0%	xm6
work set G	90.0%	x2	90.0%	2x1	90.0%	x1	90.0%	x2	90.0%	x1			90.0%	x2	90.0%	x3	82.5%	x2	85.0%	x2			85.0%	x3	90.0%	x2+	90.0%	x1	77.5%	xm9
work set H	90.0%	x2	90.0%	2x1	90.0%	x1	90.0%	x2	90.0%	x1			90.0%	x2	90.0%	x3	90.0%	x3	90.0%	x3			90.0%	x3					67.5%	xm14

90% Training Cycles

EIGHTY SEVEN.FIVE

	PhilipenH-1 %	GR	PhilipenH-2 %	GR	PhilipenO-1 %	GR	PhilipenL-1 %	GR	PhilipenL-2 %	GR	1 set special %	GR	Advanced %	GR	Progressive %	GR	Wave %	GR	Wave-3 %	GR	Descending %	GR	Ascending %	GR	Pyramid %	GR	HPyramid %	GR	Regress %	GR
warm up 1	50.0%	1t5	50.0%	1t5	50.0%	1t5	50.0%	1t5			42.5%	x5	50.0%	1t5	35.0%	1t5	42.5%	1t5	37.5%	1t5			25.0%	1t5			30.0%	1t5	50.0%	1t5
warm up 2	62.5%	1t5	62.5%	1t5	62.5%	1t5	62.5%	1t5			57.5%	x4	62.5%	1t5	47.5%	1t5	55.0%	1t5	50.0%	1t5			37.5%	1t5			42.5%	1t5	62.5%	1t5
warm up 3	72.5%	1t5	72.5%	1t5	72.5%	1t5	72.5%	1t5			70.0%	x3	72.5%	1t5	57.5%	1t5	65.0%	1t5	60.0%	1t5			47.5%	1t5			52.5%	1t5	72.5%	1t5
warm up 4	80.0%	1t5	80.0%	1t5	80.0%	1t5	80.0%	1t5			80.0%	x2	80.0%	1t5	65.0%	1t5	72.5%	1t5	67.5%	1t5			55.0%	1t5	45.0%	1t5	60.0%	1t5	80.0%	1t5
work set A	87.5%	x4	87.5%	x2							87.5%	x5+																		
work set B			87.5%	x2																										
work set C			87.5%	x2									87.5%	x3	72.5%	x2	80.0%	x2	75.0%	x2			62.5%	x4	52.5%	x10	67.5%	x5	87.5%	x4
work set D	87.5%	x4	87.5%	x2	87.5%	x3	87.5%	x2					87.5%	x3	77.5%	x2	87.5%	x4	82.5%	x2			67.5%	x4	66.0%	x8	72.5%	x4	87.5%	x4
work set E	87.5%	x4	87.5%	x2	87.5%	x3	87.5%	x2					87.5%	x3	82.5%	x2	80.0%	x2	87.5%	x4			72.5%	x4	75.0%	x6	77.5%	x3	87.5%	x4
work set F	87.5%	x4	87.5%	x2	87.5%	x3	87.5%	x2					87.5%	x3	87.5%	x4	87.5%	x4	75.0%	x2			77.5%	x4	82.5%	x4	82.5%	x2	82.5%	xm6
work set G	87.5%	x4	87.5%	2x2	87.5%	x3	87.5%	x2					87.5%	x3	87.5%	x4	80.0%	x2	82.5%	x2			82.5%	x4	87.5%	x2+	87.5%	xm	75.0%	xm10
work set H	87.5%	x4	87.5%	2x2	87.5%	x3	87.5%	x2					87.5%	x3	87.5%	x4	87.5%	x4	87.5%	x4			87.5%	x4					65.0%	xm15

87.5% Training Cycles

85% Training Cycles

EIGHTY FIVE

	PrilipenH-1	PrilipenH-2	PrilipenO-1	PrilipenL-1	PrilipenL-2	1 set special	Advanced	Progressive	Wave	Wave-3	Descending	Ascending	Pyramid	HPyramid	Regress
warm up 1	47.5% 1t5	47.5% 1t5	47.5% 1t5	47.5% 1t5		40.0% x5	47.5% 1t5	32.5% 1t5	45.0% 1t5	36.0% 1t5		22.5% 1t5		27.5% 1t5	47.5% 1t5
warm up 2	60.0% 1t5	60.0% 1t5	60.0% 1t5	60.0% 1t5		56.0% x4	60.0% 1t5	45.0% 1t5	57.5% 1t5	47.5% 1t5		35.0% 1t5		40.0% 1t5	60.0% 1t5
warm up 3	70.0% 1t5	70.0% 1t5	70.0% 1t5	70.0% 1t5		67.5% x3	70.0% 1t5	55.0% 1t5	67.5% 1t5	57.5% 1t5		45.0% 1t5		50.0% 1t5	70.0% 1t5
warm up 4	77.5% 1t5	77.5% 1t5	77.5% 1t5	77.5% 1t5		77.5% x2	77.5% 1t5	62.5% 1t5	70.0% 1t5	66.0% 1t5		52.5% 1t5	45.0% 1t5	57.5% 1t5	77.5% 1t5
work set A		85.0% x2				85.0% x6+	85.0% x3	70.0% x2	77.5% x2	72.5% x2		60.0% x4	50.0% x10	65.0% x5	85.0% x4
work set B		85.0% x2					85.0% x3	75.0% x2	85.0% x4	80.0% x2		65.0% x4	62.5% x8	70.0% x4	85.0% x4
work set C		85.0% x2					85.0% x3	80.0% x2	77.5% x2	85.0% x4		70.0% x4	72.5% x6	75.0% x3	85.0% x4
work set D	85.0% x4	85.0% x2	85.0% x3	85.0% x2			85.0% x3	85.0% x4	85.0% x4	72.5% x2		75.0% x4	80.0% x4	80.0% x2	80.0% xm8
work set E	85.0% x4	85.0% x2	85.0% x3	85.0% x2			85.0% x3	85.0% x4	77.5% x2	80.0% x2		80.0% x4	85.0% x2+	85.0% xm	72.5% xm12
work set F	85.0% x4	85.0% x2	85.0% x3	85.0% x2			85.0% x3	85.0% x4	85.0% x4	72.5% x2		85.0% x4			62.5% xm15
work set G	85.0% x4	85.0% 2x2	85.0% x3	85.0% x2			85.0% x3	85.0% x4	77.5% x2	80.0% x2					
work set H	85.0% x4	85.0% 2x2	85.0% x3	85.0% x2			85.0% x3	85.0% x4	85.0% x4	85.0% x4					

82.5% Training Cycles

EIGHTY TWO.FIVE

	PrilipenH-1	PrilipenH-2	PrilipenO-1	PrilipenL-1	PrilipenL-2	1 set special	Advanced	Progressive	Wave	Wave-3	Descending	Ascending	Pyramid	HPyramid	Regress
warm up 1	45.0% 1t5	45.0% 1t5	45.0% 1t5	45.0% 1t5		37.5% x5	45.0% 1t5	30.0% 1t5	37.5% 1t5	32.5% 1t5		20.0% 1t5		35.0% 1t5	45.0% 1t5
warm up 2	57.5% 1t5	57.5% 1t5	57.5% 1t5	57.5% 1t5		52.5% x4	57.5% 1t5	42.5% 1t5	50.0% 1t5	45.0% 1t5		32.5% 1t5		47.5% 1t5	57.5% 1t5
warm up 3	67.5% 1t5	67.5% 1t5	67.5% 1t5	67.5% 1t5		65.0% x3	67.5% 1t5	52.5% 1t5	60.0% 1t5	55.0% 1t5		42.5% 1t5		55.0% 1t5	67.5% 1t5
warm up 4	75.0% 1t5	75.0% 1t5	75.0% 1t5	75.0% 1t5		75.0% x2	75.0% 1t5	60.0% 1t5	67.5% 1t5	62.5% 1t5		50.0% 1t5			75.0% 1t5
work set A		82.5% x2				82.5% x7+	82.5% x4	67.5% x3	75.0% x3	70.0% x3		57.5% x5	47.5% x10	62.5% x5	82.5% x5
work set B		82.5% x2					82.5% x4	72.5% x3	82.5% x5	77.5% x3		62.5% x5	60.0% x8	67.5% x4	82.5% x5
work set C		82.5% x2					82.5% x4	77.5% x3	75.0% x3	82.5% x5		67.5% x5	70.0% x6	72.5% x3	82.5% x5
work set D	82.5% x4	82.5% x2	82.5% x3	82.5% x2			82.5% x4	82.5% x5	82.5% x5	70.0% x3		72.5% x5	77.5% x4	77.5% x2	77.5% xm8
work set E	82.5% x4	82.5% x2	82.5% x3	82.5% x2			82.5% x4	82.5% x5	75.0% x3	77.5% x3		77.5% x5	82.5% x2+	82.5% xm	70.0% xm13
work set F	82.5% x4	82.5% x2	82.5% x3	82.5% x2			82.5% x4	82.5% x5	82.5% x5	82.5% x5		82.5% x5			60.0% xm15
work set G	82.5% x4	82.5% 2x2	82.5% x3	82.5% x2			82.5% x4	82.5% x5	75.0% x3	77.5% x3					
work set H	82.5% x4	82.5% 2x2	82.5% x3	82.5% x2			82.5% x4	82.5% x5	82.5% x5	82.5% x5					

EIGHTY — 80% Training Cycles

	PrilipenH-1	PrilipenH-2	PrilipenO-1	PrilipenL-1	PrilipenL-2	1 set special	Advanced	Progressive	Wave	Wave-3	Descending	Ascending	Pyramid	HPyramid ↑	Regress △
warm up 1	42.5% 1t5	42.5% 1t5	42.5% 1t5	42.5% 1t5		35.0% x5	42.5% 1t5	27.5% 1t5	35.0% 1t5	30.0% 1t5				22.5% 1t5	42.5% 1t5
warm up 2	55.0% 1t5	55.0% 1t5	55.0% 1t5	55.0% 1t5		50.0% x4	55.0% 1t5	40.0% 1t5	47.5% 1t5	42.5% 1t5		30.0% 1t5		35.0% 1t5	55.0% 1t5
warm up 3	65.0% 1t5	65.0% 1t5	65.0% 1t5	65.0% 1t5		62.5% x3	65.0% 1t5	50.0% 1t5	57.5% 1t5	52.5% 1t5		40.0% 1t5		45.0% 1t5	65.0% 1t5
warm up 4	72.5% 1t5	72.5% 1t5	72.5% 1t5	72.5% 1t5		72.5% x2	72.5% 1t5	57.5% 1t5	65.0% 1t5	60.0% 1t5		47.5% 1t5		52.5% 1t5	72.5% 1t5
work set A		80.0% x2				80.0% x8+									
work set B		80.0% x2													
work set C		80.0% x2					80.0% x5	65.0% x3	72.5% x3	67.5% x3		56.0% x6	45.0% x10	60.0% x5	80.0% x6
work set D	80.0% x4	80.0% x2	80.0% x3	80.0% x2			80.0% x5	70.0% x3	80.0% x6	75.0% x6		60.0% x6	57.5% x8	65.0% x4	80.0% x6
work set E	80.0% x4	80.0% x2	80.0% x3	80.0% x2			80.0% x5	75.0% x3	72.5% x3	67.5% x3		65.0% x6	67.5% x6	70.0% x3	80.0% x6
work set F	80.0% x4	80.0% x2	80.0% x3	80.0% x2			80.0% x5	80.0% x6	80.0% x6	75.0% x3		70.0% x6	75.0% x4	75.0% x2	75.0% xm10
work set G	80.0% x4	80.0% 2x2	80.0% x3	80.0% x2			80.0% x5	80.0% x6	72.5% x3	72.5% x3		75.0% x6			
work set H	80.0% x4	80.0% 2x2	80.0% x3	80.0% x2			80.0% x5	80.0% x6	80.0% x6	80.0% x6		80.0% x6	80.0% x2+	80.0% xm	67.5% xm13

SEVENTY SEVEN.FIVE — 77.5% Training Cycles

	PrilipenH-1	PrilipenH-2	PrilipenH-3	PrilipenO-1	PrilipenO-2	PrilipenL-1	PrilipenL-2	PrilipenL-3	1 set special	Advanced	Progressive	Descending	Regress △
warm up 1	40.0% 1t5	40.0% 1t5	40.0% 1t5	40.0% 1t5	40.0% 1t5	40.0% 1t5	40.0% 1t5	40.0% 1t5	42.5% x5	40.0% 1t5	25.0% 1t5	40.0% 1t5	40.0% 1t5
warm up 2	52.5% 1t5	52.5% 1t5	52.5% 1t5	52.5% 1t5	52.5% 1t5	52.5% 1t5	52.5% 1t5	52.5% 1t5	55.0% x4	52.5% 1t5	37.5% 1t5	52.5% 1t5	52.5% 1t5
warm up 3	62.5% 1t5	62.5% 1t5	62.5% 1t5	62.5% 1t5	62.5% 1t5	62.5% 1t5	62.5% 1t5	62.5% 1t5	65.0% x3	62.5% 1t5	47.5% 1t5	62.5% 1t5	62.5% 1t5
warm up 4	70.0% 1t5	70.0% 1t5	70.0% 1t5	70.0% 1t5	70.0% 1t5	70.0% 1t5	70.0% 1t5	70.0% 1t5	72.5% x2	70.0% 1t5	55.0% 1t5	70.0% 1t5	70.0% 1t5
work set A			77.5% x3						77.5% x9+				
work set B			77.5% x3										
work set C		77.5% x4	77.5% x3		77.5% x3					77.5% x6	62.5% x4	77.5% x8	77.5% x7
work set D		77.5% x4	77.5% x3		77.5% x3			77.5% x3		77.5% x6	67.5% x4	75.0% x8	77.5% x7
work set E	77.5% x6	77.5% x4	77.5% x3	77.5% x6	77.5% x3			77.5% x3		77.5% x6	72.5% x4	72.5% x8	77.5% x7
work set F	77.5% x6	77.5% x4	77.5% x3	77.5% x6	77.5% x3	77.5% x6		77.5% x3		77.5% x6	77.5% x7	70.0% x8	72.5% xm12
work set G	77.5% x6	77.5% x4	77.5% x3	77.5% x6	77.5% x3	77.5% x6		77.5% x3		77.5% x6	77.5% x7	67.5% x8	65.0% xm15
work set H	77.5% x6	77.5% x4	77.5% x3	77.5% x6	77.5% x3	77.5% x6		77.5% x3		77.5% x6	77.5% x7	65.0% x8	

80% Training Cycles

77.5% Training Cycles

SEVENTY FIVE

75% Training Cycles

	PrilipenH-1		PrilipenH-2		PrilipenH-3		PrilipenO-1		PrilipenO-2		PrilipenL-1		PrilipenL-2		PrilipenL-3		1 set special		Advanced		Progressive		Descending		Regress △	
	%	GR	%	GR	%	GR	%	GR	%	GR	%	GR	%	GR	%	GR	%	GR	%	GR	%	GR	%	GR	%	GR
warm up 1	37.5%	1t5	37.5%	1t5	37.5%	1t5	37.5%	1t5	37.5%	1t5	37.5%	1t5	37.5%	1t5	37.5%	1t5	42.5%	x5	37.5%	1t5	22.5%	1t5	37.5%	1t5	37.5%	1t5
warm up 2	50.0%	1t5	50.0%	1t5	50.0%	1t5	50.0%	1t5	50.0%	1t5	50.0%	1t5	50.0%	1t5	50.0%	1t5	55.0%	x4	50.0%	1t5	36.0%	1t5	50.0%	1t5	50.0%	1t5
warm up 3	60.0%	1t5	60.0%	1t5	60.0%	1t5	60.0%	1t5	60.0%	1t5	60.0%	1t5	60.0%	1t5	60.0%	1t5	65.0%	x3	60.0%	1t5	45.0%	1t5	60.0%	1t5	60.0%	1t5
warm up 4	67.5%	1t5	67.5%	1t5	67.5%	1t5	67.5%	1t5	67.5%	1t5	67.5%	1t5	67.5%	1t5	67.5%	1t5	72.5%	x2	67.5%	1t5	52.5%	1t5	67.5%	1t5	67.5%	1t5
work set A			75.0%	x3	75.0%	x3											75.0%	x10+								
work set B			75.0%	x3	75.0%	x3																				
work set C			75.0%	x4	75.0%	x3			75.0%	x3											60.0%	x4	75.0%	x8	75.0%	x7
work set D			75.0%	x4	75.0%	x3			75.0%	x3											65.0%	x4	72.5%	x8	75.0%	x7
work set E	75.0%	x6	75.0%	x4	75.0%	x3	75.0%	x6	75.0%	x3					75.0%	x3			75.0%	x6	70.0%	x4	70.0%	x8	75.0%	x7
work set F	75.0%	x6	75.0%	x4	75.0%	x3	75.0%	x6	75.0%	x3	75.0%	x6	75.0%	x4	75.0%	x3			75.0%	x6	75.0%	x7	67.5%	x8	70.0%	xm12
work set G	75.0%	x6	75.0%	x4	75.0%	x3	75.0%	x6	75.0%	x3	75.0%	x6	75.0%	x4	75.0%	x3			75.0%	x6	75.0%	x7	65.0%	x8	62.5%	xm15
work set H	75.0%	x6	75.0%	x4	75.0%	x3	75.0%	x6	75.0%	x3	75.0%	x6	75.0%	x4	75.0%	x3			75.0%	x6	75.0%	x7	62.5%	x8		

SEVENTY TWO.FIVE

72.5% Training Cycles

	PrilipenH-1		PrilipenH-2		PrilipenH-3		PrilipenO-1		PrilipenO-2		PrilipenL-1		PrilipenL-2		PrilipenL-3		1 set special		Advanced		Progressive		Descending		Regress △	
	%	GR	%	GR	%	GR	%	GR	%	GR	%	GR	%	GR	%	GR	%	GR	%	GR	%	GR	%	GR	%	GR
warm up 1	35.0%	1t5	35.0%	1t5	35.0%	1t5	35.0%	1t5	35.0%	1t5	35.0%	1t5	35.0%	1t5	35.0%	1t5	42.5%	x5	35.0%	1t5	20.0%	1t5	35.0%	1t5	35.0%	1t5
warm up 2	47.5%	1t5	47.5%	1t5	47.5%	1t5	47.5%	1t5	47.5%	1t5	47.5%	1t5	47.5%	1t5	47.5%	1t5	55.0%	x4	47.5%	1t5	32.5%	1t5	47.5%	1t5	47.5%	1t5
warm up 3	57.5%	1t5	57.5%	1t5	57.5%	1t5	57.5%	1t5	57.5%	1t5	57.5%	1t5	57.5%	1t5	57.5%	1t5	65.0%	x3	57.5%	1t5	42.5%	1t5	57.5%	1t5	57.5%	1t5
warm up 4	65.0%	1t5	65.0%	1t5	65.0%	1t5	65.0%	1t5	65.0%	1t5	65.0%	1t5	65.0%	1t5	65.0%	1t5	72.5%	x2	65.0%	1t5	50.0%	1t5	65.0%	1t5	65.0%	1t5
work set A			72.5%	x3	72.5%	x3											72.5%	x12+								
work set B			72.5%	x3	72.5%	x3																				
work set C			72.5%	x4	72.5%	x3			72.5%	x3											57.5%	x5	72.5%	x10	72.5%	x10
work set D			72.5%	x4	72.5%	x3			72.5%	x3											62.5%	x5	70.0%	x10	72.5%	x10
work set E	72.5%	x6	72.5%	x4	72.5%	x3	72.5%	x6	72.5%	x3					72.5%	x3			72.5%	x8	67.5%	x5	67.5%	x10	72.5%	x10
work set F	72.5%	x6	72.5%	x4	72.5%	x3	72.5%	x6	72.5%	x3	72.5%	x6	72.5%	x4	72.5%	x3			72.5%	x8	72.5%	x10	65.0%	x10	67.5%	xm12
work set G	72.5%	x6	72.5%	x4	72.5%	x3	72.5%	x6	72.5%	x3	72.5%	x6	72.5%	x4	72.5%	x3			72.5%	x8	72.5%	x10	62.5%	x10	60.0%	xm15
work set H	72.5%	x6	72.5%	x4	72.5%	x3	72.5%	x6	72.5%	x3	72.5%	x6	72.5%	x4	72.5%	x3			72.5%	x8	72.5%	x10	60.0%	x10		

SEVENTY

70% Training Cycles

	PhilipenH-1 %	GR	PhilipenH-2 %	GR	PhilipenH-3 %	GR	PhilipenO-1 %	GR	PhilipenO-2 %	GR	PhilipenL-1 %	GR	PhilipenL-2 %	GR	PhilipenL-3 %	GR	1 set special %	GR	Advanced %	GR	Progressive %	GR	Descending %	GR	Regress △ %	GR
warm up 1	32.5%	1t5	32.5%	1t5	32.5%	1t5	32.5%	1t5	32.5%	1t5	32.5%	1t5	32.5%	1t5	32.5%	1t5	42.5%	x5	32.5%	1t5			32.5%	1t5	32.5%	1t5
warm up 2	45.0%	1t5	45.0%	1t5	45.0%	1t5	45.0%	1t5	45.0%	1t5	45.0%	1t5	45.0%	1t5	45.0%	1t5	55.0%	x4	45.0%	1t5	30.0%	1t5	45.0%	1t5	45.0%	1t5
warm up 3	55.0%	1t5	55.0%	1t5	55.0%	1t5	55.0%	1t5	55.0%	1t5	55.0%	1t5	55.0%	1t5	55.0%	1t5	65.0%	x3	55.0%	1t5	40.0%	1t5	55.0%	1t5	55.0%	1t5
warm up 4	62.5%	1t5	62.5%	1t5	62.5%	1t5	62.5%	1t5	62.5%	1t5	62.5%	1t5	62.5%	1t5	62.5%	1t5	72.5%	x2	62.5%	1t5	47.5%	1t5	62.5%	1t5	62.5%	1t5
work set A					70.0%	x3											70.0%	x13+								
work set B					70.0%	x3																				
work set C			70.0%	x4	70.0%	x3			70.0%	x3									70.0%	x8	55.0%	x5	70.0%	x10	70.0%	x10
work set D			70.0%	x4	70.0%	x3			70.0%	x3									70.0%	x8	60.0%	x5	67.5%	x10	70.0%	x10
work set E	70.0%	x6	70.0%	x4	70.0%	x3			70.0%	x3			70.0%	x4	70.0%	x3			70.0%	x8	65.0%	x5	65.0%	x10	70.0%	x10
work set F	70.0%	x6	70.0%	x4	70.0%	x3	70.0%	x6	70.0%	x3	70.0%	x6	70.0%	x4	70.0%	x3			70.0%	x8	70.0%	x10	62.5%	x10	65.0%	xm12
work set G	70.0%	x6	70.0%	x4	70.0%	x3	70.0%	x6	70.0%	x3	70.0%	x6	70.0%	x4	70.0%	x3			70.0%	x8	70.0%	x10	60.0%	x10		
work set H	70.0%	x6	70.0%	x4	70.0%	x3	70.0%	x6	70.0%	x3	70.0%	x6	70.0%	x4	70.0%	x3			70.0%	x8	70.0%	x10	57.5%	x10		

SIXTY SEVEN.FIVE

67.5% Training Cycles

	PhilipenH-1 %	GR	PhilipenH-2 %	GR	PhilipenH-3 %	GR	PhilipenO-1 %	GR	PhilipenO-2 %	GR	PhilipenO-3 %	GR	PhilipenL-1 %	GR	PhilipenL-2 %	GR	1 set special %	GR	Advanced %	GR	Progressive %	GR	Descending %	GR
warm up 1	30.0%	1t5	30.0%	1t5	30.0%	1t5	30.0%	1t5	30.0%	1t5	30.0%	1t5	30.0%	1t5	30.0%	1t5	42.5%	x5	30.0%	1t5			30.0%	1t5
warm up 2	42.5%	1t5	42.5%	1t5	42.5%	1t5	42.5%	1t5	42.5%	1t5	42.5%	1t5	42.5%	1t5	42.5%	1t5	55.0%	x4	42.5%	1t5	27.5%	1t5	42.5%	1t5
warm up 3	52.5%	1t5	52.5%	1t5	52.5%	1t5	52.5%	1t5	52.5%	1t5	52.5%	1t5	52.5%	1t5	52.5%	1t5	65.0%	x3	52.5%	1t5	37.5%	1t5	52.5%	1t5
warm up 4	60.0%	1t5	60.0%	1t5	60.0%	1t5	60.0%	1t5	60.0%	1t5	60.0%	1t5	60.0%	1t5	60.0%	1t5	72.5%	x2	60.0%	1t5	45.0%	1t5	60.0%	1t5
work set A					67.5%	x3					67.5%	x3					67.5%	x14+						
work set B					67.5%	x3					67.5%	x3												
work set C			67.5%	x5	67.5%	x3			67.5%	x4	67.5%	x3			67.5%	x3			67.5%	x10	52.5%	x6	67.5%	x12
work set D	67.5%	x6	67.5%	x5	67.5%	x3			67.5%	x4	67.5%	x3			67.5%	x3			67.5%	x10	57.5%	x6	65.0%	x12
work set E	67.5%	x6	67.5%	x5	67.5%	x3	67.5%	x6	67.5%	x4	67.5%	x3			67.5%	x3			67.5%	x10	62.5%	x6	62.5%	x12
work set F	67.5%	x6	67.5%	x5	67.5%	x3	67.5%	x6	67.5%	x4	67.5%	x3	67.5%	x6	67.5%	x3			67.5%	x10	67.5%	x12	60.0%	x12
work set G	67.5%	x6	67.5%	x5	67.5%	2x3	67.5%	x6	67.5%	x4	67.5%	x3	67.5%	x6	67.5%	x3			67.5%	x10	67.5%	x12	57.5%	x12
work set H	67.5%	x6	67.5%	x5	67.5%	2x3	67.5%	x6	67.5%	x4	67.5%	x3	67.5%	x6	67.5%	x3			67.5%	x10	67.5%	x12	55.0%	x12

SIXTY FIVE — 65% Training Cycles

	PrilipenH-1 %	GR	PrilipenH-2 %	GR	PrilipenH-3 %	GR	PrilipenO-1 %	GR	PrilipenO-2 %	GR	PrilipenO-3 %	GR	PrilipenL-1 %	GR	PrilipenL-2 %	GR	1 set special %	GR	Advanced %	GR	Progressive %	GR	Descending %	GR
warm up 1	27.5%	1t5			27.5%	1t5	27.5%	1t5	27.5%	1t5	27.5%	1t5	27.5%	1t5	27.5%	1t5	42.5%	x5	27.5%	1t5			27.5%	1t5
warm up 2	40.0%	1t5			40.0%	1t5	40.0%	1t5	40.0%	1t5	40.0%	1t5	40.0%	1t5	40.0%	1t5	55.0%	x4	40.0%	1t5	25.0%	1t5	40.0%	1t5
warm up 3	50.0%	1t5			50.0%	1t5	50.0%	1t5	50.0%	1t5	50.0%	1t5	50.0%	1t5	50.0%	1t5	65.0%	x3	50.0%	1t5	35.0%	1t5	50.0%	1t5
warm up 4	57.5%	1t5			57.5%	1t5	57.5%	1t5	57.5%	1t5	57.5%	1t5	57.5%	1t5	57.5%	1t5	72.5%	x2	57.5%	1t5	42.5%	1t5	57.5%	1t5
work set A					65.0%	x3					65.0%	x3					66.0%	x15+						
work set B					65.0%	x3					65.0%	x3												
work set C			65.0%	x5	65.0%	x3			65.0%	x4	65.0%	x3			65.0%	x3					50.0%	x6	65.0%	x12
work set D	65.0%	x6	65.0%	x5	65.0%	x3			65.0%	x4	65.0%	x3			65.0%	x3			65.0%	x10	55.0%	x6	62.5%	x12
work set E	65.0%	x6	65.0%	x5	65.0%	x3	65.0%	x6	65.0%	x4	65.0%	x3			65.0%	x3			65.0%	x10	60.0%	x6	60.0%	x12
work set F	65.0%	x6	65.0%	x5	65.0%	x3	65.0%	x6	65.0%	x4	65.0%	x3	65.0%	x6	65.0%	x3			65.0%	x10	65.0%	x12	57.5%	x12
work set G	65.0%	x6	65.0%	x5	65.0%	2x3	65.0%	x6	65.0%	x4	65.0%	x3	65.0%	x6	65.0%	x3			65.0%	x10	65.0%	x12	55.0%	x12
work set H	65.0%	x6	65.0%	x5	65.0%	2x3	65.0%	x6	65.0%	x4	65.0%	x3	65.0%	x6	65.0%	x3			65.0%	x10	65.0%	x12	52.5%	x12

65% Training Cycles

SIXTY TWO.FIVE — 62.5% Training Cycles

	PrilipenH-1 %	GR	PrilipenH-2 %	GR	PrilipenH-3 %	GR	PrilipenO-1 %	GR	PrilipenO-2 %	GR	PrilipenO-3 %	GR	PrilipenL-1 %	GR	PrilipenL-2 %	GR	1 set special %	GR	Advanced %	GR	Progressive %	GR	Descending %	GR
warm up 1	25.0%	1t5			25.0%	1t5	25.0%	1t5	25.0%	1t5	25.0%	1t5	25.0%	1t5	25.0%	1t5	42.5%	x5	25.0%	1t5			25.0%	1t5
warm up 2	37.5%	1t5			37.5%	1t5	37.5%	1t5	37.5%	1t5	37.5%	1t5	37.5%	1t5	37.5%	1t5	56.0%	x4	37.5%	1t5	27.5%	1t5	37.5%	1t5
warm up 3	47.5%	1t5			47.5%	1t5	47.5%	1t5	47.5%	1t5	47.5%	1t5	47.5%	1t5	47.5%	1t5	65.0%	x3	47.5%	1t5	37.5%	1t5	47.5%	1t5
warm up 4	55.0%	1t5			55.0%	1t5	55.0%	1t5	55.0%	1t5	55.0%	1t5	55.0%	1t5	55.0%	1t5	72.5%	x2	55.0%	1t5	45.0%	1t5	55.0%	1t5
work set A					62.5%	x3					62.5%	x3					62.5%	x15+						
work set B					62.5%	x3					62.5%	x3												
work set C			62.5%	x5	62.5%	x3			62.5%	x4	62.5%	x3			62.5%	x3			62.5%	x12	52.5%	x8	62.5%	x15
work set D	62.5%	x6	62.5%	x5	62.5%	x3			62.5%	x4	62.5%	x3			62.5%	x3			62.5%	x12	57.5%	x8	60.0%	x15
work set E	62.5%	x6	62.5%	x5	62.5%	x3	62.5%	x6	62.5%	x4	62.5%	x3			62.5%	x3			62.5%	x12	62.5%	x15	57.5%	x15
work set F	62.5%	x6	62.5%	x5	62.5%	x3	62.5%	x6	62.5%	x4	62.5%	x3	62.5%	x6	62.5%	x3			62.5%	x12	62.5%	x15	55.0%	x15
work set G	62.5%	x6	62.5%	x5	62.5%	2x3	62.5%	x6	62.5%	x4	62.5%	x3	62.5%	x6	62.5%	x3			62.5%	x12	62.5%	x15	52.5%	x15
work set H	62.5%	x6	62.5%	x5	62.5%	2x3	62.5%	x6	62.5%	x4	62.5%	x3	62.5%	x6	62.5%	x3			62.5%	x12	62.5%	x15	50.0%	x15

62.5% Training Cycles

SIXTY

	PriilipenH-1		PriilipenH-2		PriilipenH-3		PriilipenO-1		PriilipenO-2		PriilipenO-3		PriilipenL-1		PriilipenL-2		1 set special		Advanced		Progressive		Descending	
	%	GR	%	GR	%	GR	%	GR	%	GR	%	GR	%	GR	%	GR	%	GR	%	GR	%	GR	%	GR
warm up 1	22.5%	1t5	22.5%	1t5	22.5%	1t5	22.5%	1t5	22.5%	1t5	22.5%	1t5	22.5%	1t5	22.5%	1t5	42.5%	x5	22.5%	1t5			22.5%	1t5
warm up 2	35.0%	1t5	35.0%	1t5	35.0%	1t5	35.0%	1t5	35.0%	1t5	35.0%	1t5	35.0%	1t5	35.0%	1t5	55.0%	x4	35.0%	1t5	25.0%	1t5	35.0%	1t5
warm up 3	45.0%	1t5	45.0%	1t5	45.0%	1t5	45.0%	1t5	45.0%	1t5	45.0%	1t5	45.0%	1t5	45.0%	1t5	65.0%	x3	45.0%	1t5	35.0%	1t5	45.0%	1t5
warm up 4	52.5%	1t5	52.5%	1t5	52.5%	1t5	52.5%	1t5	52.5%	1t5	52.5%	1t5	52.5%	1t5	52.5%	1t5	72.5%	x2	52.5%	1t5	42.5%	1t5	52.5%	1t5
work set A					60.0%	x3					60.0%	x3					60.0%	x15+						
work set B					60.0%	x3					60.0%	x3												
work set C	60.0%	x6	60.0%	x5	60.0%	x3			60.0%	x4	60.0%	x3			60.0%	x3			60.0%	x12			60.0%	x15
work set D	60.0%	x6	60.0%	x5	60.0%	x3			60.0%	x4	60.0%	x3			60.0%	x3			60.0%	x12	50.0%	x8	57.5%	x15
work set E	60.0%	x6	60.0%	x5	60.0%	x3	60.0%	x6	60.0%	x4	60.0%	x3			60.0%	x3			60.0%	x12	55.0%	x8	55.0%	x15
work set F	60.0%	x6	60.0%	x5	60.0%	x3	60.0%	x6	60.0%	x4	60.0%	x3			60.0%	x3			60.0%	x12	60.0%	x15	52.5%	x15
work set G	60.0%	x6	60.0%	x5	60.0%	2x3	60.0%	x6	60.0%	x4	60.0%	x3	60.0%	x6	60.0%	x3			60.0%	x12	60.0%	x15	50.0%	x15
work set H	60.0%	x6	60.0%	x5	60.0%	2x3	60.0%	x6	60.0%	x4	60.0%	x3	60.0%	x6	60.0%	x3			60.0%	x12	60.0%	x15	47.5%	x15

60% Training Cycles

General Conditioning (LOWER UPPER BODY)

	Base	Load	Load	UnLoad
Weekly %	62.5%	65.0%	67.5%	60.0%
differential	[-] 5%	[-] 5%	Top %	[-] 7.5%
WORK SETS	3 sets	3 sets	3 sets	3 sets
TOP SETS	3 sets	3 sets	3 sets	3 sets
Weeks #	WK 1	WK 2	WK 3	WK 4
wu-a	27.5% 1t5	30.0% 1t5	32.5% 1t5	15.0% 1t5
wu-b	40.0% 1t5	42.5% 1t5	45.0% 1t5	30.0% 1t5
wu-c	50.0% 1t5	52.5% 1t5	55.0% 1t5	42.5% 1t5
wu-d	57.5% 1t5	60.0% 1t5	62.5% 1t5	52.5% 1t5
w1	62.5% x10	65.0% x10	67.5% x10	60.0% x8
w2	62.5% x10	65.0% x10	67.5% x10	60.0% x8
w3	62.5% x10	65.0% x10	67.5% x10	60.0% x8
w4				
w5				
w6				

General Conditioning (TOTAL BODY)

	Base	Load	Load	UnLoad
Weekly %	62.5%	65.0%	67.5%	60.0%
differential	[-] 5%	[-] 5%	Top %	[-] 7.5%
WORK SETS	3 sets	3 sets	3 sets	3 sets
TOP SETS	3 sets	3 sets	3 sets	3 sets
Weeks #	WK 1	WK 2	WK 3	WK 4
wu-a	27.5% 1t5	30.0% 1t5	32.5% 1t5	15.0% 1t5
wu-b	40.0% 1t5	42.5% 1t5	45.0% 1t5	30.0% 1t5
wu-c	50.0% 1t5	52.5% 1t5	55.0% 1t5	42.5% 1t5
wu-d	57.5% 1t5	60.0% 1t5	62.5% 1t5	52.5% 1t5
w1	62.5% x6	65.0% x6	67.5% x6	60.0% x4
w2	62.5% x6	65.0% x6	67.5% x6	60.0% x4
w3	62.5% x6	65.0% x6	67.5% x6	60.0% x4
w4				
w5				
w6				

General Conditioning 4-week Cycle – Traditional – Total, Lower, Upper

STRENGTH ENDURANCE — TOTAL BODY (Left)

	Base	Load	Load	UnLoad
Weekly %	67.5%	72.5%	77.5%	70.0%
differential	[-] 10%	[-] 5%	Top %	[-] 7.5%
WORK SETS	5 sets	6 sets	6 sets	4 sets
TOP SETS	5 sets	6 sets	6 sets	4 sets
Weeks #	WK 1	WK 2	WK 3	WK 4
wu-a	30.0% 1t5	35.0% 1t5	40.0% 1t5	32.5% 1t5
wu-b	42.5% 1t5	47.5% 1t5	52.5% 1t5	45.0% 1t5
wu-c	52.5% 1t5	57.5% 1t5	62.5% 1t5	55.0% 1t5
wu-d	60.0% 1t5	65.0% 1t5	70.0% 1t5	62.5% 1t5
wA				
wB				
wC	67.5% X6	72.5% X6	77.5% X5	70.0% X3
wD	65.0% X6	70.0% X6	75.0% X5	67.5% X3
wE	62.5% X6	67.5% X6	72.5% X5	65.0% X3
wF	60.0% X6	65.0% X6	70.0% X5	62.5% X3
wG	57.5% X6	62.5% X6	67.5% X5	
wH		60.0% X6	65.0% X5	

STRENGTH ENDURANCE — TOTAL BODY (Right)

	Base	Load	Load	UnLoad
Weekly %	65.0%	70.0%	75.0%	67.5%
differential	[-] 10%	[-] 5%	Top %	[-] 7.5%
WORK SETS	5 sets	6 sets	6 sets	4 sets
TOP SETS	5 sets	6 sets	6 sets	4 sets
Weeks #	WK 1	WK 2	WK 3	WK 4
wu-a	27.5% 1t5	32.5% 1t5	37.5% 1t5	30.0% 1t5
wu-b	40.0% 1t5	45.0% 1t5	50.0% 1t5	42.5% 1t5
wu-c	50.0% 1t5	55.0% 1t5	60.0% 1t5	52.5% 1t5
wu-d	57.5% 1t5	62.5% 1t5	67.5% 1t5	60.0% 1t5
wA				
wB				
wC	65.0% X6	70.0% X6	75.0% X6	67.5% X3
wD	62.5% X6	67.5% X6	72.5% X6	65.0% X3
wE	60.0% X6	65.0% X6	70.0% X6	62.5% X3
wF	57.5% X6	62.5% X6	67.5% X6	60.0% X3
wG	55.0% X6	60.0% X6	65.0% X6	
wH		57.5% X6	62.5% X6	

77.5% Strength Endurance 4-week Cycles – Traditional – Total

75% Strength Endurance 4-week Cycles – Traditional – Total

STRENGTH ENDURANCE — TOTAL / BODY (72.5%)

	Base	Load	Load	UnLoad
Weekly %	62.5%	67.5%	72.5%	65.0%
differential	[-] 10%	[-] 5%	Top %	[-] 7.5%
WORK SETS	5 sets	6 sets	6 sets	4 sets
TOP SETS	5 sets	6 sets	6 sets	4 sets
Weeks #	WK 1	WK 2	WK 3	WK 4
wu-a	25.0% 1t5	30.0% 1t5	35.0% 1t5	27.5% 1t5
wu-b	37.5% 1t5	42.5% 1t5	47.5% 1t5	40.0% 1t5
wu-c	47.5% 1t5	52.5% 1t5	57.5% 1t5	50.0% 1t5
wu-d	55.0% 1t5	60.0% 1t5	65.0% 1t5	57.5% 1t5
wA				
wB				
wC	62.5% X6	67.5% X6	72.5% X6	65.0% X3
wD	60.0% X6	65.0% X6	70.0% X6	62.5% X3
wE	57.5% X6	62.5% X6	67.5% X6	60.0% X3
wF	55.0% X6	60.0% X6	65.0% X6	57.5% X3
wG	52.5% X6	57.5% X6	62.5% X6	
wH		55.0% X6	60.0% X6	

72.5% Strength Endurance 4-week Cycles – Traditional – Total

STRENGTH ENDURANCE — TOTAL / BODY (70%)

	Base	Load	Load	UnLoad
Weekly %	60.0%	65.0%	70.0%	62.5%
differential	[-] 10%	[-] 5%	Top %	[-] 7.5%
WORK SETS	5 sets	6 sets	6 sets	4 sets
TOP SETS	5 sets	6 sets	6 sets	4 sets
Weeks #	WK 1	WK 2	WK 3	WK 4
wu-a	22.5% 1t5	27.5% 1t5	32.5% 1t5	25.0% 1t5
wu-b	35.0% 1t5	40.0% 1t5	45.0% 1t5	37.5% 1t5
wu-c	45.0% 1t5	50.0% 1t5	55.0% 1t5	47.5% 1t5
wu-d	52.5% 1t5	57.5% 1t5	62.5% 1t5	55.0% 1t5
wA				
wB				
wC	60.0% X6	65.0% X6	70.0% X6	62.5% X3
wD	57.5% X6	62.5% X6	67.5% X6	60.0% X3
wE	55.0% X6	60.0% X6	65.0% X6	57.5% X3
wF	52.5% X6	57.5% X6	62.5% X6	55.0% X3
wG	50.0% X6	55.0% X6	60.0% X6	
wH		52.5% X6	57.5% X6	

70% Strength Endurance 4-week Cycles – Traditional – Total

STRENGTH ENDURANCE — LOWER UPPER BODY

	Base	Load	Load	UnLoad
Weekly %	67.5%	72.5%	77.5%	70.0%
differential	[-] 10%	[-] 5%	Top %	[-] 7.5%
WORK SETS	5 sets	6 sets	6 sets	4 sets
TOP SETS	5 sets	6 sets	6 sets	4 sets
Weeks #	WK 1	WK 2	WK 3	WK 4
wu-a	30.0% 1t5	35.0% 1t5	40.0% 1t5	32.5% 1t5
wu-b	42.5% 1t5	47.5% 1t5	52.5% 1t5	45.0% 1t5
wu-c	52.5% 1t5	57.5% 1t5	62.5% 1t5	55.0% 1t5
wu-d	60.0% 1t5	65.0% 1t5	70.0% 1t5	62.5% 1t5
wA				
wB				
wC	67.5% x12	72.5% x10	77.5% x8	70.0% x8
wD	65.0% x12	70.0% x10	75.0% x8	67.5% x8
wE	62.5% x12	67.5% x10	72.5% x8	65.0% x8
wF	60.0% x12	65.0% x10	70.0% x8	62.5% x8
wG	57.5% x12	62.5% x10	67.5% x8	
wH		60.0% x10	65.0% x8	

77.5% Strength Endurance 4-week Cycles
– Traditional – Lower, Upper

STRENGTH ENDURANCE — LOWER UPPER BODY

	Base	Load	Load	UnLoad
Weekly %	65.0%	70.0%	75.0%	67.5%
differential	[-] 10%	[-] 5%	Top %	[-] 7.5%
WORK SETS	5 sets	6 sets	6 sets	4 sets
TOP SETS	5 sets	6 sets	6 sets	4 sets
Weeks #	WK 1	WK 2	WK 3	WK 4
wu-a	27.5% 1t5	32.5% 1t5	37.5% 1t5	30.0% 1t5
wu-b	40.0% 1t5	45.0% 1t5	50.0% 1t5	42.5% 1t5
wu-c	50.0% 1t5	55.0% 1t5	60.0% 1t5	52.5% 1t5
wu-d	57.5% 1t5	62.5% 1t5	67.5% 1t5	60.0% 1t5
wA				
wB				
wC	65.0% x12	70.0% x10	75.0% x8	67.5% x10
wD	62.5% x12	67.5% x10	72.5% x8	65.0% x10
wE	60.0% x12	65.0% x10	70.0% x8	62.5% x10
wF	57.5% x12	62.5% x10	67.5% x8	60.0% x10
wG	55.0% x12	60.0% x10	65.0% x8	
wH		57.5% x10	62.5% x8	

75% Strength Endurance 4-week Cycles
– Traditional – Lower, Upper

STRENGTH ENDURANCE — LOWER UPPER BODY

	Base	Load	Load	UnLoad
Weekly %	62.5%	67.5%	72.5%	65.0%
differential	[-] 10%	[-] 5%	Top %	[-] 7.5%
WORK SETS	5 sets	6 sets	6 sets	4 sets
TOP SETS	5 sets	6 sets	6 sets	4 sets
Weeks #	WK 1	WK 2	WK 3	WK 4
wu-a	25.0% 1t5	30.0% 1t5	35.0% 1t5	27.5% 1t5
wu-b	37.5% 1t5	42.5% 1t5	47.5% 1t5	40.0% 1t5
wu-c	47.5% 1t5	52.5% 1t5	57.5% 1t5	50.0% 1t5
wu-d	55.0% 1t5	60.0% 1t5	65.0% 1t5	57.5% 1t5
wA				
wB				
wC	62.5% x15	67.5% x12	72.5% x10	65.0% x10
wD	60.0% x15	65.0% x12	70.0% x10	62.5% x10
wE	57.5% x15	62.5% x12	67.5% x10	60.0% x10
wF	55.0% x15	60.0% x12	65.0% x10	57.5% x10
wG	52.5% x15	57.5% x12	62.5% x10	
wH		55.0% x12	60.0% x10	

72.5% Strength Endurance 4-week Cycles – Traditional – Lower, Upper

STRENGTH ENDURANCE — LOWER UPPER BODY

	Base	Load	Load	UnLoad
Weekly %	60.0%	65.0%	70.0%	62.5%
differential	[-] 10%	[-] 5%	Top %	[-] 7.5%
WORK SETS	5 sets	6 sets	6 sets	4 sets
TOP SETS	5 sets	6 sets	6 sets	4 sets
Weeks #	WK 1	WK 2	WK 3	WK 4
wu-a	22.5% 1t5	27.5% 1t5	32.5% 1t5	25.0% 1t5
wu-b	35.0% 1t5	40.0% 1t5	45.0% 1t5	37.5% 1t5
wu-c	45.0% 1t5	50.0% 1t5	55.0% 1t5	47.5% 1t5
wu-d	52.5% 1t5	57.5% 1t5	62.5% 1t5	55.0% 1t5
wA				
wB				
wC	60.0% x15	65.0% x12	70.0% x10	62.5% x12
wD	57.5% x15	62.5% x12	67.5% x10	60.0% x12
wE	55.0% x15	60.0% x12	65.0% x10	57.5% x12
wF	52.5% x15	57.5% x12	62.5% x10	55.0% x12
wG	50.0% x15	55.0% x12	60.0% x10	
wH		52.5% x12	57.5% x10	

70% Strength Endurance 4-week Cycles – Traditional – Lower, Upper

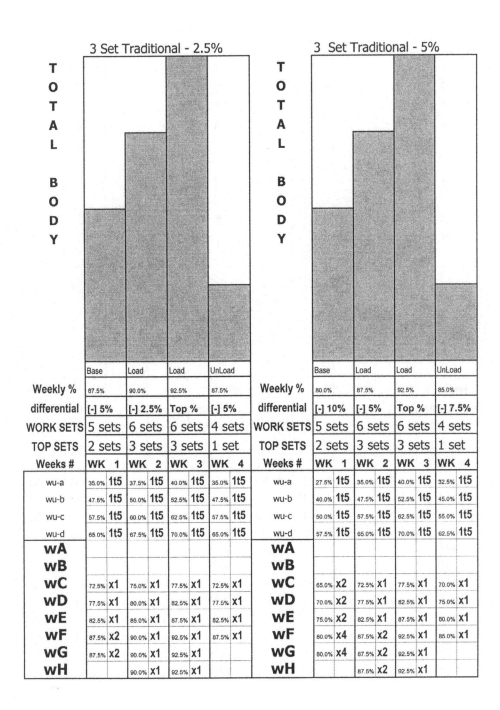

3 Set Traditional - 2.5% (TOTAL BODY)

	Base	Load	Load	UnLoad
Weekly %	87.5%	90.0%	92.5%	87.5%
differential	[-] 5%	[-] 2.5%	Top %	[-] 5%
WORK SETS	5 sets	6 sets	6 sets	4 sets
TOP SETS	2 sets	3 sets	3 sets	1 set
Weeks #	WK 1	WK 2	WK 3	WK 4
wu-a	35.0% 1t5	37.5% 1t5	40.0% 1t5	35.0% 1t5
wu-b	47.5% 1t5	50.0% 1t5	52.5% 1t5	47.5% 1t5
wu-c	57.5% 1t5	60.0% 1t5	62.5% 1t5	57.5% 1t5
wu-d	65.0% 1t5	67.5% 1t5	70.0% 1t5	65.0% 1t5
wA				
wB				
wC	72.5% x1	75.0% x1	77.5% x1	72.5% x1
wD	77.5% x1	80.0% x1	82.5% x1	77.5% x1
wE	82.5% x1	85.0% x1	87.5% x1	82.5% x1
wF	87.5% x2	90.0% x1	92.5% x1	87.5% x1
wG	87.5% x2	90.0% x1	92.5% x1	
wH		90.0% x1	92.5% x1	

3 Set Traditional - 5% (TOTAL BODY)

	Base	Load	Load	UnLoad
Weekly %	80.0%	87.5%	92.5%	85.0%
differential	[-] 10%	[-] 5%	Top %	[-] 7.5%
WORK SETS	5 sets	6 sets	6 sets	4 sets
TOP SETS	2 sets	3 sets	3 sets	1 set
Weeks #	WK 1	WK 2	WK 3	WK 4
wu-a	27.5% 1t5	35.0% 1t5	40.0% 1t5	32.5% 1t5
wu-b	40.0% 1t5	47.5% 1t5	52.5% 1t5	45.0% 1t5
wu-c	50.0% 1t5	57.5% 1t5	62.5% 1t5	55.0% 1t5
wu-d	57.5% 1t5	65.0% 1t5	70.0% 1t5	62.5% 1t5
wA				
wB				
wC	65.0% x2	72.5% x1	77.5% x1	70.0% x1
wD	70.0% x2	77.5% x1	82.5% x1	75.0% x1
wE	75.0% x2	82.5% x1	87.5% x1	80.0% x1
wF	80.0% x4	87.5% x2	92.5% x1	85.0% x1
wG	80.0% x4	87.5% x2	92.5% x1	
wH		87.5% x2	92.5% x1	

Developmental Strength 4-week Cycles – 92.5% Traditional 3 set – Total

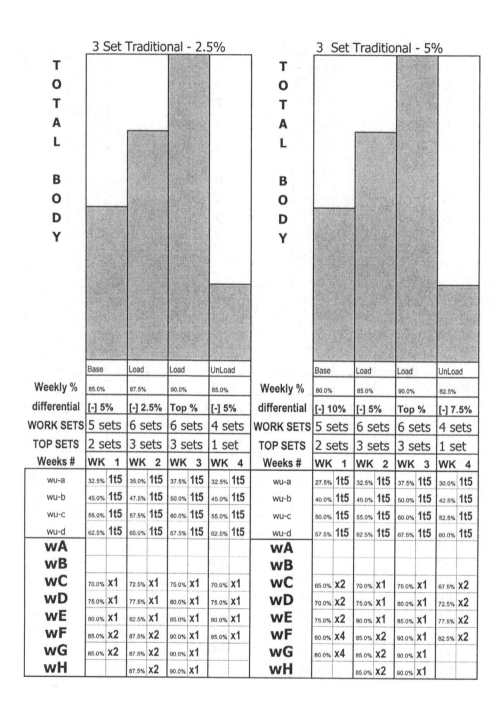

3 Set Traditional - 2.5%

TOTAL BODY

	WK 1 (Base)		WK 2 (Load)		WK 3 (Load)		WK 4 (UnLoad)	
Weekly %	85.0%		87.5%		90.0%		85.0%	
differential	[-] 5%		[-] 2.5%		Top %		[-] 5%	
WORK SETS	5 sets		6 sets		6 sets		4 sets	
TOP SETS	2 sets		3 sets		3 sets		1 set	
Weeks #								
wu-a	32.5%	1t5	35.0%	1t5	37.5%	1t5	32.5%	1t5
wu-b	45.0%	1t5	47.5%	1t5	50.0%	1t5	45.0%	1t5
wu-c	55.0%	1t5	57.5%	1t5	60.0%	1t5	55.0%	1t5
wu-d	62.5%	1t5	65.0%	1t5	67.5%	1t5	62.5%	1t5
wA								
wB								
wC	70.0%	x1	72.5%	x1	75.0%	x1	70.0%	x1
wD	75.0%	x1	77.5%	x1	80.0%	x1	75.0%	x1
wE	80.0%	x1	82.5%	x1	85.0%	x1	80.0%	x1
wF	85.0%	x2	87.5%	x2	90.0%	x1	85.0%	x1
wG	85.0%	x2	87.5%	x2	90.0%	x1		
wH			87.5%	x2	90.0%	x1		

3 Set Traditional - 5%

TOTAL BODY

	WK 1 (Base)		WK 2 (Load)		WK 3 (Load)		WK 4 (UnLoad)	
Weekly %	80.0%		85.0%		90.0%		82.5%	
differential	[-] 10%		[-] 5%		Top %		[-] 7.5%	
WORK SETS	5 sets		6 sets		6 sets		4 sets	
TOP SETS	2 sets		3 sets		3 sets		1 set	
Weeks #								
wu-a	27.5%	1t5	32.5%	1t5	37.5%	1t5	30.0%	1t5
wu-b	40.0%	1t5	45.0%	1t5	50.0%	1t5	42.5%	1t5
wu-c	50.0%	1t5	55.0%	1t5	60.0%	1t5	52.5%	1t5
wu-d	57.5%	1t5	62.5%	1t5	67.5%	1t5	60.0%	1t5
wA								
wB								
wC	65.0%	x2	70.0%	x1	75.0%	x1	67.5%	x2
wD	70.0%	x2	75.0%	x1	80.0%	x1	72.5%	x2
wE	75.0%	x2	80.0%	x1	85.0%	x1	77.5%	x2
wF	80.0%	x4	85.0%	x2	90.0%	x1	82.5%	x2
wG	80.0%	x4	85.0%	x2	90.0%	x1		
wH			85.0%	x2	90.0%	x1		

Developmental Strength 4-week Cycles – 90% Traditional 3 set – Total

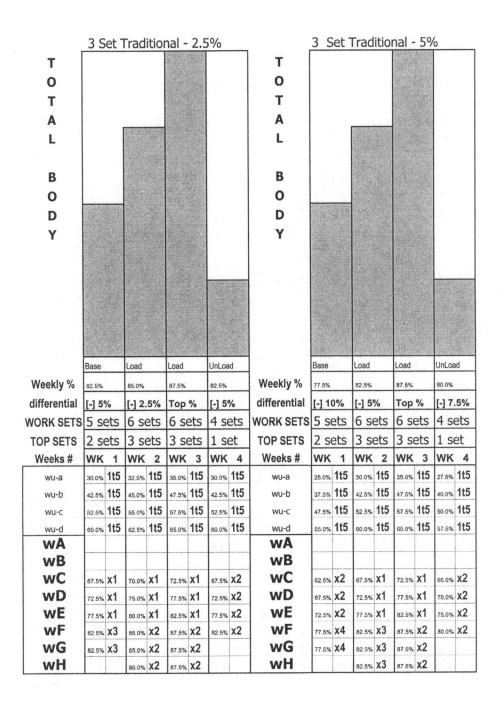

3 Set Traditional - 2.5% | **3 Set Traditional - 5%**

TOTAL BODY

	Base	Load	Load	UnLoad
Weekly %	82.5%	85.0%	87.5%	82.5%
differential	[-] 5%	[-] 2.5%	Top %	[-] 5%
WORK SETS	5 sets	6 sets	6 sets	4 sets
TOP SETS	2 sets	3 sets	3 sets	1 set
Weeks #	WK 1	WK 2	WK 3	WK 4
wu-a	30.0% 1t5	32.5% 1t5	35.0% 1t5	30.0% 1t5
wu-b	42.5% 1t5	45.0% 1t5	47.5% 1t5	42.5% 1t5
wu-c	52.5% 1t5	55.0% 1t5	57.5% 1t5	52.5% 1t5
wu-d	60.0% 1t5	62.5% 1t5	65.0% 1t5	60.0% 1t5
wA				
wB				
wC	67.5% X1	70.0% X1	72.5% X1	67.5% X2
wD	72.5% X1	75.0% X1	77.5% X1	72.5% X2
wE	77.5% X1	80.0% X1	82.5% X1	77.5% X2
wF	82.5% X3	85.0% X2	87.5% X2	82.5% X2
wG	82.5% X3	85.0% X2	87.5% X2	
wH		85.0% X2	87.5% X2	

TOTAL BODY

	Base	Load	Load	UnLoad
Weekly %	77.5%	82.5%	87.5%	80.0%
differential	[-] 10%	[-] 5%	Top %	[-] 7.5%
WORK SETS	5 sets	6 sets	6 sets	4 sets
TOP SETS	2 sets	3 sets	3 sets	1 set
Weeks #	WK 1	WK 2	WK 3	WK 4
wu-a	25.0% 1t5	30.0% 1t5	35.0% 1t5	27.5% 1t5
wu-b	37.5% 1t5	42.5% 1t5	47.5% 1t5	40.0% 1t5
wu-c	47.5% 1t5	52.5% 1t5	57.5% 1t5	50.0% 1t5
wu-d	55.0% 1t5	60.0% 1t5	65.0% 1t5	57.5% 1t5
wA				
wB				
wC	62.5% X2	67.5% X1	72.5% X1	65.0% X2
wD	67.5% X2	72.5% X1	77.5% X1	70.0% X2
wE	72.5% X2	77.5% X1	82.5% X1	75.0% X2
wF	77.5% X4	82.5% X3	87.5% X2	80.0% X2
wG	77.5% X4	82.5% X3	87.5% X2	
wH		82.5% X3	87.5% X2	

Developmental Strength 4-week Cycles – 87.5% Traditional 3 set – Total

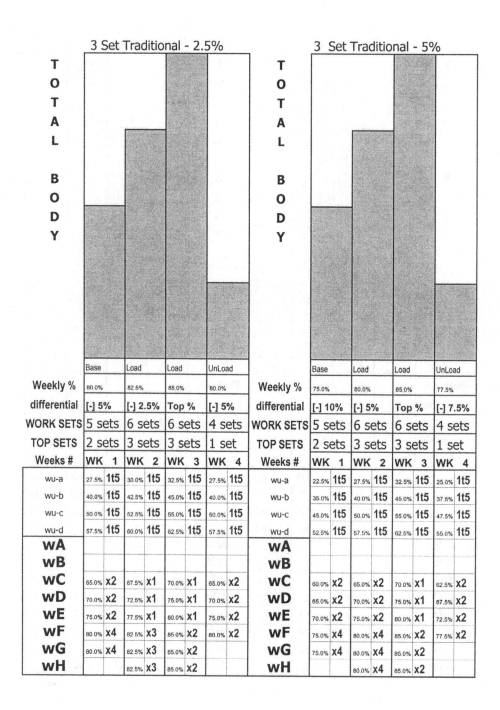

3 Set Traditional - 2.5% (TOTAL BODY)

	Base	Load	Load	UnLoad
Weekly %	80.0%	82.5%	85.0%	80.0%
differential	[-] 5%	[-] 2.5%	Top %	[-] 5%
WORK SETS	5 sets	6 sets	6 sets	4 sets
TOP SETS	2 sets	3 sets	3 sets	1 set
Weeks #	WK 1	WK 2	WK 3	WK 4
wu-a	27.5% 1t5	30.0% 1t5	32.5% 1t5	27.5% 1t5
wu-b	40.0% 1t5	42.5% 1t5	45.0% 1t5	40.0% 1t5
wu-c	50.0% 1t5	52.5% 1t5	55.0% 1t5	50.0% 1t5
wu-d	57.5% 1t5	60.0% 1t5	62.5% 1t5	57.5% 1t5
wA				
wB				
wC	65.0% x2	67.5% x1	70.0% x1	65.0% x2
wD	70.0% x2	72.5% x1	75.0% x1	70.0% x2
wE	75.0% x2	77.5% x1	80.0% x1	75.0% x2
wF	80.0% x4	82.5% x3	85.0% x2	80.0% x2
wG	80.0% x4	82.5% x3	85.0% x2	
wH		82.5% x3	85.0% x2	

3 Set Traditional - 5% (TOTAL BODY)

	Base	Load	Load	UnLoad
Weekly %	75.0%	80.0%	85.0%	77.5%
differential	[-] 10%	[-] 5%	Top %	[-] 7.5%
WORK SETS	5 sets	6 sets	6 sets	4 sets
TOP SETS	2 sets	3 sets	3 sets	1 set
Weeks #	WK 1	WK 2	WK 3	WK 4
wu-a	22.5% 1t5	27.5% 1t5	32.5% 1t5	25.0% 1t5
wu-b	35.0% 1t5	40.0% 1t5	45.0% 1t5	37.5% 1t5
wu-c	45.0% 1t5	50.0% 1t5	55.0% 1t5	47.5% 1t5
wu-d	52.5% 1t5	57.5% 1t5	62.5% 1t5	55.0% 1t5
wA				
wB				
wC	60.0% x2	65.0% x2	70.0% x1	62.5% x2
wD	65.0% x2	70.0% x2	75.0% x1	67.5% x2
wE	70.0% x2	75.0% x2	80.0% x1	72.5% x2
wF	75.0% x4	80.0% x4	85.0% x2	77.5% x2
wG	75.0% x4	80.0% x4	85.0% x2	
wH		80.0% x4	85.0% x2	

Developmental Strength 4-week Cycles – 85% Traditional 3 set – Total

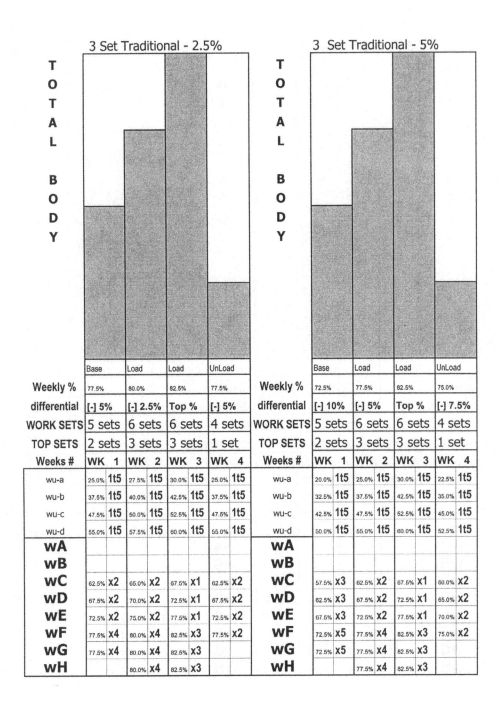

3 Set Traditional - 2.5% (TOTAL BODY)

	Base	Load	Load	UnLoad
Weekly %	77.5%	80.0%	82.5%	77.5%
differential	[-] 5%	[-] 2.5%	Top %	[-] 5%
WORK SETS	5 sets	6 sets	6 sets	4 sets
TOP SETS	2 sets	3 sets	3 sets	1 set
Weeks #	WK 1	WK 2	WK 3	WK 4
wu-a	25.0% 1t5	27.5% 1t5	30.0% 1t5	25.0% 1t5
wu-b	37.5% 1t5	40.0% 1t5	42.5% 1t5	37.5% 1t5
wu-c	47.5% 1t5	50.0% 1t5	52.5% 1t5	47.5% 1t5
wu-d	55.0% 1t5	57.5% 1t5	60.0% 1t5	55.0% 1t5
wA				
wB				
wC	62.5% x2	65.0% x2	67.5% x1	62.5% x2
wD	67.5% x2	70.0% x2	72.5% x1	67.5% x2
wE	72.5% x2	75.0% x2	77.5% x1	72.5% x2
wF	77.5% x4	80.0% x4	82.5% x3	77.5% x2
wG	77.5% x4	80.0% x4	82.5% x3	
wH		80.0% x4	82.5% x3	

3 Set Traditional - 5% (TOTAL BODY)

	Base	Load	Load	UnLoad
Weekly %	72.5%	77.5%	82.5%	75.0%
differential	[-] 10%	[-] 5%	Top %	[-] 7.5%
WORK SETS	5 sets	6 sets	6 sets	4 sets
TOP SETS	2 sets	3 sets	3 sets	1 set
Weeks #	WK 1	WK 2	WK 3	WK 4
wu-a	20.0% 1t5	25.0% 1t5	30.0% 1t5	22.5% 1t5
wu-b	32.5% 1t5	37.5% 1t5	42.5% 1t5	35.0% 1t5
wu-c	42.5% 1t5	47.5% 1t5	52.5% 1t5	45.0% 1t5
wu-d	50.0% 1t5	55.0% 1t5	60.0% 1t5	52.5% 1t5
wA				
wB				
wC	57.5% x3	62.5% x2	67.5% x1	60.0% x2
wD	62.5% x3	67.5% x2	72.5% x1	65.0% x2
wE	67.5% x3	72.5% x2	77.5% x1	70.0% x2
wF	72.5% x5	77.5% x4	82.5% x3	75.0% x2
wG	72.5% x5	77.5% x4	82.5% x3	
wH		77.5% x4	82.5% x3	

Developmental Strength 4-week Cycles – 82.5% Traditional 3 set – Total

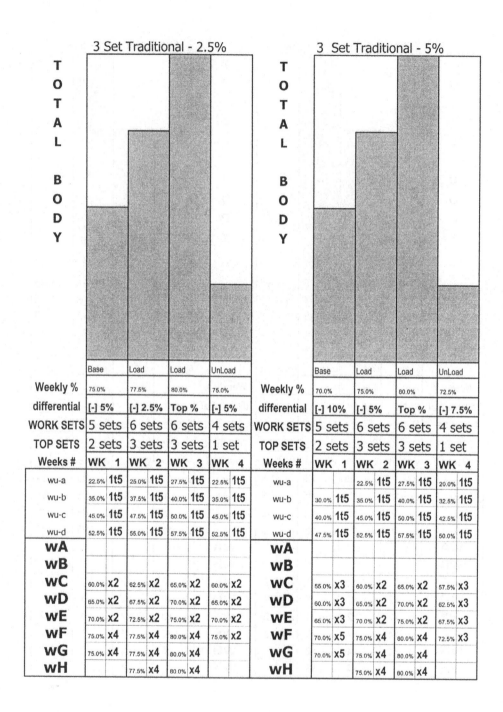

Developmental Strength 4-week Cycles – 80% Traditional 3 set – Total

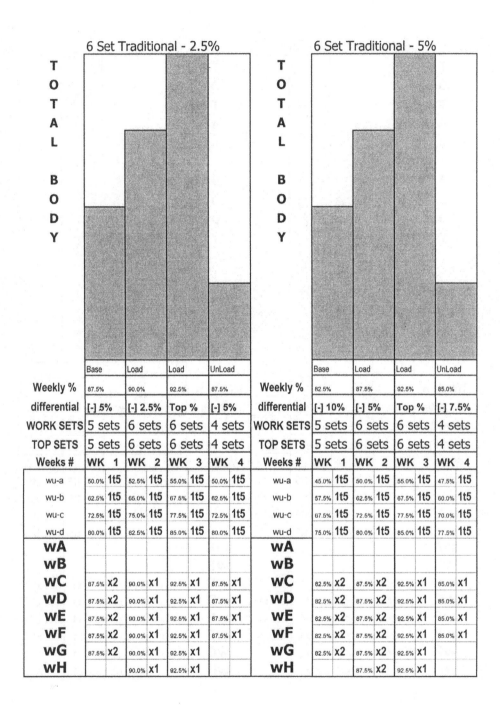

6 Set Traditional - 2.5% (TOTAL BODY)

	Base	Load	Load	UnLoad
Weekly %	87.5%	90.0%	92.5%	87.5%
differential	[-] 5%	[-] 2.5%	Top %	[-] 5%
WORK SETS	5 sets	6 sets	6 sets	4 sets
TOP SETS	5 sets	6 sets	6 sets	4 sets
Weeks #	WK 1	WK 2	WK 3	WK 4
wu-a	50.0% 1t5	52.5% 1t5	55.0% 1t5	50.0% 1t5
wu-b	62.5% 1t5	65.0% 1t5	67.5% 1t5	62.5% 1t5
wu-c	72.5% 1t5	75.0% 1t5	77.5% 1t5	72.5% 1t5
wu-d	80.0% 1t5	82.5% 1t5	85.0% 1t5	80.0% 1t5
wA				
wB				
wC	87.5% x2	90.0% x1	92.5% x1	87.5% x1
wD	87.5% x2	90.0% x1	92.5% x1	87.5% x1
wE	87.5% x2	90.0% x1	92.5% x1	87.5% x1
wF	87.5% x2	90.0% x1	92.5% x1	87.5% x1
wG	87.5% x2	90.0% x1	92.5% x1	
wH		90.0% x1	92.5% x1	

6 Set Traditional - 5% (TOTAL BODY)

	Base	Load	Load	UnLoad
Weekly %	82.5%	87.5%	92.5%	85.0%
differential	[-] 10%	[-] 5%	Top %	[-] 7.5%
WORK SETS	5 sets	6 sets	6 sets	4 sets
TOP SETS	5 sets	6 sets	6 sets	4 sets
Weeks #	WK 1	WK 2	WK 3	WK 4
wu-a	45.0% 1t5	50.0% 1t5	55.0% 1t5	47.5% 1t5
wu-b	57.5% 1t5	62.5% 1t5	67.5% 1t5	60.0% 1t5
wu-c	67.5% 1t5	72.5% 1t5	77.5% 1t5	70.0% 1t5
wu-d	75.0% 1t5	80.0% 1t5	85.0% 1t5	77.5% 1t5
wA				
wB				
wC	82.5% x2	87.5% x2	92.5% x1	85.0% x1
wD	82.5% x2	87.5% x2	92.5% x1	85.0% x1
wE	82.5% x2	87.5% x2	92.5% x1	85.0% x1
wF	82.5% x2	87.5% x2	92.5% x1	85.0% x1
wG	82.5% x2	87.5% x2	92.5% x1	
wH		87.5% x2	92.5% x1	

Developmental Strength 4-week Cycles – 92.5% Traditional 6 set – Total

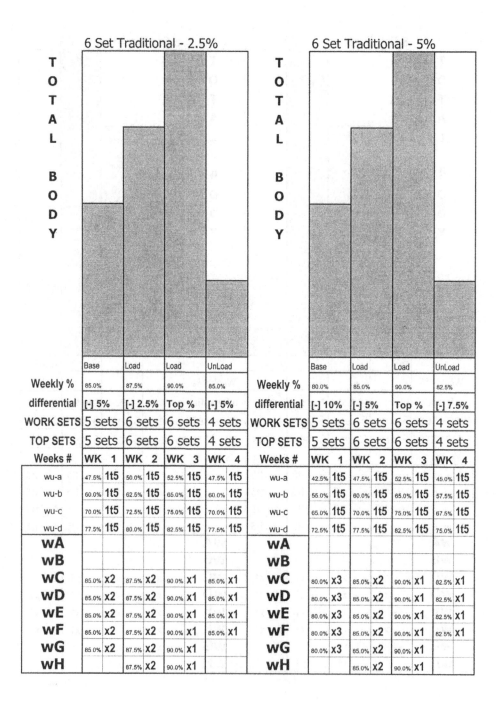

6 Set Traditional - 2.5% — TOTAL BODY

	Base	Load	Load	UnLoad
Weekly %	85.0%	87.5%	90.0%	85.0%
differential	[-] 5%	[-] 2.5%	Top %	[-] 5%
WORK SETS	5 sets	6 sets	6 sets	4 sets
TOP SETS	5 sets	6 sets	6 sets	4 sets
Weeks #	WK 1	WK 2	WK 3	WK 4
wu-a	47.5% 1t5	50.0% 1t5	52.5% 1t5	47.5% 1t5
wu-b	60.0% 1t5	62.5% 1t5	65.0% 1t5	60.0% 1t5
wu-c	70.0% 1t5	72.5% 1t5	75.0% 1t5	70.0% 1t5
wu-d	77.5% 1t5	80.0% 1t5	82.5% 1t5	77.5% 1t5
wA				
wB				
wC	85.0% x2	87.5% x2	90.0% x1	85.0% x1
wD	85.0% x2	87.5% x2	90.0% x1	85.0% x1
wE	85.0% x2	87.5% x2	90.0% x1	85.0% x1
wF	85.0% x2	87.5% x2	90.0% x1	85.0% x1
wG	85.0% x2	87.5% x2	90.0% x1	
wH		87.5% x2	90.0% x1	

6 Set Traditional - 5% — TOTAL BODY

	Base	Load	Load	UnLoad
Weekly %	80.0%	85.0%	90.0%	82.5%
differential	[-] 10%	[-] 5%	Top %	[-] 7.5%
WORK SETS	5 sets	6 sets	6 sets	4 sets
TOP SETS	5 sets	6 sets	6 sets	4 sets
Weeks #	WK 1	WK 2	WK 3	WK 4
wu-a	42.5% 1t5	47.5% 1t5	52.5% 1t5	45.0% 1t5
wu-b	55.0% 1t5	60.0% 1t5	65.0% 1t5	57.5% 1t5
wu-c	65.0% 1t5	70.0% 1t5	75.0% 1t5	67.5% 1t5
wu-d	72.5% 1t5	77.5% 1t5	82.5% 1t5	75.0% 1t5
wA				
wB				
wC	80.0% x3	85.0% x2	90.0% x1	82.5% x1
wD	80.0% x3	85.0% x2	90.0% x1	82.5% x1
wE	80.0% x3	85.0% x2	90.0% x1	82.5% x1
wF	80.0% x3	85.0% x2	90.0% x1	82.5% x1
wG	80.0% x3	85.0% x2	90.0% x1	
wH		85.0% x2	90.0% x1	

Developmental Strength 4-week Cycles – 90% Traditional 6 set – Total

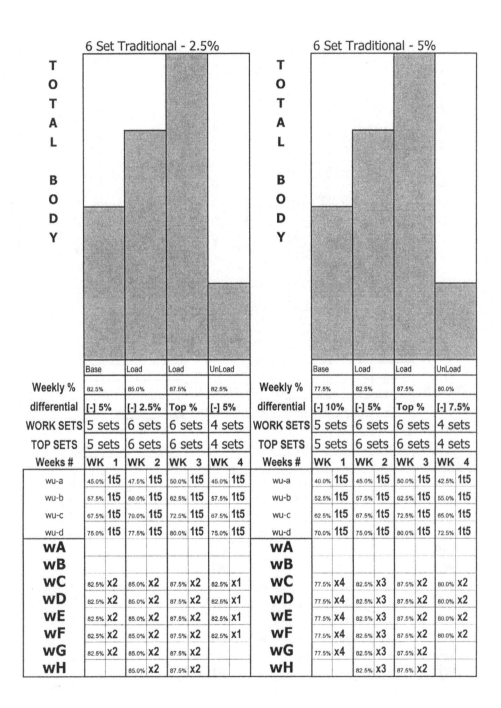

6 Set Traditional - 2.5% — TOTAL BODY

	Base	Load	Load	UnLoad
Weekly %	82.5%	85.0%	87.5%	82.5%
differential	[-] 5%	[-] 2.5%	Top %	[-] 5%
WORK SETS	5 sets	6 sets	6 sets	4 sets
TOP SETS	5 sets	6 sets	6 sets	4 sets
Weeks #	WK 1	WK 2	WK 3	WK 4
wu-a	45.0% 1t5	47.5% 1t5	50.0% 1t5	45.0% 1t5
wu-b	57.5% 1t5	60.0% 1t5	62.5% 1t5	57.5% 1t5
wu-c	67.5% 1t5	70.0% 1t5	72.5% 1t5	67.5% 1t5
wu-d	75.0% 1t5	77.5% 1t5	80.0% 1t5	75.0% 1t5
wA				
wB				
wC	82.5% X2	85.0% X2	87.5% X2	82.5% X1
wD	82.5% X2	85.0% X2	87.5% X2	82.5% X1
wE	82.5% X2	85.0% X2	87.5% X2	82.5% X1
wF	82.5% X2	85.0% X2	87.5% X2	82.5% X1
wG	82.5% X2	85.0% X2	87.5% X2	
wH		85.0% X2	87.5% X2	

6 Set Traditional - 5% — TOTAL BODY

	Base	Load	Load	UnLoad
Weekly %	77.5%	82.5%	87.5%	80.0%
differential	[-] 10%	[-] 5%	Top %	[-] 7.5%
WORK SETS	5 sets	6 sets	6 sets	4 sets
TOP SETS	5 sets	6 sets	6 sets	4 sets
Weeks #	WK 1	WK 2	WK 3	WK 4
wu-a	40.0% 1t5	45.0% 1t5	50.0% 1t5	42.5% 1t5
wu-b	52.5% 1t5	57.5% 1t5	62.5% 1t5	55.0% 1t5
wu-c	62.5% 1t5	67.5% 1t5	72.5% 1t5	65.0% 1t5
wu-d	70.0% 1t5	75.0% 1t5	80.0% 1t5	72.5% 1t5
wA				
wB				
wC	77.5% X4	82.5% X3	87.5% X2	80.0% X2
wD	77.5% X4	82.5% X3	87.5% X2	80.0% X2
wE	77.5% X4	82.5% X3	87.5% X2	80.0% X2
wF	77.5% X4	82.5% X3	87.5% X2	80.0% X2
wG	77.5% X4	82.5% X3	87.5% X2	
wH		82.5% X3	87.5% X2	

Developmental Strength 4-week Cycles – 87.5% Traditional 6 set – Total

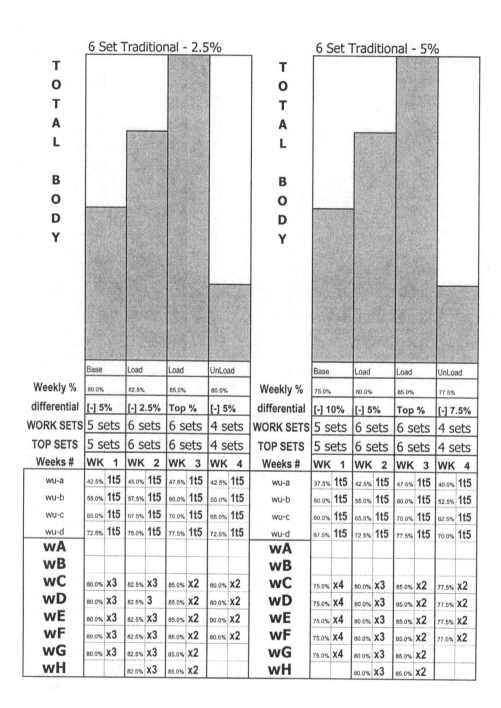

6 Set Traditional - 2.5%

TOTAL BODY	Base	Load	Load	UnLoad
Weekly %	80.0%	82.5%	85.0%	80.0%
differential	[-] 5%	[-] 2.5%	Top %	[-] 5%
WORK SETS	5 sets	6 sets	6 sets	4 sets
TOP SETS	5 sets	6 sets	6 sets	4 sets
Weeks #	WK 1	WK 2	WK 3	WK 4
wu-a	42.5% 1t5	45.0% 1t5	47.5% 1t5	42.5% 1t5
wu-b	55.0% 1t5	57.5% 1t5	60.0% 1t5	55.0% 1t5
wu-c	65.0% 1t5	67.5% 1t5	70.0% 1t5	65.0% 1t5
wu-d	72.5% 1t5	75.0% 1t5	77.5% 1t5	72.5% 1t5
wA				
wB				
wC	80.0% X3	82.5% X3	85.0% X2	80.0% X2
wD	80.0% X3	82.5% 3	85.0% X2	80.0% X2
wE	80.0% X3	82.5% X3	85.0% X2	80.0% X2
wF	80.0% X3	82.5% X3	85.0% X2	80.0% X2
wG	80.0% X3	82.5% X3	85.0% X2	
wH		82.5% X3	85.0% X2	

6 Set Traditional - 5%

TOTAL BODY	Base	Load	Load	UnLoad
Weekly %	75.0%	80.0%	85.0%	77.5%
differential	[-] 10%	[-] 5%	Top %	[-] 7.5%
WORK SETS	5 sets	6 sets	6 sets	4 sets
TOP SETS	5 sets	6 sets	6 sets	4 sets
Weeks #	WK 1	WK 2	WK 3	WK 4
wu-a	37.5% 1t5	42.5% 1t5	47.5% 1t5	40.0% 1t5
wu-b	50.0% 1t5	55.0% 1t5	60.0% 1t5	52.5% 1t5
wu-c	60.0% 1t5	65.0% 1t5	70.0% 1t5	62.5% 1t5
wu-d	67.5% 1t5	72.5% 1t5	77.5% 1t5	70.0% 1t5
wA				
wB				
wC	75.0% X4	80.0% X3	85.0% X2	77.5% X2
wD	75.0% X4	80.0% X3	85.0% X2	77.5% X2
wE	75.0% X4	80.0% X3	85.0% X2	77.5% X2
wF	75.0% X4	80.0% X3	85.0% X2	77.5% X2
wG	75.0% X4	80.0% X3	85.0% X2	
wH		80.0% X3	85.0% X2	

Developmental Strength 4-week Cycles – 85% Traditional 6 set – Total

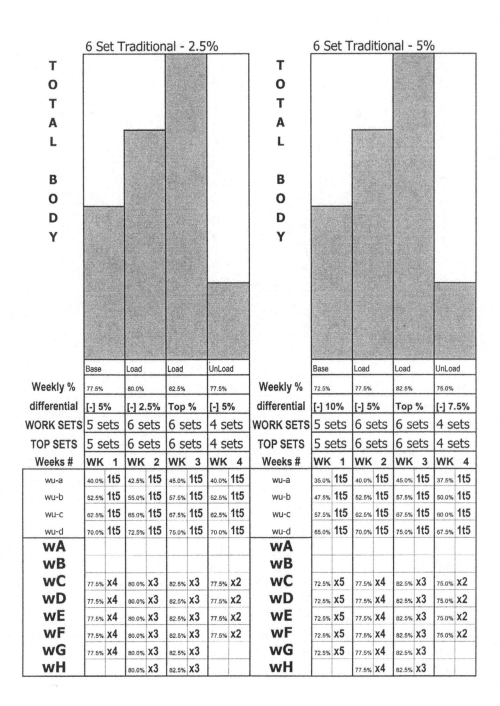

6 Set Traditional - 2.5% (TOTAL BODY)

	Base	Load	Load	UnLoad
Weekly %	77.5%	80.0%	82.5%	77.5%
differential	[-] 5%	[-] 2.5%	Top %	[-] 5%
WORK SETS	5 sets	6 sets	6 sets	4 sets
TOP SETS	5 sets	6 sets	6 sets	4 sets
Weeks #	WK 1	WK 2	WK 3	WK 4
wu-a	40.0% 1t5	42.5% 1t5	45.0% 1t5	40.0% 1t5
wu-b	52.5% 1t5	55.0% 1t5	57.5% 1t5	52.5% 1t5
wu-c	62.5% 1t5	65.0% 1t5	67.5% 1t5	62.5% 1t5
wu-d	70.0% 1t5	72.5% 1t5	75.0% 1t5	70.0% 1t5
wA				
wB				
wC	77.5% x4	80.0% x3	82.5% x3	77.5% x2
wD	77.5% x4	80.0% x3	82.5% x3	77.5% x2
wE	77.5% x4	80.0% x3	82.5% x3	77.5% x2
wF	77.5% x4	80.0% x3	82.5% x3	77.5% x2
wG	77.5% x4	80.0% x3	82.5% x3	
wH		80.0% x3	82.5% x3	

6 Set Traditional - 5% (TOTAL BODY)

	Base	Load	Load	UnLoad
Weekly %	72.5%	77.5%	82.5%	75.0%
differential	[-] 10%	[-] 5%	Top %	[-] 7.5%
WORK SETS	5 sets	6 sets	6 sets	4 sets
TOP SETS	5 sets	6 sets	6 sets	4 sets
Weeks #	WK 1	WK 2	WK 3	WK 4
wu-a	35.0% 1t5	40.0% 1t5	45.0% 1t5	37.5% 1t5
wu-b	47.5% 1t5	52.5% 1t5	57.5% 1t5	50.0% 1t5
wu-c	57.5% 1t5	62.5% 1t5	67.5% 1t5	60.0% 1t5
wu-d	65.0% 1t5	70.0% 1t5	75.0% 1t5	67.5% 1t5
wA				
wB				
wC	72.5% x5	77.5% x4	82.5% x3	75.0% x2
wD	72.5% x5	77.5% x4	82.5% x3	75.0% x2
wE	72.5% x5	77.5% x4	82.5% x3	75.0% x2
wF	72.5% x5	77.5% x4	82.5% x3	75.0% x2
wG	72.5% x5	77.5% x4	82.5% x3	
wH		77.5% x4	82.5% x3	

Developmental Strength 4-week Cycles – 82.5% Traditional 6 set – Total

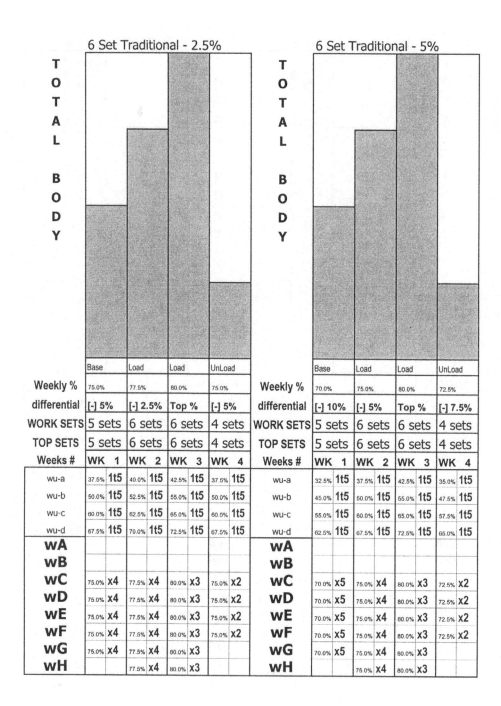

6 Set Traditional - 2.5% — TOTAL BODY

	Base		Load		Load		UnLoad	
Weekly %	75.0%		77.5%		80.0%		75.0%	
differential	[-] 5%		[-] 2.5%		Top %		[-] 5%	
WORK SETS	5 sets		6 sets		6 sets		4 sets	
TOP SETS	5 sets		6 sets		6 sets		4 sets	
Weeks #	WK 1		WK 2		WK 3		WK 4	
wu-a	37.5%	1t5	40.0%	1t5	42.5%	1t5	37.5%	1t5
wu-b	50.0%	1t5	52.5%	1t5	55.0%	1t5	50.0%	1t5
wu-c	60.0%	1t5	62.5%	1t5	65.0%	1t5	60.0%	1t5
wu-d	67.5%	1t5	70.0%	1t5	72.5%	1t5	67.5%	1t5
wA								
wB								
wC	75.0%	x4	77.5%	x4	80.0%	x3	75.0%	x2
wD	75.0%	x4	77.5%	x4	80.0%	x3	75.0%	x2
wE	75.0%	x4	77.5%	x4	80.0%	x3	75.0%	x2
wF	75.0%	x4	77.5%	x4	80.0%	x3	75.0%	x2
wG	75.0%	x4	77.5%	x4	80.0%	x3		
wH			77.5%	x4	80.0%	x3		

6 Set Traditional - 5% — TOTAL BODY

	Base		Load		Load		UnLoad	
Weekly %	70.0%		75.0%		80.0%		72.5%	
differential	[-] 10%		[-] 5%		Top %		[-] 7.5%	
WORK SETS	5 sets		6 sets		6 sets		4 sets	
TOP SETS	5 sets		6 sets		6 sets		4 sets	
Weeks #	WK 1		WK 2		WK 3		WK 4	
wu-a	32.5%	1t5	37.5%	1t5	42.5%	1t5	35.0%	1t5
wu-b	45.0%	1t5	50.0%	1t5	55.0%	1t5	47.5%	1t5
wu-c	55.0%	1t5	60.0%	1t5	65.0%	1t5	57.5%	1t5
wu-d	62.5%	1t5	67.5%	1t5	72.5%	1t5	65.0%	1t5
wA								
wB								
wC	70.0%	x5	75.0%	x4	80.0%	x3	72.5%	x2
wD	70.0%	x5	75.0%	x4	80.0%	x3	72.5%	x2
wE	70.0%	x5	75.0%	x4	80.0%	x3	72.5%	x2
wF	70.0%	x5	75.0%	x4	80.0%	x3	72.5%	x2
wG	70.0%	x5	75.0%	x4	80.0%	x3		
wH			75.0%	x4	80.0%	x3		

Developmental Strength 4-week Cycles – 80% Traditional 6 set – Total

3 Set Traditional - 2.5% — LOWER UPPER BODY

	Base	Load	Load	UnLoad
Weekly %	87.5%	90.0%	92.5%	87.5%
differential	[-] 5%	[-] 2.5%	Top %	[-] 5%
WORK SETS	5 sets	6 sets	6 sets	4 sets
TOP SETS	2 sets	3 sets	3 sets	1 set
Weeks #	WK 1	WK 2	WK 3	WK 4
wu-a	35.0% 1t5	37.5% 1t5	40.0% 1t5	35.0% 1t5
wu-b	47.5% 1t5	50.0% 1t5	52.5% 1t5	47.5% 1t5
wu-c	57.5% 1t5	60.0% 1t5	62.5% 1t5	57.5% 1t5
wu-d	65.0% 1t5	67.5% 1t5	70.0% 1t5	65.0% 1t5
wA				
wB				
wC	72.5% x2	75.0% x1	77.5% x1	72.5% x2
wD	77.5% x2	80.0% x1	82.5% x1	77.5% x2
wE	82.5% x2	85.0% x1	87.5% x1	82.5% x2
wF	87.5% x4	90.0% x3	92.5% x3	87.5% x2
wG	87.5% x4	90.0% x3	92.5% x3	
wH		90.0% x3	92.5% x3	

3 Set Traditional - 5% — LOWER UPPER BODY

	Base	Load	Load	UnLoad
Weekly %	80.0%	87.5%	92.5%	85.0%
differential	[-] 10%	[-] 5%	Top %	[-] 7.5%
WORK SETS	5 sets	6 sets	6 sets	4 sets
TOP SETS	2 sets	3 sets	3 sets	1 set
Weeks #	WK 1	WK 2	WK 3	WK 4
wu-a	27.5% 1t5	35.0% 1t5	40.0% 1t5	32.5% 1t5
wu-b	40.0% 1t5	47.5% 1t5	52.5% 1t5	45.0% 1t5
wu-c	50.0% 1t5	57.5% 1t5	62.5% 1t5	55.0% 1t5
wu-d	57.5% 1t5	65.0% 1t5	70.0% 1t5	62.5% 1t5
wA				
wB				
wC	65.0% x3	72.5% x2	77.5% x1	70.0% x2
wD	70.0% x3	77.5% x2	82.5% x1	75.0% x2
wE	75.0% x3	82.5% x2	87.5% x1	80.0% x2
wF	80.0% x6	87.5% x4	92.5% x3	85.0% x2
wG	80.0% x6	87.5% x4	92.5% x3	
wH		87.5% x4	92.5% x3	

Developmental Strength 4-week Cycles – 92.5% Traditional 3 set – Lower, Upper

3 Set Traditional - 2.5%

LOWER UPPER BODY

	Base	Load	Load	UnLoad
Weekly %	85.0%	87.5%	90.0%	85.0%
differential	[-] 5%	[-] 2.5%	Top %	[-] 5%
WORK SETS	5 sets	6 sets	6 sets	4 sets
TOP SETS	2 sets	3 sets	3 sets	1 set
Weeks #	WK 1	WK 2	WK 3	WK 4
wu-a	32.5% 1t5	35.0% 1t5	37.5% 1t5	32.5% 1t5
wu-b	45.0% 1t5	47.5% 1t5	50.0% 1t5	45.0% 1t5
wu-c	55.0% 1t5	57.5% 1t5	60.0% 1t5	55.0% 1t5
wu-d	62.5% 1t5	65.0% 1t5	67.5% 1t5	62.5% 1t5
wA				
wB				
wC	70.0% x2	72.5% x2	75.0% x1	70.0% x2
wD	75.0% x2	77.5% x2	80.0% x1	75.0% x2
wE	80.0% x2	82.5% x2	85.0% x1	80.0% x2
wF	85.0% x4	87.5% x4	90.0% x3	85.0% x2
wG	85.0% x4	87.5% x4	90.0% x3	
wH		87.5% x4	90.0% x3	

3 Set Traditional - 5%

LOWER UPPER BODY

	Base	Load	Load	UnLoad
Weekly %	80.0%	85.0%	90.0%	82.5%
differential	[-] 10%	[-] 5%	Top %	[-] 7.5%
WORK SETS	5 sets	6 sets	6 sets	4 sets
TOP SETS	2 sets	3 sets	3 sets	1 set
Weeks #	WK 1	WK 2	WK 3	WK 4
wu-a	27.5% 1t5	32.5% 1t5	37.5% 1t5	30.0% 1t5
wu-b	40.0% 1t5	45.0% 1t5	50.0% 1t5	42.5% 1t5
wu-c	50.0% 1t5	55.0% 1t5	60.0% 1t5	52.5% 1t5
wu-d	57.5% 1t5	62.5% 1t5	67.5% 1t5	60.0% 1t5
wA				
wB				
wC	65.0% x3	70.0% x2	75.0% x1	67.5% x3
wD	70.0% x3	75.0% x2	80.0% x1	72.5% x3
wE	75.0% x3	80.0% x2	85.0% x1	77.5% x3
wF	80.0% x6	85.0% x4	90.0% x3	82.5% x3
wG	80.0% x6	85.0% x4	90.0% x3	
wH		85.0% x4	90.0% x3	

Developmental Strength 4-week Cycles – 90% Traditional 3 set – Lower, Upper

3 Set Traditional - 2.5%

LOWER UPPER BODY

	Base	Load	Load	UnLoad
Weekly %	82.5%	85.0%	87.5%	82.5%
differential	[-] 5%	[-] 2.5%	Top %	[-] 5%
WORK SETS	5 sets	6 sets	6 sets	4 sets
TOP SETS	2 sets	3 sets	3 sets	1 set
Weeks #	WK 1	WK 2	WK 3	WK 4
wu-a	30.0% 1t5	32.5% 1t5	35.0% 1t5	30.0% 1t5
wu-b	42.5% 1t5	45.0% 1t5	47.5% 1t5	42.5% 1t5
wu-c	52.5% 1t5	55.0% 1t5	57.5% 1t5	52.5% 1t5
wu-d	60.0% 1t5	62.5% 1t5	65.0% 1t5	60.0% 1t5
wA				
wB				
wC	67.5% x3	70.0% x2	72.5% x2	67.5% x3
wD	72.5% x3	75.0% x2	77.5% x2	72.5% x3
wE	77.5% x3	80.0% x2	82.5% x2	77.5% x3
wF	82.5% x5	85.0% x4	87.5% x4	82.5% x3
wG	82.5% x5	85.0% x4	87.5% x4	
wH		85.0% x4	87.5% x4	

3 Set Traditional - 5%

LOWER UPPER BODY

	Base	Load	Load	UnLoad
Weekly %	77.5%	82.5%	87.5%	80.0%
differential	[-] 10%	[-] 5%	Top %	[-] 7.5%
WORK SETS	5 sets	6 sets	6 sets	4 sets
TOP SETS	2 sets	3 sets	3 sets	1 set
Weeks #	WK 1	WK 2	WK 3	WK 4
wu-a	25.0% 1t5	30.0% 1t5	35.0% 1t5	27.5% 1t5
wu-b	37.5% 1t5	42.5% 1t5	47.5% 1t5	40.0% 1t5
wu-c	47.5% 1t5	52.5% 1t5	57.5% 1t5	50.0% 1t5
wu-d	55.0% 1t5	60.0% 1t5	65.0% 1t5	57.5% 1t5
wA				
wB				
wC	62.5% x4	67.5% x3	72.5% x2	65.0% x3
wD	67.5% x4	72.5% x3	77.5% x2	70.0% x3
wE	72.5% x4	77.5% x3	82.5% x2	75.0% x3
wF	77.5% x7	82.5% x5	87.5% x4	80.0% x3
wG	77.5% x7	82.5% x5	87.5% x4	
wH		82.5% x5	87.5% x4	

Developmental Strength 4-week Cycles – 87.5% Traditional 3 set – Lower, Upper

3 Set Traditional - 2.5%

LOWER UPPER BODY

	Base	Load	Load	UnLoad
Weekly %	80.0%	82.5%	85.0%	80.0%
differential	[-] 5%	[-] 2.5%	Top %	[-] 5%
WORK SETS	5 sets	6 sets	6 sets	4 sets
TOP SETS	2 sets	3 sets	3 sets	1 set
Weeks #	WK 1	WK 2	WK 3	WK 4
wu-a	27.5% 1t5	30.0% 1t5	32.5% 1t5	27.5% 1t5
wu-b	40.0% 1t5	42.5% 1t5	45.0% 1t5	40.0% 1t5
wu-c	50.0% 1t5	52.5% 1t5	55.0% 1t5	50.0% 1t5
wu-d	57.5% 1t5	60.0% 1t5	62.5% 1t5	57.5% 1t5
wA				
wB				
wC	65.0% x3	67.5% x3	70.0% x2	65.0% x3
wD	70.0% x3	72.5% x3	75.0% x2	70.0% x3
wE	75.0% x3	77.5% x3	80.0% x2	75.0% x3
wF	80.0% x6	82.5% x5	85.0% x4	80.0% x3
wG	80.0% x6	82.5% x5	85.0% x4	
wH		82.5% x5	85.0% x4	

3 Set Traditional - 5%

LOWER UPPER BODY

	Base	Load	Load	UnLoad
Weekly %	75.0%	80.0%	85.0%	77.5%
differential	[-] 10%	[-] 5%	Top %	[-] 7.5%
WORK SETS	5 sets	6 sets	6 sets	4 sets
TOP SETS	2 sets	3 sets	3 sets	1 set
Weeks #	WK 1	WK 2	WK 3	WK 4
wu-a	22.5% 1t5	27.5% 1t5	32.5% 1t5	25.0% 1t5
wu-b	35.0% 1t5	40.0% 1t5	45.0% 1t5	37.5% 1t5
wu-c	45.0% 1t5	50.0% 1t5	55.0% 1t5	47.5% 1t5
wu-d	52.5% 1t5	57.5% 1t5	62.5% 1t5	55.0% 1t5
wA				
wB				
wC	60.0% x4	65.0% x3	70.0% x2	62.5% x4
wD	65.0% x4	70.0% x3	75.0% x2	67.5% x4
wE	70.0% x4	75.0% x3	80.0% x2	72.5% x4
wF	75.0% x7	80.0% x6	85.0% x4	77.5% x4
wG	75.0% x7	80.0% x6	85.0% x4	
wH		80.0% x6	85.0% x4	

Developmental Strength 4-week Cycles – 85% Traditional 3 set – Lower, Upper

3 Set Traditional - 2.5%

LOWER UPPER BODY

	Base	Load	Load	UnLoad
Weekly %	77.5%	80.0%	82.5%	77.5%
differential	[-] 5%	[-] 2.5%	Top %	[-] 5%
WORK SETS	5 sets	6 sets	6 sets	4 sets
TOP SETS	2 sets	3 sets	3 sets	1 set
Weeks #	WK 1	WK 2	WK 3	WK 4
wu-a	25.0% 1t5	27.5% 1t5	30.0% 1t5	25.0% 1t5
wu-b	37.5% 1t5	40.0% 1t5	42.5% 1t5	37.5% 1t5
wu-c	47.5% 1t5	50.0% 1t5	52.5% 1t5	47.5% 1t5
wu-d	55.0% 1t5	57.5% 1t5	60.0% 1t5	55.0% 1t5
wA				
wB				
wC	62.5% X4	65.0% X3	67.5% X3	62.5% X4
wD	67.5% X4	70.0% X3	72.5% X3	67.5% X4
wE	72.5% X4	75.0% X3	77.5% X3	72.5% X4
wF	77.5% X7	80.0% X6	82.5% X5	77.5% X4
wG	77.5% X7	80.0% X6	82.5% X5	
wH		80.0% X6	82.5% X5	

3 Set Traditional - 5%

LOWER UPPER BODY

	Base	Load	Load	UnLoad
Weekly %	72.5%	77.5%	82.5%	75.0%
differential	[-] 10%	[-] 5%	Top %	[-] 7.5%
WORK SETS	5 sets	6 sets	6 sets	4 sets
TOP SETS	2 sets	3 sets	3 sets	1 set
Weeks #	WK 1	WK 2	WK 3	WK 4
wu-a	20.0% 1t5	25.0% 1t5	30.0% 1t5	22.5% 1t5
wu-b	32.5% 1t5	37.5% 1t5	42.5% 1t5	35.0% 1t5
wu-c	42.5% 1t5	47.5% 1t5	52.5% 1t5	45.0% 1t5
wu-d	50.0% 1t5	55.0% 1t5	60.0% 1t5	52.5% 1t5
wA				
wB				
wC	57.5% X5	62.5% X4	67.5% X3	60.0% X4
wD	62.5% X5	67.5% X4	72.5% X3	65.0% X4
wE	67.5% X5	72.5% X4	77.5% X3	70.0% X4
wF	72.5% X10	77.5% X7	82.5% X5	75.0% X4
wG	72.5% X10	77.5% X7	82.5% X5	
wH		77.5% X7	82.5% X5	

Developmental Strength 4-week Cycles – 82.5% Traditional 3 set – Lower, Upper

3 Set Traditional - 2.5%

LOWER UPPER BODY	Base	Load	Load	UnLoad
Weekly %	75.0%	77.5%	80.0%	75.0%
differential	[-] 5%	[-] 2.5%	Top %	[-] 5%
WORK SETS	5 sets	6 sets	6 sets	4 sets
TOP SETS	2 sets	3 sets	3 sets	1 set
Weeks #	WK 1	WK 2	WK 3	WK 4
wu-a	22.5% 1t5	25.0% 1t5	27.5% 1t5	22.5% 1t5
wu-b	35.0% 1t5	37.5% 1t5	40.0% 1t5	35.0% 1t5
wu-c	45.0% 1t5	47.5% 1t5	50.0% 1t5	45.0% 1t5
wu-d	52.5% 1t5	55.0% 1t5	57.5% 1t5	52.5% 1t5
wA				
wB				
wC	60.0% X4	62.5% X4	65.0% X3	60.0% X4
wD	65.0% X4	67.5% X4	70.0% X3	65.0% X4
wE	70.0% X4	72.5% X4	75.0% X3	70.0% X4
wF	75.0% X7	77.5% X7	80.0% X6	75.0% X4
wG	75.0% X7	77.5% X7	80.0% X6	
wH		77.5% X7	80.0% X6	

3 Set Traditional - 5%

LOWER UPPER BODY	Base	Load	Load	UnLoad
Weekly %	70.0%	75.0%	80.0%	72.5%
differential	[-] 10%	[-] 5%	Top %	[-] 7.5%
WORK SETS	5 sets	6 sets	6 sets	4 sets
TOP SETS	2 sets	3 sets	3 sets	1 set
Weeks #	WK 1	WK 2	WK 3	WK 4
wu-a		22.5% 1t5	27.5% 1t5	20.0% 1t5
wu-b	30.0% 1t5	35.0% 1t5	40.0% 1t5	32.5% 1t5
wu-c	40.0% 1t5	45.0% 1t5	50.0% 1t5	42.5% 1t5
wu-d	47.5% 1t5	52.5% 1t5	57.5% 1t5	50.0% 1t5
wA				
wB				
wC	55.0% X5	60.0% X4	65.0% X3	57.5% X5
wD	60.0% X5	65.0% X4	70.0% X3	62.5% X5
wE	65.0% X5	70.0% X4	75.0% X3	67.5% X5
wF	70.0% X10	75.0% X7	80.0% X6	72.5% X5
wG	70.0% X10	75.0% X7	80.0% X6	
wH		75.0% X7	80.0% X6	

Developmental Strength 4-week Cycles – 80% Traditional 3 set – Lower, Upper

6 Set Traditional - 2.5%

	Base	Load	Load	UnLoad
Weekly %	87.5%	90.0%	92.5%	87.5%
differential	[-] 5%	[-] 2.5%	Top %	[-] 5%
WORK SETS	5 sets	6 sets	6 sets	4 sets
TOP SETS	5 sets	6 sets	6 sets	4 sets
Weeks #	WK 1	WK 2	WK 3	WK 4
wu-a	50.0% 1t5	52.5% 1t5	55.0% 1t5	50.0% 1t5
wu-b	62.5% 1t5	65.0% 1t5	67.5% 1t5	62.5% 1t5
wu-c	72.5% 1t5	75.0% 1t5	77.5% 1t5	72.5% 1t5
wu-d	80.0% 1t5	82.5% 1t5	85.0% 1t5	80.0% 1t5
wA				
wB				
wC	87.5% X3	90.0% X2	92.5% X2	87.5% X2
wD	87.5% X3	90.0% X2	92.5% X2	87.5% X2
wE	87.5% X3	90.0% X2	92.5% X2	87.5% X2
wF	87.5% X3	90.0% X2	92.5% X2	87.5% X2
wG	87.5% X3	90.0% X2	92.5% X2	
wH		90.0% X2	92.5% X2	

6 Set Traditional - 5%

	Base	Load	Load	UnLoad
Weekly %	82.5%	87.5%	92.5%	85.0%
differential	[-] 10%	[-] 5%	Top %	[-] 7.5%
WORK SETS	5 sets	6 sets	6 sets	4 sets
TOP SETS	5 sets	6 sets	6 sets	4 sets
Weeks #	WK 1	WK 2	WK 3	WK 4
wu-a	45.0% 1t5	50.0% 1t5	55.0% 1t5	47.5% 1t5
wu-b	57.5% 1t5	62.5% 1t5	67.5% 1t5	60.0% 1t5
wu-c	67.5% 1t5	72.5% 1t5	77.5% 1t5	70.0% 1t5
wu-d	75.0% 1t5	80.0% 1t5	85.0% 1t5	77.5% 1t5
wA				
wB				
wC	82.5% X4	87.5% X3	92.5% X2	85.0% X2
wD	82.5% X4	87.5% X3	92.5% X2	85.0% X2
wE	82.5% X4	87.5% X3	92.5% X2	85.0% X2
wF	82.5% X4	87.5% X3	92.5% X2	85.0% X2
wG	82.5% X4	87.5% X3	92.5% X2	
wH		87.5% X3	92.5% X2	

LOWER UPPER BODY

Developmental Strength 4-week Cycles – 92.5% Traditional 6 set – Lower, Upper

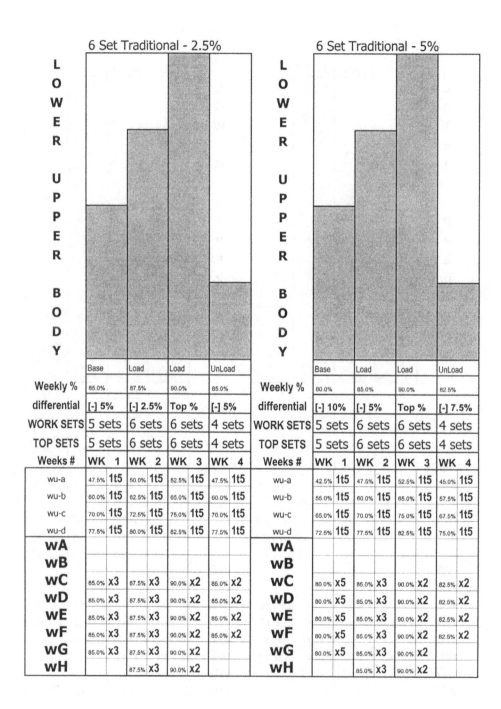

6 Set Traditional - 2.5% (LOWER UPPER BODY)

	Base	Load	Load	UnLoad
Weekly %	85.0%	87.5%	90.0%	85.0%
differential	[-] 5%	[-] 2.5%	Top %	[-] 5%
WORK SETS	5 sets	6 sets	6 sets	4 sets
TOP SETS	5 sets	6 sets	6 sets	4 sets
Weeks #	WK 1	WK 2	WK 3	WK 4
wu-a	47.5% 1t5	50.0% 1t5	52.5% 1t5	47.5% 1t5
wu-b	60.0% 1t5	62.5% 1t5	65.0% 1t5	60.0% 1t5
wu-c	70.0% 1t5	72.5% 1t5	75.0% 1t5	70.0% 1t5
wu-d	77.5% 1t5	80.0% 1t5	82.5% 1t5	77.5% 1t5
wA				
wB				
wC	85.0% X3	87.5% X3	90.0% X2	85.0% X2
wD	85.0% X3	87.5% X3	90.0% X2	85.0% X2
wE	85.0% X3	87.5% X3	90.0% X2	85.0% X2
wF	85.0% X3	87.5% X3	90.0% X2	85.0% X2
wG	85.0% X3	87.5% X3	90.0% X2	
wH		87.5% X3	90.0% X2	

6 Set Traditional - 5% (LOWER UPPER BODY)

	Base	Load	Load	UnLoad
Weekly %	80.0%	85.0%	90.0%	82.5%
differential	[-] 10%	[-] 5%	Top %	[-] 7.5%
WORK SETS	5 sets	6 sets	6 sets	4 sets
TOP SETS	5 sets	6 sets	6 sets	4 sets
Weeks #	WK 1	WK 2	WK 3	WK 4
wu-a	42.5% 1t5	47.5% 1t5	52.5% 1t5	45.0% 1t5
wu-b	55.0% 1t5	60.0% 1t5	65.0% 1t5	57.5% 1t5
wu-c	65.0% 1t5	70.0% 1t5	75.0% 1t5	67.5% 1t5
wu-d	72.5% 1t5	77.5% 1t5	82.5% 1t5	75.0% 1t5
wA				
wB				
wC	80.0% X5	85.0% X3	90.0% X2	82.5% X2
wD	80.0% X5	85.0% X3	90.0% X2	82.5% X2
wE	80.0% X5	85.0% X3	90.0% X2	82.5% X2
wF	80.0% X5	85.0% X3	90.0% X2	82.5% X2
wG	80.0% X5	85.0% X3	90.0% X2	
wH		85.0% X3	90.0% X2	

Developmental Strength 4-week Cycles – 90% Traditional 6 set – Lower, Upper

6 Set Traditional - 2.5%

LOWER UPPER BODY

	Base	Load	Load	UnLoad
Weekly %	82.5%	85.0%	87.5%	82.5%
differential	[-] 5%	[-] 2.5%	Top %	[-] 5%
WORK SETS	5 sets	6 sets	6 sets	4 sets
TOP SETS	5 sets	6 sets	6 sets	4 sets
Weeks #	WK 1	WK 2	WK 3	WK 4
wu-a	45.0% 1t5	47.5% 1t5	50.0% 1t5	45.0% 1t5
wu-b	57.5% 1t5	60.0% 1t5	62.5% 1t5	57.5% 1t5
wu-c	67.5% 1t5	70.0% 1t5	72.5% 1t5	67.5% 1t5
wu-d	75.0% 1t5	77.5% 1t5	80.0% 1t5	75.0% 1t5
wA				
wB				
wC	82.5% X4	85.0% X3	87.5% X3	82.5% X2
wD	82.5% X4	85.0% X3	87.5% X3	82.5% X2
wE	82.5% X4	85.0% X3	87.5% X3	82.5% X2
wF	82.5% X4	85.0% X3	87.5% X3	82.5% X2
wG	82.5% X4	85.0% X3	87.5% X3	
wH		85.0% X3	87.5% X3	

6 Set Traditional - 5%

LOWER UPPER BODY

	Base	Load	Load	UnLoad
Weekly %	77.5%	82.5%	87.5%	80.0%
differential	[-] 10%	[-] 5%	Top %	[-] 7.5%
WORK SETS	5 sets	6 sets	6 sets	4 sets
TOP SETS	5 sets	6 sets	6 sets	4 sets
Weeks #	WK 1	WK 2	WK 3	WK 4
wu-a	40.0% 1t5	45.0% 1t5	50.0% 1t5	42.5% 1t5
wu-b	52.5% 1t5	57.5% 1t5	62.5% 1t5	55.0% 1t5
wu-c	62.5% 1t5	67.5% 1t5	72.5% 1t5	65.0% 1t5
wu-d	70.0% 1t5	75.0% 1t5	80.0% 1t5	72.5% 1t5
wA				
wB				
wC	77.5% X6	82.5% X4	87.5% X3	80.0% X3
wD	77.5% X6	82.5% X4	87.5% X3	80.0% X3
wE	77.5% X6	82.5% X4	87.5% X3	80.0% X3
wF	77.5% X6	82.5% X4	87.5% X3	80.0% X3
wG	77.5% X6	82.5% X4	87.5% X3	
wH		82.5% X4	87.5% X3	

Developmental Strength 4-week Cycles – 87.5% Traditional 6 set – Lower, Upper

6 Set Traditional - 2.5%

LOWER UPPER BODY

	Base	Load	Load	UnLoad
Weekly %	80.0%	82.5%	85.0%	80.0%
differential	[-] 5%	[-] 2.5%	Top %	[-] 5%
WORK SETS	5 sets	6 sets	6 sets	4 sets
TOP SETS	5 sets	6 sets	6 sets	4 sets
Weeks #	WK 1	WK 2	WK 3	WK 4
wu-a	42.5% 1t5	45.0% 1t5	47.5% 1t5	42.5% 1t5
wu-b	55.0% 1t5	57.5% 1t5	60.0% 1t5	55.0% 1t5
wu-c	65.0% 1t5	67.5% 1t5	70.0% 1t5	65.0% 1t5
wu-d	72.5% 1t5	75.0% 1t5	77.5% 1t5	72.5% 1t5
wA				
wB				
wC	80.0% X5	82.5% X4	85.0% X3	80.0% X3
wD	80.0% X5	82.5% X4	85.0% X3	80.0% X3
wE	80.0% X5	82.5% X4	85.0% X3	80.0% X3
wF	80.0% X5	82.5% X4	85.0% X3	80.0% X3
wG	80.0% X5	82.5% X4	85.0% X3	
wH		82.5% X4	85.0% X3	

6 Set Traditional - 5%

LOWER UPPER BODY

	Base	Load	Load	UnLoad
Weekly %	75.0%	80.0%	85.0%	77.5%
differential	[-] 10%	[-] 5%	Top %	[-] 7.5%
WORK SETS	5 sets	6 sets	6 sets	4 sets
TOP SETS	5 sets	6 sets	6 sets	4 sets
Weeks #	WK 1	WK 2	WK 3	WK 4
wu-a	37.5% 1t5	42.5% 1t5	47.5% 1t5	40.0% 1t5
wu-b	50.0% 1t5	55.0% 1t5	60.0% 1t5	52.5% 1t5
wu-c	60.0% 1t5	65.0% 1t5	70.0% 1t5	62.5% 1t5
wu-d	67.5% 1t5	72.5% 1t5	77.5% 1t5	70.0% 1t5
wA				
wB				
wC	75.0% X6	80.0% X5	85.0% X3	77.5% X3
wD	75.0% X6	80.0% X5	85.0% X3	77.5% X3
wE	75.0% X6	80.0% X5	85.0% X3	77.5% X3
wF	75.0% X6	80.0% X5	85.0% X3	77.5% X3
wG	75.0% X6	80.0% X5	85.0% X3	
wH		80.0% X5	85.0% X3	

Developmental Strength 4-week Cycles – 85% Traditional 6 set – Lower, Upper

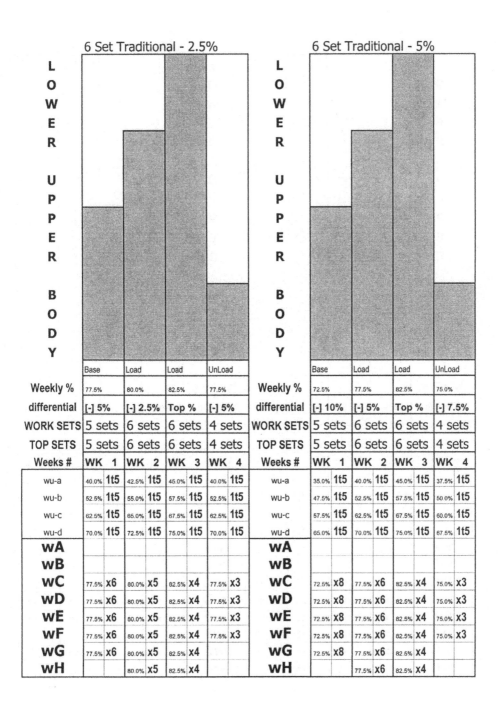

6 Set Traditional - 2.5%

LOWER UPPER BODY

	Base	Load	Load	UnLoad
Weekly %	77.5%	80.0%	82.5%	77.5%
differential	[-] 5%	[-] 2.5%	Top %	[-] 5%
WORK SETS	5 sets	6 sets	6 sets	4 sets
TOP SETS	5 sets	6 sets	6 sets	4 sets
Weeks #	WK 1	WK 2	WK 3	WK 4
wu-a	40.0% 1t5	42.5% 1t5	45.0% 1t5	40.0% 1t5
wu-b	52.5% 1t5	55.0% 1t5	57.5% 1t5	52.5% 1t5
wu-c	62.5% 1t5	65.0% 1t5	67.5% 1t5	62.5% 1t5
wu-d	70.0% 1t5	72.5% 1t5	75.0% 1t5	70.0% 1t5
wA				
wB				
wC	77.5% x6	80.0% x5	82.5% x4	77.5% x3
wD	77.5% x6	80.0% x5	82.5% x4	77.5% x3
wE	77.5% x6	80.0% x5	82.5% x4	77.5% x3
wF	77.5% x6	80.0% x5	82.5% x4	77.5% x3
wG	77.5% x6	80.0% x5	82.5% x4	
wH		80.0% x5	82.5% x4	

6 Set Traditional - 5%

LOWER UPPER BODY

	Base	Load	Load	UnLoad
Weekly %	72.5%	77.5%	82.5%	75.0%
differential	[-] 10%	[-] 5%	Top %	[-] 7.5%
WORK SETS	5 sets	6 sets	6 sets	4 sets
TOP SETS	5 sets	6 sets	6 sets	4 sets
Weeks #	WK 1	WK 2	WK 3	WK 4
wu-a	35.0% 1t5	40.0% 1t5	45.0% 1t5	37.5% 1t5
wu-b	47.5% 1t5	52.5% 1t5	57.5% 1t5	50.0% 1t5
wu-c	57.5% 1t5	62.5% 1t5	67.5% 1t5	60.0% 1t5
wu-d	65.0% 1t5	70.0% 1t5	75.0% 1t5	67.5% 1t5
wA				
wB				
wC	72.5% x8	77.5% x6	82.5% x4	75.0% x3
wD	72.5% x8	77.5% x6	82.5% x4	75.0% x3
wE	72.5% x8	77.5% x6	82.5% x4	75.0% x3
wF	72.5% x8	77.5% x6	82.5% x4	75.0% x3
wG	72.5% x8	77.5% x6	82.5% x4	
wH		77.5% x6	82.5% x4	

Developmental Strength 4-week Cycles – 82.5% Traditional 6 set – Lower, Upper

6 Set Traditional - 2.5%

LOWER UPPER BODY

	Base	Load	Load	UnLoad
Weekly %	75.0%	77.5%	80.0%	75.0%
differential	[-] 5%	[-] 2.5%	Top %	[-] 5%
WORK SETS	5 sets	6 sets	6 sets	4 sets
TOP SETS	5 sets	6 sets	6 sets	4 sets
Weeks #	WK 1	WK 2	WK 3	WK 4
wu-a	37.5% 1t5	40.0% 1t5	42.5% 1t5	37.5% 1t5
wu-b	50.0% 1t5	52.5% 1t5	55.0% 1t5	50.0% 1t5
wu-c	60.0% 1t5	62.5% 1t5	65.0% 1t5	60.0% 1t5
wu-d	67.5% 1t5	70.0% 1t5	72.5% 1t5	67.5% 1t5
wA				
wB				
wC	75.0% x6	77.5% x6	80.0% x5	75.0% x3
wD	75.0% x6	77.5% x6	80.0% x5	75.0% x3
wE	75.0% x6	77.5% x6	80.0% x5	75.0% x3
wF	75.0% x6	77.5% x6	80.0% x5	75.0% x3
wG	75.0% x6	77.5% x6	80.0% x5	
wH		77.5% x6	80.0% x5	

6 Set Traditional - 5%

LOWER UPPER BODY

	Base	Load	Load	UnLoad
Weekly %	70.0%	75.0%	80.0%	72.5%
differential	[-] 10%	[-] 5%	Top %	[-] 7.5%
WORK SETS	5 sets	6 sets	6 sets	4 sets
TOP SETS	5 sets	6 sets	6 sets	4 sets
Weeks #	WK 1	WK 2	WK 3	WK 4
wu-a	32.5% 1t5	37.5% 1t5	42.5% 1t5	35.0% 1t5
wu-b	45.0% 1t5	50.0% 1t5	55.0% 1t5	47.5% 1t5
wu-c	55.0% 1t5	60.0% 1t5	65.0% 1t5	57.5% 1t5
wu-d	62.5% 1t5	67.5% 1t5	72.5% 1t5	65.0% 1t5
wA				
wB				
wC	70.0% x8	75.0% x6	80.0% x5	72.5% x4
wD	70.0% x8	75.0% x6	80.0% x5	72.5% x4
wE	70.0% x8	75.0% x6	80.0% x5	72.5% x4
wF	70.0% x8	75.0% x6	80.0% x5	72.5% x4
wG	70.0% x8	75.0% x6	80.0% x5	
wH		75.0% x6	80.0% x5	

Developmental Strength 4-week Cycles – 80% Traditional 6 set – Lower, Upper

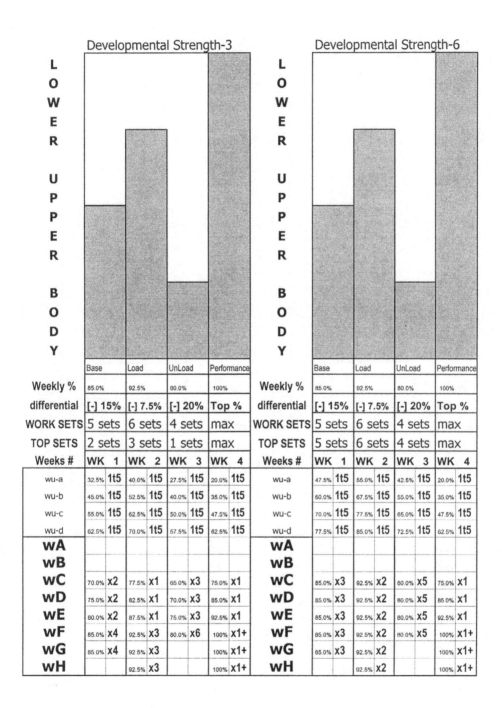

Developmental Strength-3 (Lower / Upper Body)

	Base	Load	UnLoad	Performance
Weekly %	85.0%	92.5%	80.0%	100%
differential	[-] 15%	[-] 7.5%	[-] 20%	Top %
WORK SETS	5 sets	6 sets	4 sets	max
TOP SETS	2 sets	3 sets	1 sets	max
Weeks #	WK 1	WK 2	WK 3	WK 4
wu-a	32.5% 1t5	40.0% 1t5	27.5% 1t5	20.0% 1t5
wu-b	45.0% 1t5	52.5% 1t5	40.0% 1t5	35.0% 1t5
wu-c	55.0% 1t5	62.5% 1t5	50.0% 1t5	47.5% 1t5
wu-d	62.5% 1t5	70.0% 1t5	57.5% 1t5	62.5% 1t5
wA				
wB				
wC	70.0% x2	77.5% x1	65.0% x3	75.0% x1
wD	75.0% x2	82.5% x1	70.0% x3	85.0% x1
wE	80.0% x2	87.5% x1	75.0% x3	92.5% x1
wF	85.0% x4	92.5% x3	80.0% x6	100% x1+
wG	85.0% x4	92.5% x3		100% x1+
wH		92.5% x3		100% x1+

Developmental Strength-6 (Lower / Upper Body)

	Base	Load	UnLoad	Performance
Weekly %	85.0%	92.5%	80.0%	100%
differential	[-] 15%	[-] 7.5%	[-] 20%	Top %
WORK SETS	5 sets	6 sets	4 sets	max
TOP SETS	5 sets	6 sets	4 sets	max
Weeks #	WK 1	WK 2	WK 3	WK 4
wu-a	47.5% 1t5	55.0% 1t5	42.5% 1t5	20.0% 1t5
wu-b	60.0% 1t5	67.5% 1t5	55.0% 1t5	35.0% 1t5
wu-c	70.0% 1t5	77.5% 1t5	65.0% 1t5	47.5% 1t5
wu-d	77.5% 1t5	85.0% 1t5	72.5% 1t5	62.5% 1t5
wA				
wB				
wC	85.0% x3	92.5% x2	80.0% x5	75.0% x1
wD	85.0% x3	92.5% x2	80.0% x5	85.0% x1
wE	85.0% x3	92.5% x2	80.0% x5	92.5% x1
wF	85.0% x3	92.5% x2	80.0% x5	100% x1+
wG	85.0% x3	92.5% x2		100% x1+
wH		92.5% x2		100% x1+

Developmental Strength 4-week Cycles – 100% Performance – Lower, Upper

Developmental Strength-3

	Base	Load	UnLoad	Performance
Weekly %	80.0%	87.5%	75.0%	95%
differential	[-] 15%	[-] 7.5%	[-] 20%	Top %
WORK SETS	5 sets	6 sets	4 sets	max
TOP SETS	2 sets	3 sets	1 sets	max
Weeks #	WK 1	WK 2	WK 3	WK 4
wu-a	27.5% 1t5	35.0% 1t5	22.5% 1t5	
wu-b	40.0% 1t5	47.5% 1t5	35.0% 1t5	20.0% 1t5
wu-c	50.0% 1t5	57.5% 1t5	45.0% 1t5	32.5% 1t5
wu-d	57.5% 1t5	65.0% 1t5	52.5% 1t5	45.0% 1t5
wA				
wB				
wC	65.0% x3	72.5% x2	60.0% x4	57.5% x1
wD	70.0% x3	77.5% x2	65.0% x4	70.0% x1
wE	75.0% x3	82.5% x2	70.0% x4	87.5% x1
wF	80.0% x6	87.5% x4	75.0% x7	95.0% x2
wG	80.0% x6	87.5% x4		95.0% x2
wH		87.5% x4		95.0% x2

Developmental Strength-6

	Base	Load	UnLoad	Performance
Weekly %	80.0%	87.5%	75.0%	95%
differential	[-] 15%	[-] 7.5%	[-] 20%	Top %
WORK SETS	5 sets	6 sets	4 sets	max
TOP SETS	5 sets	6 sets	4 sets	max
Weeks #	WK 1	WK 2	WK 3	WK 4
wu-a	42.5% 1t5	50.0% 1t5	37.5% 1t5	
wu-b	55.0% 1t5	62.5% 1t5	50.0% 1t5	20.0% 1t5
wu-c	65.0% 1t5	72.5% 1t5	60.0% 1t5	32.5% 1t5
wu-d	72.5% 1t5	80.0% 1t5	67.5% 1t5	45.0% 1t5
wA				
wB				
wC	80.0% x5	87.5% x3	75.0% x6	57.5% x1
wD	80.0% x5	87.5% x3	75.0% x6	70.0% x1
wE	80.0% x5	87.5% x3	75.0% x6	87.5% x1
wF	80.0% x5	87.5% x3	75.0% x6	95.0% x2
wG	80.0% x5	87.5% x3		95.0% x2
wH		87.5% x3		95.0% x2

Developmental Strength 4-week Cycles – 95% Performance – Lower, Upper

Developmental Strength-3

L O W E R

U P P E R

B O D Y

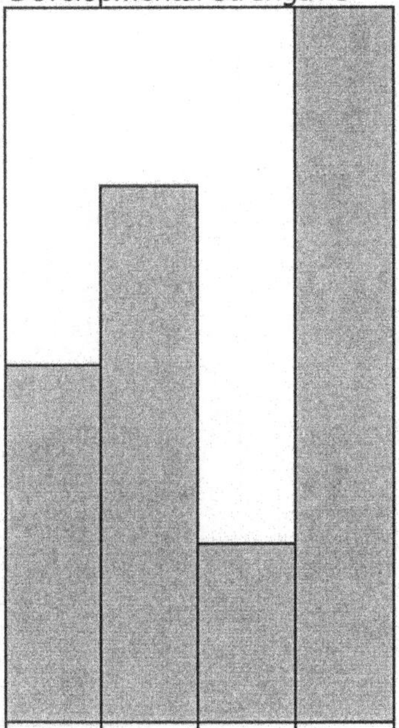

	Base		Load		UnLoad		Performance	
Weekly %	77.5%		85.0%		72.5%		92.5%	
differential	[-] 15%		[-] 7.5%		[-] 20%		Top %	
WORK SETS	5 sets		6 sets		4 sets		max	
TOP SETS	2 sets		3 sets		1 sets		max	
Weeks #	WK 1		WK 2		WK 3		WK 4	
wu-a	25.0%	1t5	32.5%	1t5	20.0%	1t5	40.0%	1t5
wu-b	37.5%	1t5	45.0%	1t5	32.5%	1t5	52.5%	1t5
wu-c	47.5%	1t5	55.0%	1t5	42.5%	1t5	62.5%	1t5
wu-d	55.0%	1t5	62.5%	1t5	50.0%	1t5	70.0%	1t5
wA								
wB								
wC	62.5%	x4	70.0%	x2	57.5%	x5	77.5%	x1
wD	67.5%	x4	75.0%	x2	62.5%	x5	82.5%	x1
wE	72.5%	x4	80.0%	x2	67.5%	x5	87.5%	x1
wF	77.5%	x7	85.0%	x4	72.5%	x10	92.5%	x3
wG	77.5%	x7	85.0%	x4			92.5%	x3
wH			85.0%	x4			92.5%	x3

Developmental Strength-6

L O W E R

U P P E R

B O D Y

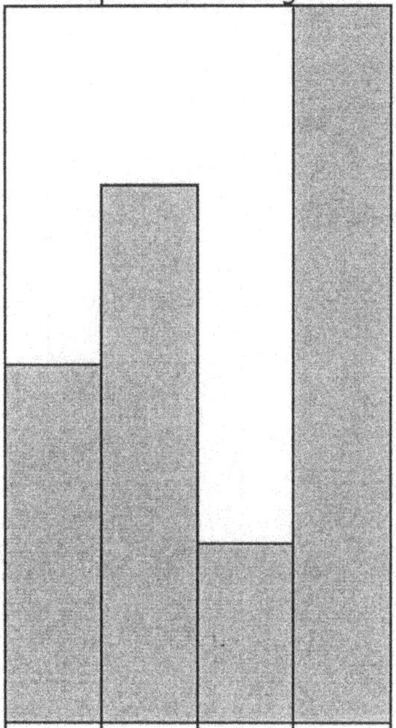

	Base		Load		UnLoad		Performance	
Weekly %	77.5%		85.0%		72.5%		92.5%	
differential	[-] 15%		[-] 7.5%		[-] 20%		Top %	
WORK SETS	5 sets		6 sets		4 sets		max	
TOP SETS	5 sets		6 sets		4 sets		max	
Weeks #	WK 1		WK 2		WK 3		WK 4	
wu-a	40.0%	1t5	47.5%	1t5	35.0%	1t5	55.0%	1t5
wu-b	52.5%	1t5	60.0%	1t5	47.5%	1t5	67.5%	1t5
wu-c	62.5%	1t5	70.0%	1t5	57.5%	1t5	77.5%	1t5
wu-d	70.0%	1t5	77.5%	1t5	65.0%	1t5	85.0%	1t5
wA								
wB								
wC	77.5%	x6	85.0%	x3	72.5%	x8	92.5%	x2
wD	77.5%	x6	85.0%	x3	72.5%	x8	92.5%	x2
wE	77.5%	x6	85.0%	x3	72.5%	x8	92.5%	x2
wF	77.5%	x6	85.0%	x3	72.5%	x8	92.5%	x2
wG	77.5%	x6	85.0%	x3			92.5%	x2
wH			85.0%	x3			92.5%	x2

Developmental Strength 4-week Cycles – 92.5% Performance – Lower, Upper

Developmental Strength-3

	Base	Load	UnLoad	Performance
Weekly %	75.0%	82.5%	70.0%	90%
differential	[-] 15%	[-] 7.5%	[-] 20%	Top %
WORK SETS	5 sets	6 sets	4 sets	max
TOP SETS	2 sets	3 sets	1 sets	max
Weeks #	WK 1	WK 2	WK 3	WK 4
wu-a	25.0% 1t5	30.0% 1t5		37.5% 1t5
wu-b	37.5% 1t5	42.5% 1t5	30.0% 1t5	50.0% 1t5
wu-c	47.5% 1t5	52.5% 1t5	40.0% 1t5	60.0% 1t5
wu-d	55.0% 1t5	60.0% 1t5	47.5% 1t5	67.5% 1t5
wA				
wB				
wC	62.5% x4	67.5% x3	55.0% x5	75.0% x1
wD	67.5% x4	72.5% x3	60.0% x5	80.0% x1
wE	72.5% x4	77.5% x3	65.0% x5	85.0% x1
wF	77.5% x7	82.5% x5	70.0% x10	90.0% x3
wG	77.5% x7	82.5% x5		90.0% x3
wH		82.5% x5		90.0% x3

Developmental Strength-6

	Base	Load	UnLoad	Performance
Weekly %	75.0%	82.5%	70.0%	90%
differential	[-] 15%	[-] 7.5%	[-] 20%	Top %
WORK SETS	5 sets	6 sets	4 sets	max
TOP SETS	5 sets	6 sets	4 sets	max
Weeks #	WK 1	WK 2	WK 3	WK 4
wu-a	40.0% 1t5	45.0% 1t5	32.5% 1t5	52.5% 1t5
wu-b	52.5% 1t5	57.5% 1t5	45.0% 1t5	65.0% 1t5
wu-c	62.5% 1t5	67.5% 1t5	55.0% 1t5	75.0% 1t5
wu-d	70.0% 1t5	75.0% 1t5	62.5% 1t5	82.5% 1t5
wA				
wB				
wC	77.5% x6	82.5% x4	70.0% x8	90.0% x2
wD	77.5% x6	82.5% x4	70.0% x8	90.0% x2
wE	77.5% x6	82.5% x4	70.0% x8	90.0% x2
wF	77.5% x6	82.5% x4	70.0% x8	90.0% x2
wG	77.5% x6	82.5% x4		90.0% x2
wH		82.5% x4		90.0% x2

Developmental Strength 4-week Cycles – 90% Performance – Lower, Upper

Developmental Strength-3

L O W E R   U P P E R   B O D Y

	Base	Load	UnLoad	Performance
Weekly %	72.5%	80.0%	67.5%	87.5%
differential	[-] 15%	[-] 7.5%	[-] 20%	Top %
WORK SETS	5 sets	6 sets	4 sets	max
TOP SETS	2 sets	3 sets	1 sets	max
Weeks #	WK 1	WK 2	WK 3	WK 4
wu-a	20.0% 1t5	30.0% 1t5		35.0% 1t5
wu-b	32.5% 1t5	42.5% 1t5	27.5% 1t5	47.5% 1t5
wu-c	42.5% 1t5	52.5% 1t5	37.5% 1t5	57.5% 1t5
wu-d	50.0% 1t5	60.0% 1t5	45.0% 1t5	65.0% 1t5
wA				
wB				
wC	57.5% x5	65.0% x3	52.5% x6	72.5% x2
wD	62.5% x5	70.0% x3	57.5% x6	77.5% x2
wE	67.5% x5	75.0% x3	62.5% x6	82.5% x2
wF	72.5% x10	80.0% x5	67.5% x12	87.5% x4
wG	72.5% x10	80.0% x5		87.5% x4
wH		80.0% x5		87.5% x4

Developmental Strength-6

L O W E R   U P P E R   B O D Y

	Base	Load	UnLoad	Performance
Weekly %	72.5%	80.0%	67.5%	87.5%
differential	[-] 15%	[-] 7.5%	[-] 20%	Top %
WORK SETS	5 sets	6 sets	4 sets	max
TOP SETS	5 sets	6 sets	4 sets	max
Weeks #	WK 1	WK 2	WK 3	WK 4
wu-a	35.0% 1t5	45.0% 1t5	30.0% 1t5	50.0% 1t5
wu-b	47.5% 1t5	57.5% 1t5	42.5% 1t5	62.5% 1t5
wu-c	57.5% 1t5	67.5% 1t5	52.5% 1t5	72.5% 1t5
wu-d	65.0% 1t5	75.0% 1t5	60.0% 1t5	80.0% 1t5
wA				
wB				
wC	72.5% x8	80.0% x4	67.5% x10	87.5% x3
wD	72.5% x8	80.0% x4	67.5% x10	87.5% x3
wE	72.5% x8	80.0% x4	67.5% x10	87.5% x3
wF	72.5% x8	80.0% x4	67.5% x10	87.5% x3
wG	72.5% x8	80.0% x4		87.5% x3
wH		80.0% x4		87.5% x3

Developmental Strength 4-week Cycles – 87.5% Performance – Lower, Upper

Developmental Strength-3

	Base	Load	UnLoad	Performance
Weekly %	70.0%	77.5%	65.0%	85%
differential	[-] 15%	[-] 7.5%	[-] 20%	Top %
WORK SETS	5 sets	6 sets	4 sets	max
TOP SETS	2 sets	3 sets	1 sets	max
Weeks #	WK 1	WK 2	WK 3	WK 4
wu-a		25.0% 1t5		32.5% 1t5
wu-b	30.0% 1t5	37.5% 1t5	25.0% 1t5	45.0% 1t5
wu-c	40.0% 1t5	47.5% 1t5	35.0% 1t5	55.0% 1t5
wu-d	47.5% 1t5	55.0% 1t5	42.5% 1t5	62.5% 1t5
wA				
wB				
wC	55.0% x5	62.5% x4	50.0% x6	70.0% x2
wD	60.0% x5	67.5% x4	55.0% x6	75.0% x2
wE	65.0% x5	72.5% x4	60.0% x6	80.0% x2
wF	70.0% x10	77.5% x7	65.0% x12	85.0% x4
wG	70.0% x10	77.5% x7		85.0% x4
wH		77.5% x7		85.0% x4

Developmental Strength-6

	Base	Load	UnLoad	Performance
Weekly %	70.0%	77.5%	65.0%	85%
differential	[-] 15%	[-] 7.5%	[-] 20%	Top %
WORK SETS	5 sets	6 sets	4 sets	max
TOP SETS	5 sets	6 sets	4 sets	max
Weeks #	WK 1	WK 2	WK 3	WK 4
wu-a	32.5% 1t5	40.0% 1t5	27.5% 1t5	47.5% 1t5
wu-b	45.0% 1t5	52.5% 1t5	40.0% 1t5	60.0% 1t5
wu-c	55.0% 1t5	62.5% 1t5	50.0% 1t5	70.0% 1t5
wu-d	62.5% 1t5	70.0% 1t5	57.5% 1t5	77.5% 1t5
wA				
wB				
wC	70.0% x8	77.5% x6	65.0% x10	85.0% x3
wD	70.0% x8	77.5% x6	65.0% x10	85.0% x3
wE	70.0% x8	77.5% x6	65.0% x10	85.0% x3
wF	70.0% x8	77.5% x6	65.0% x10	85.0% x3
wG	70.0% x8	77.5% x6		85.0% x3
wH		77.5% x6		85.0% x3

Developmental Strength 4-week Cycles – 85% Performance – Lower, Upper

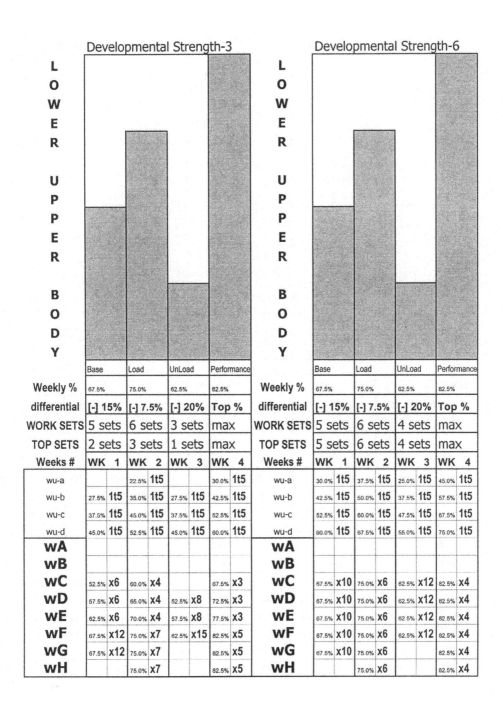

Developmental Strength-3

LOWER UPPER BODY

	Base	Load	UnLoad	Performance
Weekly %	67.5%	75.0%	62.5%	82.5%
differential	[-] 15%	[-] 7.5%	[-] 20%	Top %
WORK SETS	5 sets	6 sets	3 sets	max
TOP SETS	2 sets	3 sets	1 sets	max

Weeks #	WK 1		WK 2		WK 3		WK 4	
wu-a			22.5%	1t5			30.0%	1t5
wu-b	27.5%	1t5	35.0%	1t5	27.5%	1t5	42.5%	1t5
wu-c	37.5%	1t5	45.0%	1t5	37.5%	1t5	52.5%	1t5
wu-d	45.0%	1t5	52.5%	1t5	45.0%	1t5	60.0%	1t5
wA								
wB								
wC	52.5%	x6	60.0%	x4			67.5%	x3
wD	57.5%	x6	65.0%	x4	52.5%	x8	72.5%	x3
wE	62.5%	x6	70.0%	x4	57.5%	x8	77.5%	x3
wF	67.5%	x12	75.0%	x7	62.5%	x15	82.5%	x5
wG	67.5%	x12	75.0%	x7			82.5%	x5
wH			75.0%	x7			82.5%	x5

Developmental Strength-6

LOWER UPPER BODY

	Base	Load	UnLoad	Performance
Weekly %	67.5%	75.0%	62.5%	82.5%
differential	[-] 15%	[-] 7.5%	[-] 20%	Top %
WORK SETS	5 sets	6 sets	4 sets	max
TOP SETS	5 sets	6 sets	4 sets	max

Weeks #	WK 1		WK 2		WK 3		WK 4	
wu-a	30.0%	1t5	37.5%	1t5	25.0%	1t5	45.0%	1t5
wu-b	42.5%	1t5	50.0%	1t5	37.5%	1t5	57.5%	1t5
wu-c	52.5%	1t5	60.0%	1t5	47.5%	1t5	67.5%	1t5
wu-d	60.0%	1t5	67.5%	1t5	55.0%	1t5	75.0%	1t5
wA								
wB								
wC	67.5%	x10	75.0%	x6	62.5%	x12	82.5%	x4
wD	67.5%	x10	75.0%	x6	62.5%	x12	82.5%	x4
wE	67.5%	x10	75.0%	x6	62.5%	x12	82.5%	x4
wF	67.5%	x10	75.0%	x6	62.5%	x12	82.5%	x4
wG	67.5%	x10	75.0%	x6			82.5%	x4
wH			75.0%	x6			82.5%	x4

Developmental Strength 4-week Cycles – 82.5% Performance – Lower, Upper

Developmental Strength-3

LOWER UPPER BODY

	Base		Load		UnLoad		Performance	
Weekly %	65.0%		72.5%		60.0%		80%	
differential	[-] 15%		[-] 7.5%		[-] 20%		Top %	
WORK SETS	5 sets		6 sets		3 sets		max	
TOP SETS	2 sets		3 sets		1 sets		max	
Weeks #	WK 1		WK 2		WK 3		WK 4	
wu-a			20.0%	1t5			27.5%	1t5
wu-b	25.0%	1t5	32.5%	1t5	25.0%	1t5	40.0%	1t5
wu-c	35.0%	1t5	42.5%	1t5	35.0%	1t5	50.0%	1t5
wu-d	42.5%	1t5	50.0%	1t5	42.5%	1t5	57.5%	1t5
wA								
wB								
wC	50.0%	x6	57.5%	x5			65.0%	x3
wD	55.0%	x6	62.5%	x5	50.0%	x8	70.0%	x3
wE	60.0%	x6	67.5%	x5	55.0%	x8	75.0%	x3
wF	65.0%	x12	72.5%	x10	60.0%	x15	80.0%	x6
wG	65.0%	x12	72.5%	x10			80.0%	x6
wH			72.5%	x10			80.0%	x6

Developmental Strength-6

LOWER UPPER BODY

	Base		Load		UnLoad		Performance	
Weekly %	65.0%		72.5%		60.0%		80%	
differential	[-] 15%		[-] 7.5%		[-] 20%		Top %	
WORK SETS	5 sets		6 sets		4 sets		max	
TOP SETS	5 sets		6 sets		4 sets		max	
Weeks #	WK 1		WK 2		WK 3		WK 4	
wu-a	27.5%	1t5	35.0%	1t5	22.5%	1t5	42.5%	1t5
wu-b	40.0%	1t5	47.5%	1t5	35.0%	1t5	55.0%	1t5
wu-c	50.0%	1t5	57.5%	1t5	45.0%	1t5	65.0%	1t5
wu-d	57.5%	1t5	65.0%	1t5	52.5%	1t5	72.5%	1t5
wA								
wB								
wC	65.0%	x10	72.5%	x8	60.0%	x12	80.0%	x5
wD	65.0%	x10	72.5%	x8	60.0%	x12	80.0%	x5
wE	65.0%	x10	72.5%	x8	60.0%	x12	80.0%	x5
wF	65.0%	x10	72.5%	x8	60.0%	x12	80.0%	x5
wG	65.0%	x10	72.5%	x8			80.0%	x5
wH			72.5%	x8			80.0%	x5

Developmental Strength 4-week Cycles – 80% Performance – Lower, Upper

Prilepin - Developmental Strength (100% Performance)

	Base	Load	Load	Performance
Weekly %	85.0%	92.5%	80.0%	100%
differential	[-] 15%	[-] 7.5%	[-] 20%	Top %
WORK SETS	8 sets	10 sets	6 sets	max
TOP SETS	8 sets	10 sets	6 sets	max
Weeks #	WK 1	WK 2	WK 3	WK 4
wu-a	47.5% 1t5	55.0% 1t5	42.5% 1t5	32.5% 1t5
wu-b	60.0% 1t5	67.5% 1t5	55.0% 1t5	47.5% 1t5
wu-c	70.0% 1t5	77.5% 1t5	65.0% 1t5	60.0% 1t5
wu-d	77.5% 1t5	85.0% 1t5	72.5% 1t5	70.0% 1t5
wA	85.0% x2	92.5% x1		
wB	85.0% x2	92.5% x1		
wC	85.0% x2	92.5% x1	80.0% x2	77.5% x1
wD	85.0% x2	92.5% x1	80.0% x2	85.0% x1
wE	85.0% x2	92.5% x1	80.0% x2	92.5% x1
wF	85.0% x2	92.5% x1	80.0% x2	100% x1+
wG	85.0% x2	92.5% 2x1	80.0% x2	100% x1+
wH	85.0% x2	92.5% 2x1	80.0% x2	100% x1+

Prilepin Developmental 4-week Cycles – 100% Performance

Prilepin - Developmental Strength (95% Performance)

	Base	Load	Load	Performance
Weekly %	80.0%	87.5%	75.0%	95%
differential	[-] 15%	[-] 7.5%	[-] 20%	Top %
WORK SETS	8 sets	10 sets	6 sets	max
TOP SETS	8 sets	10 sets	6 sets	max
Weeks #	WK 1	WK 2	WK 3	WK 4
wu-a	42.5% 1t5	50.0% 1t5	37.5% 1t5	27.5% 1t5
wu-b	55.0% 1t5	62.5% 1t5	50.0% 1t5	40.0% 1t5
wu-c	65.0% 1t5	72.5% 1t5	60.0% 1t5	52.5% 1t5
wu-d	72.5% 1t5	80.0% 1t5	67.5% 1t5	62.5% 1t5
wA	80.0% x2	87.5% x2		
wB	80.0% x2	87.5% x2		
wC	80.0% x2	87.5% x2	75.0% x3	70.0% x1
wD	80.0% x2	87.5% x2	75.0% x3	75.0% x1
wE	80.0% x2	87.5% x2	75.0% x3	87.5% x1
wF	80.0% x2	87.5% x2	75.0% x3	95.0% x1
wG	80.0% x2	87.5% 2x2	75.0% x3	95.0% x1
wH	80.0% x2	87.5% 2x2	75.0% x3	95.0% x1

Prilepin Developmental 4-week Cycles – 95% Performance

Prilepin - Developmental Strength

	Base	Load	Load	Performance
Weekly %	77.5%	85.0%	72.5%	92.5%
differential	[-] 15%	[-] 7.5%	[-] 20%	Top %
WORK SETS	8 sets	10 sets	6 sets	max
TOP SETS	8 sets	10 sets	6 sets	max
Weeks #	WK 1	WK 2	WK 3	WK 4
wu-a	40.0% 1t5	47.5% 1t5	35.0% 1t5	55.0% 1t5
wu-b	52.5% 1t5	60.0% 1t5	47.5% 1t5	67.5% 1t5
wu-c	62.5% 1t5	70.0% 1t5	57.5% 1t5	77.5% 1t5
wu-d	70.0% 1t5	77.5% 1t5	65.0% 1t5	85.0% 1t5
wA	77.5% x3	85.0% x2		92.5% x1
wB	77.5% x3	85.0% x2		92.5% x1
wC	77.5% x3	85.0% x2	72.5% x3	92.5% x1
wD	77.5% x3	85.0% x2	72.5% x3	92.5% x1
wE	77.5% x3	85.0% x2	72.5% x3	92.5% x1
wF	77.5% x3	85.0% x2	72.5% x3	92.5% x1
wG	77.5% x3	85.0% 2x2	72.5% x3	92.5% 2x1
wH	77.5% x3	85.0% 2x2	72.5% x3	92.5% 2x1

Prilepin Developmental 4-week Cycles – 92.5% Performance

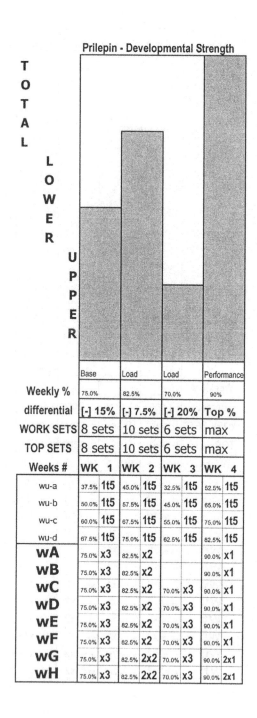

Prilepin - Developmental Strength

	Base	Load	Load	Performance
Weekly %	75.0%	82.5%	70.0%	90%
differential	[-] 15%	[-] 7.5%	[-] 20%	Top %
WORK SETS	8 sets	10 sets	6 sets	max
TOP SETS	8 sets	10 sets	6 sets	max
Weeks #	WK 1	WK 2	WK 3	WK 4
wu-a	37.5% 1t5	45.0% 1t5	32.5% 1t5	52.5% 1t5
wu-b	50.0% 1t5	57.5% 1t5	45.0% 1t5	65.0% 1t5
wu-c	60.0% 1t5	67.5% 1t5	55.0% 1t5	75.0% 1t5
wu-d	67.5% 1t5	75.0% 1t5	62.5% 1t5	82.5% 1t5
wA	75.0% x3	82.5% x2		90.0% x1
wB	75.0% x3	82.5% x2		90.0% x1
wC	75.0% x3	82.5% x2	70.0% x3	90.0% x1
wD	75.0% x3	82.5% x2	70.0% x3	90.0% x1
wE	75.0% x3	82.5% x2	70.0% x3	90.0% x1
wF	75.0% x3	82.5% x2	70.0% x3	90.0% x1
wG	75.0% x3	82.5% 2x2	70.0% x3	90.0% 2x1
wH	75.0% x3	82.5% 2x2	70.0% x3	90.0% 2x1

Prilepin Developmental 4-week Cycles – 90% Performance

Prilepin - Developmental Strength (87.5% Performance)

T O T A L / L O W E R / U P P E R

	Base	Load	Load	Performance
Weekly %	72.5%	80.0%	67.5%	87.5%
differential	[-] 15%	[-] 7.5%	[-] 20%	Top %
WORK SETS	8 sets	10 sets	6 sets	max
TOP SETS	8 sets	10 sets	6 sets	max
Weeks #	WK 1	WK 2	WK 3	WK 4
wu-a	35.0% 1t5	42.5% 1t5	30.0% 1t5	50.0% 1t5
wu-b	47.5% 1t5	55.0% 1t5	42.5% 1t5	62.5% 1t5
wu-c	57.5% 1t5	65.0% 1t5	52.5% 1t5	72.5% 1t5
wu-d	65.0% 1t5	72.5% 1t5	60.0% 1t5	80.0% 1t5
wA	72.5% x3	80.0% x2		87.5% x2
wB	72.5% x3	80.0% x2		87.5% x2
wC	72.5% x3	80.0% x2	67.5% x3	87.5% x2
wD	72.5% x3	80.0% x2	67.5% x3	87.5% x2
wE	72.5% x3	80.0% x2	67.5% x3	87.5% x2
wF	72.5% x3	80.0% x2	67.5% x3	87.5% x2
wG	72.5% x3	80.0% 2x2	67.5% x3	87.5% 2x2
wH	72.5% x3	80.0% 2x2	67.5% x3	87.5% 2x2

Prilepin Developmental 4-week Cycles –
87.5% Performance

Prilepin - Developmental Strength (85% Performance)

T O T A L / L O W E R / U P P E R

	Base	Load	Load	Performance
Weekly %	70.0%	77.5%	65.0%	85%
differential	[-] 15%	[-] 7.5%	[-] 20%	Top %
WORK SETS	6 sets	8 sets	5 sets	max
TOP SETS	6 sets	8 sets	5 sets	max
Weeks #	WK 1	WK 2	WK 3	WK 4
wu-a	32.5% 1t5	40.0% 1t5	27.5% 1t5	47.5% 1t5
wu-b	45.0% 1t5	52.5% 1t5	40.0% 1t5	60.0% 1t5
wu-c	55.0% 1t5	62.5% 1t5	50.0% 1t5	70.0% 1t5
wu-d	62.5% 1t5	70.0% 1t5	57.5% 1t5	77.5% 1t5
wA		77.5% x3		85.0% x2
wB		77.5% x3		85.0% x2
wC	70.0% x3	77.5% x3		85.0% x2
wD	70.0% x3	77.5% x3	65.0% x3	85.0% x2
wE	70.0% x3	77.5% x3	65.0% x3	85.0% x2
wF	70.0% x3	77.5% x3	65.0% x3	85.0% x2
wG	70.0% x3	77.5% x3	65.0% x3	85.0% 2x2
wH	70.0% x3	77.5% x3	65.0% x3	85.0% 2x2

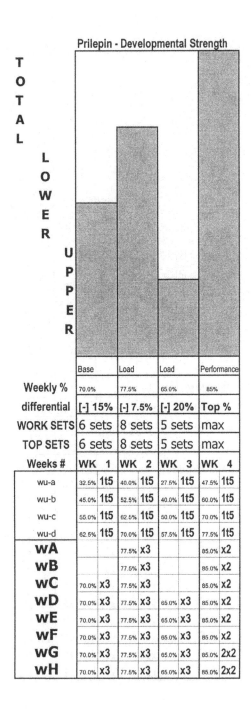

Prilepin Developmental 4-week Cycles –
85% Performance

Prilepin - Developmental Strength

	Base	Load	Load	Performance
Weekly %	67.5%	75.0%	62.5%	82.5%
differential	[-] 15%	[-] 7.5%	[-] 20%	Top %
WORK SETS	6 sets	8 sets	5 sets	max
TOP SETS	6 sets	8 sets	5 sets	max
Weeks #	WK 1	WK 2	WK 3	WK 4
wu-a	30.0% 1t5	37.5% 1t5	25.0% 1t5	45.0% 1t5
wu-b	42.5% 1t5	50.0% 1t5	37.5% 1t5	57.5% 1t5
wu-c	52.5% 1t5	60.0% 1t5	47.5% 1t5	67.5% 1t5
wu-d	60.0% 1t5	67.5% 1t5	55.0% 1t5	75.0% 1t5
wA		75.0% x3		82.5% x2
wB		75.0% x3		82.5% x2
wC	67.5% x3	75.0% x3		82.5% x2
wD	67.5% x3	75.0% x3	62.5% x3	82.5% x2
wE	67.5% x3	75.0% x3	62.5% x3	82.5% x2
wF	67.5% x3	75.0% x3	62.5% x3	82.5% x2
wG	67.5% x3	75.0% x3	62.5% x3	82.5% 2x2
wH	67.5% x3	75.0% x3	62.5% x3	82.5% 2x2

Prilepin Developmental 4-week Cycles – 82.5% Performance

Prilepin - Developmental Strength

	Base	Load	Load	Performance
Weekly %	65.0%	72.5%	60.0%	80%
differential	[-] 15%	[-] 7.5%	[-] 20%	Top %
WORK SETS	6 sets	8 sets	5 sets	max
TOP SETS	6 sets	8 sets	5 sets	max
Weeks #	WK 1	WK 2	WK 3	WK 4
wu-a	27.5% 1t5	35.0% 1t5	22.5% 1t5	42.5% 1t5
wu-b	40.0% 1t5	47.5% 1t5	35.0% 1t5	55.0% 1t5
wu-c	50.0% 1t5	57.5% 1t5	45.0% 1t5	65.0% 1t5
wu-d	57.5% 1t5	65.0% 1t5	52.5% 1t5	72.5% 1t5
wA		72.5% x3		80.0% x2
wB		72.5% x3		80.0% x2
wC	65.0% x3	72.5% x3		80.0% x2
wD	65.0% x3	72.5% x3	60.0% x3	80.0% x2
wE	65.0% x3	72.5% x3	60.0% x3	80.0% x2
wF	65.0% x3	72.5% x3	60.0% x3	80.0% x2
wG	65.0% x3	72.5% x3	60.0% x3	80.0% 2x2
wH	65.0% x3	72.5% x3	60.0% x3	80.0% 2x2

Prilepin Developmental 4-week Cycles – 80% Performance

C

Comprehensive Exercise Pool

- Total Body Exercises
- Lower Body Exercises
- Upper Body Exercises

Total Body Exercises

Sub Category	Total Body Movements
Pull and Catch	BB Clean - Deck - Power
Pull and Catch	BB Clean - Deck - Squat
Pull and Catch	BB Clean - Deck - Split
Pull and Catch	BB Clean - Hang - Power
Pull and Catch	BB Clean - Hang - Squat
Pull and Catch	BB Clean - Hang - Split
Pull and Catch	BB Clean - Rack - Power
Pull and Catch	BB Clean - Rack - Squat
Pull and Catch	BB Clean - Rack - Split
Pull and Catch	DB Clean - Deck - Power
Pull and Catch	DB Clean - Deck - Squat
Pull and Catch	DB Clean - Deck - Split
Pull and Catch	DB Clean - Hang - Power
Pull and Catch	DB Clean - Hang - Squat
Pull and Catch	DB Clean - Hang - Split
Pull and Catch	BB Snatch - Deck - Power
Pull and Catch	BB Snatch - Deck - Squat
Pull and Catch	BB Snatch - Deck - Split
Pull and Catch	BB Snatch - Hang - Power
Pull and Catch	BB Snatch - Hang - Squat
Pull and Catch	BB Snatch - Hang - Split
Pull and Catch	BB Snatch - Rack - Power
Pull and Catch	BB Snatch - Rack - Squat
Pull and Catch	BB Snatch - Rack - Split
Pull and Catch	DB SA Snatch - Deck - Power
Pull and Catch	DB SA Snatch - Deck - Split
Pull and Catch	DB SA Snatch - Hang - Power
Pull and Catch	DB SA Snatch - Hang - Split
Pull and Catch	BB SA Snatch - Hang - Power
Overhead	BB Push Press
Overhead	BB Push Jerk
Overhead	BB Split Jerk
Overhead	DB Push Press
Overhead	DB Push Jerk
Overhead	DB Split Jerk
Extension	Deadlift - Deck
Extension	Deadlift - Rack
Extension	Deadlift - Elevated
Extension	BB Clean Gr Shrug Pull - Deck
Extension	BB Clean Gr Power Pull - Deck
Extension	BB Clean Gr Shrug Pull - Hang

Sub Category	Total Body Movements
Extension	BB Clean Gr Power Pull - Hang
Extension	BB Clean Gr Shrug Pull - Rack
Extension	BB Clean Gr Power Pull - Rack
Extension	BB Snatch Gr Shrug Pull - Deck
Extension	BB Snatch Gr Power Pull - Deck
Extension	BB Snatch Gr Shrug Pull - Hang
Extension	BB Snatch Gr Power Pull - Hang
Extension	BB Snatch Gr Shrug Pull - Rack
Extension	BB Snatch Gr Power Pull - Rack
Extension	DB Shrug Pull - Deck
Extension	DB Power Pull - Deck
Extension	DB Shrug Pull - Hang
Extension	DB Power Pull - Hang
Hybrids	BB Clean to Push Press - Deck
Hybrids	BB Clean to Push Jerk - Deck
Hybrids	BB Clean to Split Jerk - Deck
Hybrids	BB Clean to Push Press - Hang
Hybrids	BB Clean to Push Jerk - Hang
Hybrids	BB Clean to Split Jerk - Hang
Hybrids	DB Clean to Push Press - Deck
Hybrids	DB Clean to Push Jerk - Deck
Hybrids	DB Clean to Split Jerk - Deck
Hybrids	DB Clean to Push Press - Hang
Hybrids	DB Clean to Push Jerk - Hang
Hybrids	DB Clean to Split Jerk - Hang
Hybrids	BB Clean to Front Squat
Hybrids	DB Clean to Front Squat
Hybrids	BB Clean to Fr Squat to P Press
Hybrids	BB Clean to Fr Squat to P Jerk
Hybrids	BB Clean to Fr Squat to S Jerk
Hybrids	DB Clean to Fr Squat to P Press
Hybrids	DB Clean to Fr Squat to P Jerk
Hybrids	DB Clean to Fr Squat to S Jerk
Technique	Snatch Balance
Technique	Pressing Snatch Balance
Technique	Heaving Snatch Balance
Alternative	Hammer Shrug Pull
Alternative	Hammer Hi Pull
Alternative	Hammer Deadlift
Alternative	Hammer Jammer
BB = Barbell	
DB = Dumbbell	

Lower Body Exercises

Sub Category	Lower Body Movements
In Place Double	BB-Squat-Back-Power Stance
In Place Double	BB-Squat-Back-Olympic Stance
In Place Double	BB-Squat-Box-Back-Power
In Place Double	BB-Squat-Box-Back-Olympic
In Place Double	BB-Squat-Front-Power Stance
In Place Double	BB-Squat-Front-Olympic Stance
In Place Double	BB-Squat-Box-Front-Power
In Place Double	BB-Squat-Box-Front-Olympic
In Place Double	BB-Squat-Zercher-Power
In Place Double	BB-Squat-Box-Zercher-Power
In Place Double	BB-Squat-Overhead-Natural
In Place Double	BB-Squat-Box-Overhead-Nat
In Place Double	BB-Squat-1/4-Jump-Vertical
In Place Double	BB-Squat-1/4-Sport-Vertical
In Place Double	BB-Squat-Midpoint-Power
In Place Double	BB-Squat-Midpoint-Olympic
In Place Single	BB-Squat-Split
In Place Double	DB-Squat-Natural
In Place Double	DB-Sumo-Squat
In Place Single	Single Leg Squat
In Place Double	Safety Bar-Squat-Power
In Place Double	Safety Bar-Squat-Olympic
In Place Double	Safety Bar-Box-Squat-Power
In Place Double	Safety Bar-Box-Squat-Olympic
In Place Double	Safety Bar-Squat-Midpoint-Pow
In Place Double	Safety Bar-Squat-Midpoint-Oly
Horizontal	BB-Lunge-Asterisk
Horizontal	DB-Lunge-Asterisk
Horizontal	BB-Lunge-Standard
Horizontal	DB-Lunge-Standard
Horizontal	BB-Lunge-Reverse
Horizontal	DB-Lunge-Reverse
Horizontal	BB-Lunge-45 degree
Horizontal	DB-Lunge-45 degree
Horizontal	BB-Lunge-Transverse
Horizontal	DB-Lunge-Transverse
Horizontal	BB-Lunge-Lateral
Horizontal	DB-Lunge-Lateral
Horizontal	BB-Lunge-Forward Walk
Horizontal	DB-Lunge-Forward Walk
Horizontal	BB-Lunge-Reverse Walk
Horizontal	DB-Lunge-Reverse Walk

Sub Category	Lower Body Movements
Horizontal	BB-Lunge-Shuffle
Horizontal	DB-Lunge-Shuffle
Horizontal	DB-Lunge-Tennis
Vertical	BB-Step Up/Down-Standard
Vertical	DB-Step Up/Down-Standard
Vertical	BB-Step Up/Down-Reverse
Vertical	DB-Step Up/Down-Reverse
Vertical	BB-Step Up/Down-45 degree
Vertical	DB-Step Up/Down-45 degree
Vertical	BB-Step Up/Down-Lateral
Vertical	DB-Step Up/Down-Lateral
Vertical	BB-Step Up/Down-Crossover
Vertical	DB-Step Up/Down-Crossover
Vertical	BB-Step Up/Down-Shuffle
Vertical	DB-Step Up/Down-Shuffle
Posterior Chain	Romanian Deadlift
Posterior Chain	Stiff Legged Deadlift
Posterior Chain	Glute Ham Raise
Posterior Chain	Back Extension
Posterior Chain	Reverse Hyperextensions
Posterior Chain	Good Mornings
Posterior Chain	Pull Thru's
Posterior Chain	Partner Leg Curl
Posterior Chain	Stability Ball Hip Lift
Posterior Chain	Stability Ball Hip Lift to Curl
Posterior Chain	Lying Leg Curl
Posterior Chain	Seated Leg Curl
Posterior Chain	Standing Leg Curl
Hybrids	Back Squat to Standing Press
Hybrids	Back Squat to Push Press
Hybrids	Back Squat to Push Jerk
Hybrids	Back Squat to Split Jerk
Hybrids	Front Squat to Standing Press
Hybrids	Front Squat to Push Press
Hybrids	Front Squat to Push Jerk
Hybrids	Front Squat to Split Jerk
Hybrids	Good Morning to Back Squat
Hybrids	Sumo Squat to Power Pull
Hybrids	DB Squat to Standing Press
Hybrids	DB Squat to Push Press
Hybrids	DB Squat to Push Jerk
Hybrids	DB Squat to Split Jerk
Hybrids	DB Squat to Lateral Raise
Hybrids	DB Squat to Front Raise
Hybrids	BB Lunge-Forward/Reverse

Sub Category	Lower Body Movements
Hybrids	BB Lunge-Reverse/Forward
Hybrids	BB Lunge-Reverse/Lateral
Hybrids	BB Lunge-Lateral/Reverse
Hybrids	BB Lunge-For/Rev walk
Hybrids	BB Lunge-Rev/For walk
Hybrids	BB Lunge-Shuffle RT/LT
Hybrids	BB Lunge-Shuffle LT/RT
Hybrids	DB Lunge-Forward/Reverse
Hybrids	DB Lunge-Reverse/Forward
Hybrids	DB Lunge-Reverse/Lateral
Hybrids	DB Lunge-Lateral/Reverse
Hybrids	DB Lunge-For/Rev walk
Hybrids	DB Lunge-Rev/For walk
Hybrids	DB Lunge-Shuffle RT/LT
Hybrids	DB Lunge-Shuffle LT/RT
Hybrids	Reverse Lunge to St U/D
Hybrids	Lateral Lunge to Lat Step U/D
Hybrids	Lat Lunge to X Over Step U/D
Hybrids	Crossover Step to Squat
Hybrids	Step Up/Down to Lateral St U/D
Hybrids	DB Lunge to Press
Hybrids	DB Walking Lunge to Press
Hybrids	DB Lunge to Curl to Press
Hybrids	DB Walking Lunge to Curl to Pr
Hybrids	DB Lateral Lunge to Press
Alternative	Bear Squat
Alternative	Leg Press
Alternative	Hammer Squat Lunge
Alternative	Hammer V Squat
Alternative	BB Hack Squat
Alternative	Leg Extension
Alternative	Hip Extension
Alternative	Hip Flexion
Alternative	Hip Adduction
Alternative	Hip Abduction
Alternative	Band Kick Backs
Alternative	Heel Raises
Alternative	Toe Raises
Alternative	Band Pull Apart
Alternative	Band Shuffles

Upper Body Exercises

Sub Category	Upper Body Movements
Horizontal Press	BB-Bench Press
Horizontal Press	DB-Bench Press
Horizontal Press	BB-Incline Press-Low
Horizontal Press	DB-Incline Press-Low
Horizontal Press	BB-Incline Press-Low
Horizontal Press	DB-Incline Press-Low
Horizontal Press	BB-Incline Press-Moderate
Horizontal Press	DB-Incline Press-Moderate
Horizontal Press	BB-Incline Press-Steep
Horizontal Press	DB-Incline Press-Steep
Horizontal Press	BB-Decline Press
Horizontal Press	DB-Decline Press
Horizontal Press	BB-Reverse Grip Bench Press
Horizontal Press	Cambered Bar Bench Press
Horizontal Press	Super Bar Bench Press
Horizontal Press	BB-1 Board Bench Press
Horizontal Press	BB-2 Board Bench Press
Horizontal Press	BB-3 Board Bench Press
Horizontal Press	BB-4 Board Bench Press
Horizontal Press	BB-5 Board Bench Press
Horizontal Press	BB-Floor Press
Horizontal Press	DB-Floor Press
Horizontal Press	Push Up
Vertical Press	BB-Standing Press-Front
Vertical Press	BB-Standing Press-Behind Head
Vertical Press	BB-Seated Press-Front
Vertical Press	BB-Seated Press-Behind Head
Vertical Press	DB-Standing Press
Vertical Press	DB Seated Press
Vertical Press	BB Bradford Press
Vertical Press	Parallel Bar Dips
Sub Category	Upper Body Movements
Horizontal Pull	BB Bent Over Row
Horizontal Pull	DB Bent Over Row
Horizontal Pull	Inverted Pull Ups
Horizontal Pull	Inverted Chin Ups
Horizontal Pull	Chest Supported Row
Horizontal Pull	Seated Row
Vertical Pull	Pull Ups
Vertical Pull	Chin Ups
Vertical Pull	Pull Downs
Vertical Pull	BB-Upright Row

Sub Category	Upper Body Movements
Vertical Pull	DB Upright Row
Flexion/Extension	BB-Extensions
Flexion/Extension	DB-Extensions
Flexion/Extension	DB Elbows Out Extension
Flexion/Extension	Pushdowns
Flexion/Extension	BB Curl
Flexion/Extension	DB Curl
Flexion/Extension	Resistance Options
Shoulder Rotation	Lateral Raise
Shoulder Rotation	Front Raise
Shoulder Rotation	Bent Over Raise
Shoulder Rotation	45 Degree Raise
Shoulder Rotation	"L" Raise
Shoulder Rotation	Empty Can
Shoulder Rotation	Internal Rotation
Shoulder Rotation	External Rotation
Shoulder Rotation	Horizontal Internal Rotation
Shoulder Rotation	Horizontal External Rotation
Shoulder Rotation	Marshall Rotation
Shoulder Rotation	Step Over
Shoulder Rotation	Scapula Push Ups
Shoulder Rotation	Bear Crawls
Shoulder Rotation	Wheel Barrow Walks
Shoulder Rotation	Seated DB Clean
Shoulder Rotation	Seated DB Snatch
Shoulder Rotation	Pulls to Face
Shoulder Rotation	Fly
Shoulder Rotation	Incline Fly
Shoulder Rotation	Reverse Fly
Shoulder Rotation	Standing Fly
Shoulder Rotation	Plate Raise
Shoulder Rotation	Shrugs
Alternative	Chest Press
Alternative	Shoulder Press
Alternative	Jammer Press
Alternative	Neider Press
Alternative	Steel Log Standing Press
Alternative	Steel Log Bench Press
Alternative	Steel Log Row
Alternative	Trap Bar Standing Press
Alternative	Wrist Flips
Alternative	Wrist Curl
Alternative	Reverse Wrist Curl
Alternative	Forearm Role Ups
Alternative	Neck

D

Developing Your Weekly Exercise Plan Step by Step

Creating Your Exercise Program

This appendix will simplify all the material in Chapter 4 by going through the five basic steps in choosing exercises for a specific program. At this time, because you have already completed your annual plan, the template and cycle you will use is already set.

An example for a 3x5 tier system program follows:

- Create an exercise pool.
- Separate exercises into three movement categories.
- Classify each exercise per movement category and label it as a specific movement:
  - ❑ Total-body exercises
  - ❑ Lower-body exercises
  - ❑ Upper-body exercises
- Rank exercises per movement category.
- Input exercises into template.
  - ❑ Input total-body exercises
  - ❑ Input lower-body exercises
  - ❑ Input upper-body exercises

Step 1 – Create an Exercise Pool

Back Squat
Bench Press
Clean from Deck
Hang Clean
High Step Up
Standard Lunge
DB Incline Press
Snatch Grip Power Pull
Snatch Grip Shrug Pull
Clean Grip Shrug Pull
Clean Grip Power Pull
DB Clean
DB Single Arm Snatch
Chin Ups
Standing Press
Grip3 Bench Press
Front Squat
Leg Press
Hammer Row
Lateral Lunge
Incline Press
DB Press
Reverse Lunge
Split Clean from Hang
Split Jerk
Push Press
Inverted Pull Up
Deadlift
Low Step Up
Overhead Squat

Step 2 – Separate into 3 Movement Categories

Total Body Movements	Lower Body Movements	Upper Body Movements
Clean from Deck	Back Squat	Bench Press
Hang Clean	High Step Up	DB Incline Press
Snatch Grip Power Pull	Standard Lunge	Chin Ups
Snatch Grip Shrug Pull	Front Squat	Standing Press
Clean Grip Shrug Pull	Leg Press	Grip3 Bench Press
Clean Grip Power Pull	Lateral Lunge	Hammer Row
DB Clean	Reverse Lunge	Incline Press
DB Single Arm Snatch	Low Step Up	DB Press
Split Clean from Hang	Overhead Squat	Inverted Pull Up
Split Jerk		
Push Press		
Deadlift		

Step 3 – Classify Each Exercise per Movement Category and Label it as a Specific Movement

Total Body Movements	Classification	Specific Movement
Clean from Deck	Supplemental	Full Pull and Catch Bilateral
Hang Clean	Foundation	Full Pull and Catch Bilateral
Snatch Grip Power Pull	Major Assistance	Extension
Snatch Grip Shrug Pull	Major Assistance	Extension
Clean Grip Shrug Pull	Major Assistance	Extension
Clean Grip Power Pull	Major Assistance	Extension
DB Clean	Major Assistance	Full Pull and Catch Unilateral
DB Single Arm Snatch	Major Assistance	Full Pull and Catch Unilateral
Split Clean from Hang	Supplemental	Full Pull and Catch Unilateral
Split Jerk	Supplemental	Full Pull and Catch Unilateral
Push Press	Major Assistance	Pushing - Press
Deadlift	Supplemental	Extension

Lower Body Movements	Classification	Specific Movement
Back Squat	Foundation	In Place Double Leg
High Step Up	Major Assistance	Vertical
Standard Lunge	Major Assistance	Horizontal
Front Squat	Supplemental	In Place Double Leg
Leg Press	Supplemental	In Place Double Leg
Lateral Lunge	Major Assistance	Horizontal
Reverse Lunge	Major Assistance	Horizontal
Low Step Up	Major Assistance	Vertical
Overhead Squat	Supplemental	In Place Double Leg

Upper Body Movements	Classification	Specific Movement
Bench Press	Foundation	Horizontal Bilateral
DB Incline Press	Major Assistance	Horizontal Unilateral
Chin Ups	Major Assistance	Vertical Bilateral
Standing Press	Major Assistance	Vertical Bilateral
Grip3 Bench Press	Supplemental	Horizontal Bilateral
Hammer Row	Major Assistance	Horizontal Unilateral
Incline Press	Supplemental	Horizontal Bilateral
DB Press	Major Assistance	Vertical Unilateral
Inverted Pull Up	Major Assistance	Horizontal Bilateral

Step 4 – Rank Each Exercise per Movement Category

Total Body Movements	Classification	Specific Movement
Clean from Deck	Supplemental	Full Pull and Catch Bilateral
Hang Clean [1]	Foundation	Full Pull and Catch Bilateral
Snatch Grip Power Pull [3]	Major Assistance	Extension
Snatch Grip Shrug Pull	Major Assistance	Extension
Clean Grip Shrug Pull [4]	Major Assistance	Extension
Clean Grip Power Pull	Major Assistance	Extension
DB Clean	Major Assistance	Full Pull and Catch Unilateral
DB Single Arm Snatch [5]	Major Assistance	Full Pull and Catch Unilateral
Split Clean from Hang	Supplemental	Full Pull and Catch Unilateral
Split Jerk [2]	Supplemental	Full Pull and Catch Unilateral
Push Press	Major Assistance	Pushing - Press
Deadlift	Supplemental	Extension

Lower Body Movements	Classification	Specific Movement
Back Squat [1]	Foundation	In Place Double Leg
High Step Up [4]	Major Assistance	Vertical
Standard Lunge [5]	Major Assistance	Horizontal
Front Squat [2]	Supplemental	In Place Double Leg
Leg Press [3]	Supplemental	In Place Double Leg
Lateral Lunge	Major Assistance	Horizontal
Reverse Lunge	Major Assistance	Horizontal
Low Step Up	Major Assistance	Vertical
Overhead Squat	Supplemental	In Place Double Leg

Upper Body Movements	Classification	Specific Movement
Bench Press [1]	Foundation	Horizontal Bilateral
DB Incline Press [2]	Major Assistance	Horizontal Unilateral
Chin Ups [4]	Major Assistance	Vertical Bilateral
Standing Press [5]	Major Assistance	Vertical Bilateral
Grip3 Bench Press	Supplemental	Horizontal Bilateral
Hammer Row	Major Assistance	Horizontal Unilateral
Incline Press	Supplemental	Horizontal Bilateral
DB Press	Major Assistance	Vertical Unilateral
Inverted Pull Up [3]	Major Assistance	Horizontal Bilateral

Step 5 – Input Exercise in Template

Input Total Body Exercises

Rotation	Session T	Rotation	Session L	Rotation	Session U
Total 1	Hang Clean	Lower 1		Upper 1	
Lower 2		Upper 2		Total 2	Split Jerk
Upper 3		Total 3	Snatch Grip Power Pull	Lower 3	
Total 4	Clean Grip Shrug Pull	Lower 4		Upper 4	
Lower 5		Upper 5		Total 5	DB Single Arm Snatch

Add Lower Body Exercises

Rotation	Session T	Rotation	Session L	Rotation	Session U
Total 1	Hang Clean	Lower 1	Back Squat	Upper 1	
Lower 2	Front Squat	Upper 2		Total 2	Split Jerk
Upper 3		Total 3	Snatch Grip Power Pull	Lower 3	Leg Press
Total 4	Clean Grip Shrug Pull	Lower 4	High Step Up	Upper 4	
Lower 5	Standard Lunge	Upper 5		Total 5	DB Single Arm Snatch

Add Upper Body Exercises

Rotation	Session T	Rotation	Session L	Rotation	Session U
Total 1	Hang Clean	Lower 1	Back Squat	Upper 1	Bench Press
Lower 2	Front Squat	Upper 2	DB Incline Press	Total 2	Split Jerk
Upper 3	Inverted Pull Up	Total 3	Snatch Grip Power Pull	Lower 3	Leg Press
Total 4	Clean Grip Shrug Pull	Lower 4	High Step Up	Upper 4	Chin Ups
Lower 5	Standard Lunge	Upper 5	Standing Press	Total 5	DB Single Arm Snatch

References

Bompa, Tudor. 1983, 1990. <u>Theory and Methodology of Training.</u> (2nd Edition). Iowa.

Bompa, Tudor. 1993. <u>Periodization of Strength</u>. Toronto, Canada.

Bompa, Tudor. 1999. <u>Periodization Training for Sports</u>. Illinois.

Boyle, M. 2001. Torso Training Manual. Massachusetts.

Boyle, M. Stability and Conditioning the Body's Torso. Video.

Brzycki, M. 1995. A Practical Approach to Strength Training. (3rd Edition). Indiana.

Davies, J. 2002. <u>Renegade Training for Football</u>. Minnesota.

Doyle, C. 1999. Professional Development. *University of Iowa*.

Drechsler, A. 1998. <u>The Weightlifting Encyclopedia</u>. New York.

Fleck, S., Kraemer, W. 1996. <u>Periodization Breakthrough</u>. New York.

Goldstein, Y. Practical Application of Speed Training Techniques in Advanced Bodybuilding Training. http://www.thinkmuscle.com

Halbert, G. 2002. Speeding Up Your Progress. *Powerlifting USA*. 25(12).

Hatfield. F. Powerlifting and Speed-Strength Training. http://www.drsquat.com

Johnston, K. & Simmons, L. 1997. Force Training, Video and Manual.

Jones, L, Eksten, F., Fleschler, P. 2001. USA Weightlifting Sports Performance Coach Manual. Colorado.

Kenn, J. 1993. Strength Training Procedures: Lecture Guide and Laboratory Manual. *Unpublished Master's Project*. Boise State University.

Kenn, J. 1994. Strength Training Program Design *Scholastic Coach*. 63(10).

Kenn, J. 1995. Sets and Reps. <u>Scholastic Coach</u>. 64(7).

Kenn, J. 1997. Program Design for the Tier System. *Strength and Conditioning*. 19(2).

Kenn, J. 1998. 30 Second Continuation Set. <u>Coach and Athletic Director</u>. 67(5).

Kenn, J. 2000. WHAT'S RIGHT – The Great Philosophical Debate. *Hard Training*. (Dec.)

Kreis, E.J. 1992. <u>Speed-Strength Training for Football</u>. Tennessee.

Koch, Fred. 1994. <u>Strength Training for Sports</u>.

Medvedyev, A.S. 1986. <u>A System of Multi-Year Training in Weightlifting</u>. Michigan.

Medvedyev, A.S. 1986. <u>A Program of Multi-Year Training in Weightlifting</u>. Michigan.

Pauletto, B. 1991. <u>Strength Training for Coaches</u>. Illinois.

Plisk, S. 1998. Accelerative Training. *Milo*. 6(1).

Poliquin, C. 1997. <u>The Poliquin Principles</u>. California.

Roman, R.A. 1986. <u>The Training of the Weightlifter</u>. Michigan.

Rooney, M. 2002. Professional Development. *Parisi School of Sport*.

Roundtable. 1986. Periodization: Part I. *National Strength and Conditioning Journal*. 8(5).

Roundtable. 1986. Periodization: Part II. *National Strength and Conditioning Journal*. 8(6).

Roundtable. 1986. Periodization: Part III. *National Strength and Conditioning Journal*. 9(1).

Simmons, L. 1990. Rehabilitation and Restoration. *Powerlifting USA*. 13(10).

Simmons, L. 1990. When Less is More: Training by Percents II. *Powerlifting USA*. 14(2).

Simmons, L. 1994. Cycling Systems. *Powerlifting USA*. 17(6).

Simmons, L. 1994. Training by Percents, Part I. *Powerlifting USA*. 17(10).

Simmons, L. 1994. What is Conjugate Training. *Powerlifting USA*. 18(5).

Simmons, L. 1995. Raising Work Capacity. *Powerlifting USA*. 18(9).

Simmons, L. 1995. Overtraining or Adaptation. *Powerlifting USA*. 18(11).
Simmons, L. 1995. Percent Training, What is it really? Part I. *Powerlifting USA*. 19(4).
Simmons, L. 1996. Percent Training, What is it really? Part II. *Powerlifting USA*. 19(6).
Simmons, L. 1996. Multi-Year Training System. *Powerlifting USA*. 19(8).
Simmons, L. 1996. Strengthening the Torso. *Powerlifting USA*. 19(10).
Simmons, L. 1996. Maximum Effort Method. *Powerlifting USA*. 19(11).
Simmons, L. 1996. Chain Reactions. *Powerlifting USA*. 19(12).
Simmons, L. 1996. Distributing the Loads. *Powerlifting USA*. 20(3).
Simmons, L. 1997. How Many Work Outs? *Powerlifting USA*. 20(7).
Simmons, L. 1997. A Weekly Schedule. *Powerlifting USA*. 20(8).
Simmons, L. 1997. Progressive Overload: Is It Progressive Disaster. *Powerlifting USA*. 21(2).
Simmons, L. 1997. You Gotta Train Heavy, The Maximum Effort Method. *Powerlifting USA*. 21(4).
Simmons, L. 1998. Principle of Variety. *Powerlifting USA*. 22(1).
Simmons, L. 1998. Speed Strength. *Powerlifting USA*. 21(7).
Simmons, L. 1998. HIT or MISS?. *Powerlifting USA*. 22(3).
Simmons, L. 1998. General Physical Preparedness. *Powerlifting USA*. 22(4).
Simmons, L. 1999. Bands and Chains *Powerlifting USA*. 22(6).
Simmons, L. 1999. Training Methodologies. *Powerlifting USA*. 22(9).
Simmons, L. 1999. The Method of Maximal Resistance. *Powerlifting USA*. 23(5).
Simmons, L. 2000. Extra Workouts. *Powerlifting USA*. 23(6).
Simmons, L. 2000. The Conjugate Method. *Powerlifting USA*. 23(8).
Simmons, L. 2001. Eccentric and Concentric Training. *Powerlifting USA*. 24(6).
Simmons, L. 2001. Developing Special Strengths. *Powerlifting USA*. 24(7).
Simmons, L. 2000. Building the Torso. *Powerlifting USA*. 24(8).
Simmons, L. 2001. Extra Workouts. *Powerlifting USA*. 24(9).
Simmons, L. 2001. The Factor of Time. *Powerlifting USA*. 24(12).
Simmons, L. 2001. Speed Cycling *Powerlifting USA*. 25(3).
Simmons, L. 2002. Don't Chase Your Tail. *Powerlifting USA*. 25(2).
Simmons, L. 2002. The Repetition Method. *Powerlifting USA*. 25(8).
Simmons, L. 2002. Training Methods. *Powerlifting USA*. 25(10).
Simmons, L. 2002. The Importance of Volume. *Powerlifting USA*. 25(11).
Siff, M. 2002. Facts and Fallacies of Fitness. (5th edition). Colorado.
Siff, M. & Verkhoshansky, Y.V. 1998. Supertraining. (3rd Edition). South Africa.
Staley, C. Quality Strength for Human Athletic Performance: A Guide to Speed Strength Training. http://www.thinkmuscle.com
Starr, B. 1996. The Strongest Shall Survive. (4th edition). Virginia.
Stone, M. & O'Bryant, H. 1987. Weight Training: A Scientific Approach. Minnesota.
Tate, Dave. 1999-present. Professional Development. Elite Fitness Systems.
Tate, Dave. 2000. Accommodating Resistance, How to use bands and chains to increase your max lifts. *Testosterone Magazine*. Issue 127, October 20, 2000. http://www.t-mag.com
Tate, Dave. 2000. The Periodization Bible Part I: The Old Testament – Linear Periodization. *Testosterone Magazine*. Issue 129. November 3, 2000. http://www.t-mag.com
Tate, Dave. 2000. The Periodization Bible Part II: The New Testament – Conjugated Periodization. *Testosterone Magazine*. Issue 133, December 8, 2000. http://www.t-mag.com
Tate, Dave. 2001. Drag Your Butt Into Shape General Physical Preparedness: Westside Style. *Testosterone Magazine*. Issue 146, March 2, 2001. http://www.t-mag.com
Tate, D. 2001. The Westside Seminar Video. *Elite Fitness Systems*. Ohio.
Verkhoshansky, Y.V. 1977. Fundamentals of Special Strength-Training in Sport. Michigan.
Verkhoshansky, Y.V. 1985. Programming and Organization of Training. Michigan

About the Author

Joe Kenn has been a strength and conditioning professional for 14 years, the last 12 on the collegiate level. In January 2003, he was named head coach of sports performance at Arizona State University, Kenn received his bachelor of science degree with an emphasis in health and sports science in December 1988 from Wake Forest University. Kenn started his career at Pine Crest School in Fort Lauderdale, Florida, and then returned to his alma mater, Wake Forest, for a brief period before heading off to Boise State University in July 1991. He designed the first tier system programs for the women's basketball and volleyball teams at BSU in 1992 while working as the graduate assistant strength and conditioning coach. Kenn completed his master's degree in education from Boise State in August 1993. He has led programs at Boise State University (May 1994-April 1999) for all sports, University of Utah (April 1999-December 2000) for all sports, and Arizona State University (January 2001-December 2002) for football.

Kenn is a certified strength and conditioning specialist through the National Strength and Conditioning Association, a certified sports performance coach, and a certified club coach from United States Weightlifting. Kenn has coached numerous successful athletes in all sports, some of whom have been able to go on to compete professionally. He has been published in several journals and publications and has spoken at the local, state, regional, and national levels. He has received numerous honors, including being named the 2002 National Strength and Conditioning Association's Collegiate Strength and Conditioning Professional of the Year.

Kenn is a former collegiate football player, having played offensive and defensive line at Wake Forest University. Kenn played for both Al Groh and ACC legend Bill Dooley. Kenn continues his lifting passion as a competitive power lifter.

Originally from Inwood, Long Island, NY, where his parents and sister reside, Kenn and his family, Angela, Joe IV, and Peter, live in Gilbert, AZ.